MW01629589

THE ILLUSTRIOUS *Women of Islām* FROM THE FIRST GENERATION

Taken from *Siyar A'lām an-Nubalā'* by Imām adh-Dhahabī
& *Al-Iṣābah fī Tamyīz aṣ-Ṣaḥābah* by Ibn Ḥajar al-'Aṣqalānī

ISBN: 978-1-5323-7598-9 (softback)
978-1-5323-8446-2 (hardback)

First Edition: Dhul-Qa'dah 1439 AH / August 2018 CE

Cover Design: Usul Design
Email: info@usuldesign.com

Translator: Rasheed Barbee

Editing & Formatting: Danielle Lebenson al-Amrikiyyah
www.amrikiyyahdesign.com

Publisher's Information:
Authentic Statements Publishing
P.O. Box 15536
Philadelphia, PA 19131
215.382.3382
215.382.3782 – Fax

Store:
5000 Locust St.(Side Entrance)
Philadelphia, PA 19139

Website: www.authenticstatements.com
E-mail: info@authenticstatements.com

Please visit our website for upcoming publications, audio/DVD online catalog, and info on events and seminars, *inshāAllāh*.

Transliteration Table

Consonants

ء	'	د	d	ض	ḍ	ك	k
ب	b	ذ	dh	ط	ṭ	ل	l
ت	t	ر	r	ظ	ẓ	م	m
ث	th	ز	z	ع	ʿ	ن	n
ج	j	س	s	غ	gh	ه	h
ح	ḥ	ش	sh	ف	f	و	w
خ	kh	ص	ṣ	ق	q	ي	y

Vowels

Short	ـَ	a	ـِ	i	ـُ	u
Long	ـَا	ā	ـِي	ī	ـُو	ū
Diphthongs	ـَيْ	ay	ـَوْ	aw		

Glyphs

ﷺ *Ṣallāllāhu ʿalayhi wa sallam* (May Allāh's praise & salutations be upon him)

ʿAlayhis-salām (Peace be upon him)

Raḍiyallāhu ʿanhu (May Allāh be pleased with him)

Raḍiyallāhu ʿanhum (May Allāh be pleased with them)

Raḍiyallāhu ʿanhumā (May Allāh be pleased with them both)

Raḍiyallāhu ʿanhā (May Allāh be pleased with her)

Raḥimahullāh (May Allāh have mercy on him)

Contents

Encyclopedia of Female Companions

INTRODUCTION

BY THE TRANSLATOR

All praises belong to Allāh, the Lord of all that exists, the Most Beneficent and the Most Merciful of those who show mercy. May Allāh exalt the rank of and send peace upon the best of mankind, Muḥammad bin 'Abdillāh, and upon his family and his Companions collectively.

As to what follows:

Allāh the Exalted selected the best men and women as Companions for the Messenger of Allāh ﷺ. Allāh the Exalted said:

﴿ اللَّهُ أَعْلَمُ حَيْثُ يَجْعَلُ رِسَالَتَهُ ﴾

Allāh knows best with whom to place His Message.

[Sūrah al-An'ām 6:124]

Ibn al-Qayyim رَحِمَهُ ٱللَّهُ said, "Allāh knows best where to place His Message, both regarding the original recipient (meaning the Messenger) and those who inherit it from him (meaning his Companions)."

The Illustrious Women of Islām is a collection of biographies of the noble Companions of the Messenger of Allāh ﷺ from among the women, extracted from two classic history books: *Siyar A'lām an-Nubalā'* by Imām adh-Dhahabī and *Al-Iṣābah fī Tamyīz aṣ-Ṣaḥābah* by Ibn Ḥajar al-'Aṣqalānī.

Siyar A'lām an-Nubalā' by Imām adh-Dhahabī is an encyclopedic book of biographies of the noble Companions of the Messenger of Allāh ﷺ and the scholars from the generations that followed them up until the era of the author, who died in 748 AH. This book recounts memoirs of those noble women closest to the Prophet ﷺ, such as his wives, nursing mothers, daughters, granddaughters, paternal aunts, paternal cousins, nursing sisters, and select women from the Muhājirūn and Anṣār.

Al-Iṣābah fī Tamyīz aṣ-Ṣaḥābah by Ibn Ḥajar al-'Aṣqalānī is the most comprehensive dictionary of the Companions of the Messenger of Allāh ﷺ. This book is arranged in alphabetical order illustrating these noble women from mankind and *jinn*. Although this translation is comprehensive, it does not include every woman regarded as a Companion. Some of the biographies are extensive, some are brief; all of them are extraordinary.

Rasheed bin Estes Barbee
Durham, North Carolina
Shawwāl 1439 / June 2018

THE ILLUSTRIOUS WOMEN OF ISLĀM FROM THE FIRST GENERATION

Taken from Siyar A'lām an-Nubalā'

THE WIVES OF THE PROPHET

1) Khadījah bint Khuwaylid

2) Sawdah bint Zam'ah

3) 'Ā'ishah bint Abī Bakr aṣ-Ṣiddīq

4) Ḥafṣah bint 'Umar bin al-Khaṭṭāb

5) Zaynab bint Khuzaymah

6) Umm Salamah Hind bint Abī Umayyah bin al-Mughīrah

7) Juwayriyah bint al-Ḥārith

8) Zaynab bint Jaḥsh

9) Umm Ḥabībah Ramlah bint Abī Sufyān

10) Ṣafiyyah bint Ḥuyayy bin Akhṭab

11) Maymūnah bint al-Ḥārith

KHADĪJAH BINT KHUWAYLID

Khadījah was the Mother of the Believers and the leader of all the women of the world during her era. She is the mother of al-Qāsim, the daughter of Khuwaylid bin Asad bin 'Abdil-'Uzzā bin Quṣayy bin Kilāb al-Qurashī al-Asadī. She is the mother of the children of the Messenger of Allāh ﷺ[1]. She was the first person to believe in him. She gave credence to him before anyone else. She made his heart firm. She took him to her uncle Waraqah. Her virtues are extraordinary. She is from those women who achieved excellence and distinction. She was intelligent, religious, modest, and noble. She is from the inhabitants of Paradise. The Prophet ﷺ used to praise her and favor her over the other Mothers of the Believers. He would go to great lengths to laud her, to the extent that 'Ā'ishah said:

مَا غِرْتُ مِنَ امْرَأَةٍ مَا غِرْتُ مِنْ خَدِيجَةَ، مِنْ كَثْرَةِ ذِكْرِ النَّبِيِّ صَلَّى اللَّهُ عَلَيْهِ وَسَلَّمَ لَهَا.

Never did I feel jealous of any woman as I felt in the case of Khadījah. This was due to the Prophet ﷺ mentioning her often.[2]

From her noble traits is that she was the first woman the Prophet ﷺ married. She bore a number of his children, and he never married another woman while married to her. He did not marry another woman until she died. She was a blessed Companion. She would spend her wealth on him. The Prophet ﷺ conducted business and trade on her behalf. Allāh ordered him to give her glad tidings of a palace in Paradise made from jewels in which there is no noise and no toil.

Jubayr bin Muṭ'im stated, "Khadījah's paternal uncle 'Amr bin Asad married her to the Messenger of Allāh ﷺ. Khadījah's father died in the war of al-Fijār[3]. [The Prophet] was 25 years old while Khadījah was 40 years old."

---

[1] **Translator's note:** Khadījah رضي الله عنها was the mother of all his children except Ibrāhīm, whose mother was Māriyah the Coptic.

[2] *Ṣaḥīḥ Muslim* 2435

[3] **Translator's note:** This war between Arab tribes began during the Pre-Islamic Days of Ignorance, 33 years before the migration, and it lasted for 10 years.

Az-Zubayr bin Bakkār said, "During the Pre-Islamic Days of Ignorance, Khadījah was known as 'the Pure One' (aṭ-Ṭāhirah); her mother was Fāṭimah bint Zā'idah al-'Āmiriyah."

Khadījah was previously married to Hālah bin Zurārah at-Tamīmī and then to 'Atīq bin 'Ābid bin 'Abdillāh, then she married the Prophet ﷺ. He was 25 years old when they married, and she was 15 years older than him.

'Ā'ishah said that Khadījah died before the prayer was made obligatory. It has been said that she passed away during the month of Ramaḍān, and she was buried in al-Ḥajūn[4] at the age of 65.

'Ā'ishah said, "When the Messenger of Allāh ﷺ would mention Khadījah, he would not grow tired of praising her and seeking forgiveness for her. One day, he mentioned her and jealousy overcame me. I said, 'Allāh has exchanged something better for you than an old woman.' I saw that this made him very upset. Thus, my temper was removed. I said to myself, 'O Allāh, if you remove the displeasure that Your Messenger has for me, I will not speak unfavorably about her again.' When the Prophet ﷺ saw how I was affected, he said, 'How can you say this? By Allāh, she believed in me when the people belied me. She accepted me when the people rejected me. And I have been granted children from her while I have not been granted children from other than her[5].' "

Al-Wāqidī[6] said, "The boycott against the clan of Banū Hāshim ended three years before the migration; then Abū Ṭālib (the uncle of the Prophet) died, and Khadījah died a month and five days before him." Al-Ḥākim said, "She died three days after Abū Ṭālib."

'Ā'ishah ﵂ said, "Never did I feel jealous of any woman as I felt in the case of Khadījah. This was due to the Prophet ﷺ mentioning

---

[4] **Translator's note:** A cemetery to the north of Masjid al-Ḥarām, and near the Masjid of the Jinn, in Makkah.

[5] Collected by aṭ-Ṭabarānī in *Al-Kabīr* (14/23).

[6] **Translator's note:** Abū 'Abdillāh Muḥammad bin 'Umar bin Wāqid al-Aslamī, an Islamic historian who died in 207 AH.

her often. He married me three years after her death, and his Lord commanded him to give her glad tidings of a palace in Paradise[7]."

Abū Hurayrah ﷺ said:

أَتَى جِبْرِيلُ النَّبِيَّ صلى الله عليه وسلم فَقَالَ يَا رَسُولَ اللَّهِ هَذِهِ خَدِيجَةُ قَدْ أَتَتْ مَعَهَا إِنَاءٌ فِيهِ إِدَامٌ أَوْ طَعَامٌ أَوْ شَرَابٌ، فَإِذَا هِيَ أَتَتْكَ فَاقْرَأْ عَلَيْهَا السَّلاَمَ مِنْ رَبِّهَا وَمِنِّي، وَبَشِّرْهَا بِبَيْتٍ فِي الْجَنَّةِ مِنْ قَصَبٍ، لاَ صَخَبَ فِيهِ وَلاَ نَصَبَ.

Jibrīl came to the Prophet ﷺ and said, "O Messenger of Allāh, Khadījah is bringing you a dish with some food or drink. When she arrives, convey to her the *salām* from her Lord and from me. And give her glad tidings of a palace in Paradise made from jewels, in which there is no noise and no toil."[8]

'Alī ﷺ said, "I heard the Messenger of Allāh ﷺ say:

خَيْرُ نِسَائِهَا خَدِيجَةُ بِنْتُ خُوَيْلِدٍ، وَخَيْرُ نِسَائِهَا مَرْيَمُ بِنْتُ عِمْرَانَ.

" 'The best woman of her era is Khadījah bint Khuwaylid, and the best woman of her era was Maryam bint 'Imrān.' "[9]

Abū Salamah and Yaḥyā bin 'Abdur-Raḥmān said, "When Khadījah died, the Prophet ﷺ received a visit from Khawlah bint Ḥakīm, the wife of 'Uthmān bin Maẓ'ūn[10]. She said, 'O Messenger of Allāh, will you not marry?' He responded, 'Who should I marry?' She said, 'Sawdah bint Zam'ah. She believed in you and follows you.' " This *ḥadīth* in its entirety is *mursal.*[11]

---

[7] *Ṣaḥīḥ al-Bukhārī* 103 and *Ṣaḥīḥ Muslim* 2435, from the *ḥadīth* of Hishām bin 'Urwah from his father.

[8] *Ṣaḥīḥ al-Bukhārī* 3820

[9] *Ṣaḥīḥ al-Bukhārī* 7/101

[10] **Translator's note:** He is the maternal uncle of Ḥafṣah bint 'Umar bin al-Khaṭṭāb, the wife of the Prophet ﷺ.

[11] **Translator's note:** A *ḥadīth* is called a "*mursal ḥadīth*" if the one who narrated it from the Prophet ﷺ is a Tābi'ī and not a Companion. Imām Abū 'Abdillāh al-Ḥākim said,

Ibn Is'ḥāq said, "Calamities came consecutively to the Messenger of Allāh with the death of Abū Ṭālib and Khadījah. And Khadījah was the epitome of honesty. Her lineage connects to the lineage of the Prophet ﷺ at Quṣayy bin Kilāb. She was a business investor, thus she presented a business opportunity to the Prophet ﷺ to take some of her wealth to Shām to conduct trade. The Prophet ﷺ went to Shām with the freed slave of Khadījah named Maysarah. He sold the product she had sent with him and increased her wealth. She sent word to him that she was interested in marrying him; thus, he married her and gave her 20 camels as a dowry."[12]

Khadījah's children from the Prophet ﷺ are: al-Qāsim, aṭ-Ṭayyib, and aṭ-Ṭāhir, who all died during their suckling years; and Ruqayyah, Zaynab, Umm Kulthūm, and Fāṭimah.

'Ā'ishah رضي الله عنها said:

أَوَّلُ مَا بُدِئَ بِهِ رَسُولُ اللَّهِ صلى الله عليه وسلم مِنَ الْوَحْيِ الرُّؤْيَا الصَّالِحَةُ فِي النَّوْمِ.

Revelation first began for the Messenger of Allāh ﷺ in the form of a good dream.[13]

She said, "Then he received the verses:

﴿ اقْرَأْ بِاسْمِ رَبِّكَ الَّذِي خَلَقَ ۝١ خَلَقَ الْإِنسَانَ مِنْ عَلَقٍ ۝٢ اقْرَأْ وَرَبُّكَ الْأَكْرَمُ ۝٣ ﴾

" 'Read, in the name of your Lord, Who has created. He created man from a clot. Read; and your Lord is the Most Generous.'

[Sūrah al-'Alaq 93:1-3]

"There is no difference of opinion among the scholars of *ḥadīth* that the *mursal ḥadīth* is one which the narrator narrated with a complete chain back to the Tābi'ī, and the Tābi'ī says, 'The Messenger of Allāh ﷺ said.' " (*Ma'rifah 'Ulūm al-Ḥadīth*). This narration is collected in *Al-Musnad* (6/211), and all the men in the chain are reliable.

[12] *Prophetic Sīrah* by Ibn Hishām

[13] *Ṣaḥīḥ al-Bukhārī* 3

"The Messenger of Allāh ﷺ returned with his heart beating severely. He entered upon Khadījah bint Khuwaylid and said, 'Cover me, cover me!' They covered him until his fear was gone, and after that he told her everything that had happened and said, 'I fear that something may happen to me.' Khadījah replied:

كَلَّا، أَبْشِرْ، فَوَاللَّهِ لَا يُخْزِيكَ اللَّهُ أَبَدًا، إِنَّكَ لَتَصِلُ الرَّحِمَ، وَتَصْدُقُ الْحَدِيثَ، وَتَحْمِلُ الْكَلَّ، وَتُعِينُ عَلَى نَوَائِبِ الْحَقِّ.

" 'Never! Receive the glad tidings. By Allāh, Allāh will never disgrace you. You keep good relations with your kin, you speak the truth, you help the poor and destitute and assist those afflicted with calamity.'

"She took him to see her uncle Waraqah bin Nawfal bin Asad. During the Pre-Islamic Period, he became a Christian and used to write the Arabic script, and he used to write of the Gospels in Arabic as much as Allāh wished him to write. He was an old man who had lost his sight. Khadījah said, 'Listen to what your nephew has to say.' Waraqah said, 'O my nephew, what did you see?' The Prophet ﷺ told him what he saw. Upon hearing this, Waraqah said:

هَذَا النَّامُوسُ الَّذِي أُنْزِلَ عَلَى مُوسَى.

" 'This is the same Nāmūs[14] whom Allāh had sent to Moses.' "[15]

Shaykh 'Izz ad-Dīn bin al-Athīr said, "The Muslims have agreed that Khadījah was the first person to enter Islām."

Az-Zuhrī said, "The first people to believe in Allāh and His Messenger were Khadījah, Abū Bakr, and 'Alī ﷺ.

Ibn Is'ḥāq narrated, "Khadījah said to the Messenger of Allāh, 'Are you able to inform me when your Companion (Jibrīl) arrives?' He

[14] **Translator's note:** Nāmūs has many meanings, including "the one who keeps a secret." Imām an-Nawawī said, "Jibrīl is called this because Allāh entrusted him with some affairs of the unseen."

[15] *Ṣaḥīḥ al-Bukhārī* 6982

said, 'Yes.' When he came, he said, 'O Khadījah, Jibrīl is here.' She said, 'Sit on your right thigh. Do you see him?' He said, 'Yes.' She said, 'Sit on your left thigh. Do you see him?' He said, 'Yes.' Then she covered him with her garment and she lay under her garment with him and said, 'Do you see him?' He replied, 'No.' She said, 'Receive the good news that, by Allāh, this is surely an angel and not a devil.' "[16] (Because the devil would not have been ashamed to look at him while he was under a woman's garment.)

Anas bin Mālik said that the Messenger of Allāh ﷺ said:

حَسْبُكَ مِنْ نِسَاءِ الْعَالَمِينَ: مَرْيَمُ ابْنَةُ عِمْرَانَ، وَخَدِيجَةُ بِنْتُ خُوَيْلِدٍ، وَفَاطِمَةُ بِنْتُ مُحَمَّدٍ، وَآسِيَةُ امْرَأَةُ فِرْعَوْنَ.

Sufficient for you among the women of mankind are Maryam bint 'Imrān, Khadījah bint Khuwaylid, Fāṭimah bint Muḥammad, and Āsiyah the wife of Pharaoh.[17]

The Messenger of Allāh said:

سَيِّدَةُ نِسَاءِ أَهْلِ الْجَنَّةِ بَعْدَ مَرْيَمَ فَاطِمَةُ، وَخَدِيجَةُ، وَامْرَأَةُ فِرْعَوْنَ آسِيَةُ.

The leaders of the women of Paradise are Maryam, Fāṭimah, Khadījah, and Āsiyah the wife of Pharaoh.[18]

'Ā'ishah said that Khadījah died before the prayer was made obligatory. Al-Wāqidī said that she passed away during the month of Ramaḍān and she was buried in al-Ḥajūn. Qatādah and 'Urwah said that she died three years prior to the migration to Madīnah.

Sawdah bint Zam'ah

The Mother of the Believers Sawdah bint Zam'ah bin Qays al-Qurashiyyah al-'Āmiriyyah.

[16] Collected by Ibn Hishām (1/238, 239).

[17] *Jāmi' at-Tirmidhī* 3878; Abū 'Īsā said that this *ḥadīth* is *ḥasan*.

[18] Collected by al-Ḥākim (3/185). **Translator's note:** Declared authentic by al-Albānī.

She was the first woman the Messenger of Allāh ﷺ married after Khadījah. He was only married to her for three years or more before he consummated his marriage with 'Ā'ishah. She was a noble, honorable woman with firm resolve.

Sawdah was previously married to as-Sakrān bin 'Amr, the brother of Suhayl bin 'Amr. She gave her days to 'Ā'ishah, showing concern for the heart of the Messenger of Allāh ﷺ[19].

She narrated *aḥādīth,* some of which have been collected in *Ṣaḥīḥ al-Bukhārī*. Ibn 'Abbās and Yaḥyā bin 'Abdillāh al-Anṣārī narrated from her.

'Ā'ishah ﵂ said:

مَا رَأَيْتُ امْرَأَةً أَحَبَّ إِلَيَّ أَنْ أَكُونَ فِي مِسْلَاخِهَا مِنْ سَوْدَةَ، مِنَ امْرَأَةٍ، فِيهَا حِدَّةٌ، فَلَمَّا كَبِرَتْ جَعَلَتْ يَوْمَهَا مِنَ النَّبِيِّ صَلَّى اللَّهُ عَلَيْهِ وَسَلَّمَ لِعَائِشَةَ.

I never saw a woman and wanted to be in her skin (wanted to be her) other than Sawdah bint Zam'ah; she was a woman with firm resolve. When she became older, she gave her days with the Prophet ﷺ to 'Ā'ishah.[20]

The Messenger of Allāh ﷺ married Sawdah during the month of Ramaḍān 10 years after he became a prophet. He migrated with her to Madīnah. She died in Madīnah during the month of Shawwāl.

Al-Wāqidī noted, "Sawdah died in Madīnah in Shawwāl in 54 AH." While Sa'īd bin Abī Hilāl said, "Sawdah ﵂ died during 'Umar's caliphate."

Ibn Sa'd said, "Sawdah and her husband (as-Sakrān bin 'Amr) accepted Islām and migrated to Abyssinia."

---

[19] **Translator's note:** Shaykh Muḥammad bin 'Abdil-Wahhāb al-'Aqīl said, "As for Sawdah: her choosing to remain with the Prophet ﷺ shows her intelligence, as she wanted to be raised on the Day of Judgment from amongst his wives ﵅."

[20] *Ṣaḥīḥ Muslim* 1463 (translation based upon the explanation of Imām an-Nawawī).

As-Sakrān bin 'Amr returned to Makkah, where he died, leaving Sawdah a widow. The Prophet ﷺ proposed to her. She said, "My affair is up to you." He told her to have a man from her family marry them, so she told Ḥāṭib bin 'Amr al-'Āmirī to marry her off. Ḥāṭib is from those who migrated and participated in Badr.

Sawdah bint Zam'ah رضي الله عنها used to make the Messenger of Allāh ﷺ laugh[21]. Sawdah said to the Messenger of Allāh ﷺ:

صَلَّيْتُ خَلْفَكَ الْبَارِحَةَ فَرَكَعْتَ بِي حَتَّى أَمْسَكْتُ بِأَنْفِي مَخَافَةَ أَنْ يَقْطُرَ الدَّمُ قَالَ: فَضَحِكَ وَكَانَتْ تُضْحِكُهُ الْأَحْيَانَ بِالشَّيْءِ.

"I prayed behind you last night, so I bowed until I had to hold my nose fearing blood would drip." Thus, he laughed. And she would make him laugh from time to time with poetry.[22]

'Ā'ishah رضي الله عنها said:

اسْتَأْذَنَتْ سَوْدَةُ لَيْلَةَ الْمُزْدَلِفَةِ، أَنْ تَدْفَعَ قَبْلَ حَطْمَةِ النَّاسِ وَكَانَتِ امْرَأَةً ثَبِطَةً - أَيْ ثَقِيلَةً - فَأَذِنَ لَهَا.

Sawdah sought permission on the night of Muzdalifah to leave before it became too crowded, because she was a heavy woman, and he gave her permission.[23]

Sawdah bint Zam'ah رضي الله عنها was a charitable woman.

Ibn Sīrīn narrated that after the death of the Messenger of Allāh ﷺ, 'Umar bin al-Khaṭṭāb sent Sawdah a sack containing *dirham*. She said, "What is this?" They said, "Money." She said, "Money in a sack disguised as dates?" So she said to a young girl, "Give me contentment." So the young girl gave all the money to the poor.[24]

---

[21] **Translator's note:** The laughing of the Messenger of Allāh ﷺ was a smile, as 'Ā'ishah said, "I have never seen the Messenger of Allāh ﷺ laughing so heartily that his uvula could be seen. He used to smile only." Collected by al-Bukhārī and Muslim.

[22] *Aṭ-Ṭabaqāt* 54/8

[23] *Ṣaḥīḥ Muslim* 1290

[24] *Aṭ-Ṭabaqāt* 56/8

Sawdah narrated five *aḥādīth* which are collected in *Al-Bukhārī* and *Muslim*, and one which is only collected in *Ṣaḥīḥ al-Bukhārī*.

Abū Wāqid al-Laythī said:

سَمِعْتُ رَسُولَ اللَّهِ صلى الله عليه وسلم يَقُولُ لأَزْوَاجِهِ فِي حَجَّةِ الْوَدَاعِ هَذِهِ ثُمَّ ظُهُورُ الْحُصْرِ.

I heard the Messenger of Allāh ﷺ saying to his wives during the Farewell Pilgrimage, "This (is the pilgrimage for you); afterwards, stick to the surface of the mats (stay at home)."[25]

TRANSLATOR'S ADDENDUM

Sawdah bint Zam'ah ﷺ said:

حَجَجْتُ وَاعْتَمَرْتُ، فَأَنَا أَقَرُّ فِي بَيْتِي كَمَا أَمَرَنِي اللَّهُ عَزَّ وَجَلَّ.

I performed Ḥajj and 'Umrah, so I remain in my home as I have been commanded to do by Allāh the Exalted.[26]

Sawdah bint Zam'ah had two brothers: Mālik bin Zam'ah and 'Abd bin Zam'ah.

As for Mālik bin Zam'ah, he was from the first and foremost to accept Islām. He migrated to Abyssinia during the second migration, then he returned to Madīnah with Ja'far bin Abī Ṭālib, and then he passed away.[27]

As for her brother 'Abd bin Zam'ah: he was not Muslim at the time Sawdah married the Messenger of Allāh, so he began to throw dirt on his head in anguish over his sister's marriage. When he accepted Islām, he wrote a poem saying, "Verily, I was foolish the day I threw dirt upon my head because the Messenger of Allāh ﷺ married

---

[25] *Sunan Abī Dāwūd* 1722

[26] Narrated by Ibn Sīrīn; collected in *Aṭ-Ṭabaqāt al-Kubrā* by Ibn Sa'd (#9703).

[27] *Accuracy in Distinguishing the Companions* by Ibn Ḥajar

Sawdah."[28]

Her brother 'Abd bin Zam'ah is also mentioned in the *ḥadīth* concerning the child of the bed. 'Ā'ishah said:

أَنَّ سَعْدَ بْنَ أَبِي وَقَّاصٍ تنازع هو وعَبْدُ بْنُ زَمْعَةَ فِي عبدٍ لزَمْعَةَ فقَالَ سَعْدٌ: يَا رَسُولَ اللَّهِ، هذا ابن أَخِي عتبة بن أبي وقاص، عهد به إليَّ فهو ابنه، وَقَالَ عَبْدُ بْنُ زَمْعَةَ: هذا أَخِي وَابْنُ أَمَةِ أَبِي وُلِدَ عَلَى فِرَاشِ أَبِي، فَرَأَى النَّبِيُّ صَلَّى اللَّهُ عَلَيْهِ وَسَلَّمَ شَبَهًا بَيِّنًا بِعُتْبَةَ، فَقَالَ: هُوَ لَكَ يَا عَبْدُ بْنَ زَمْعَةَ الْوَلَدُ لِلْفِرَاشِ. ثم قال لسودة بنت زمعة وهي إحدى أمهات المؤمنين رضي الله عنها: احْتَجِبِي عَنْهُ يَا سَوْدَةُ.

Sa'd bin Abī Waqqāṣ and 'Abd bin Zam'ah disputed concerning a slave belonging to Zam'ah. Sa'd said, "O Messenger of Allāh, this is the son of my brother, 'Utbah bin Abī Waqqāṣ, who asked me to take care of him because he is his son." 'Abd bin Zam'ah said, "This is my brother, O Messenger of Allāh, the son of my father's slave-woman who was born in my father's bed." The Messenger of Allāh ﷺ saw a clear resemblance to 'Utbah, but he said, "He is yours, O 'Abd bin Zam'ah. The child is for the (owner of the) bed." Then he said to Sawdah bint Zam'ah, who was one of the Mothers of the Believers, "Observe *ḥijāb* from him, O Sawdah."[29]

'Ā'ISHAH BINT ABĪ BAKR AṢ-ṢIDDĪQ

She is the daughter of the Imām, aṣ-Ṣiddīq, the Caliph of the Messenger of Allāh ﷺ, Abū Bakr 'Abdullāh bin Abī Quḥāfah 'Uthmān bin 'Āmir bin 'Amr bin Ka'b bin Sa'd bin Tamīm bin Murrah bin Ka'b from the tribe of Quraysh.

She is the Mother of the Believers and the most knowledgeable woman of this *ummah* without exception.

[28] *Siyar A'lām an-Nubalā'* by Imām adh-Dhahabī, p. 230.

[29] Narrated by al-Bukhārī (2053) and Muslim (1457).

Her mother is Umm Rūmān bint ʿĀmir bin ʿUwaymīr.

Abū Bakr and Umm Rūmān migrated with ʿĀ'ishah. The Prophet ﷺ married her before migration and after the death of Khadījah. That was about 10 months before the migration. Some have said it was two years prior. The marriage was consummated after the Prophet ﷺ returned from the Battle of Badr.

A great deal of good, blessed knowledge has been narrated by her and her father, and the likes of ʿUmar, Fāṭimah, Saʿd, Ḥamzah bin ʿAmr al-Aslamī, and Judāmah bint Wahb.

ʿĀ'ishah رضي الله عنها narrated 2,210 *aḥādīth*. Of these *aḥādīth*, 174 are agreed upon by al-Bukhārī and Muslim.[30]

ʿĀ'ishah رضي الله عنها is from those born into Islām. She was eight years younger than Fāṭimah. ʿĀ'ishah used to say:

لَمْ أَعْقِلْ أَبَوَيَّ إِلَّا وَهُمَا يَدِينَانِ الدِّينَ.

I do not have any recollection of my parents except that both of them practiced the religion (Islām).[31]

She recalled meeting a blind old man in Makkah who led the elephants, and he would ask for money.

She was a woman with a white complexion and she was very attractive. For this reason, she was called "the Little Red One." The Prophet ﷺ did not marry a virgin other than her and he did not love any woman like he loved her. I do not know of any woman in the *ummah* of Muḥammad ﷺ more knowledgeable than her. Some scholars say she is better than her father, but this is rejected. Allāh has placed measure in everything. We testify that she is the wife of the Prophet ﷺ in this world and in the Hereafter. So is there any greater praise than this?! Although Khadījah has some qualities not

---

[30] **Translator's note:** Shaykh ʿUthaymīn noted, "Only three Companions narrated more *aḥādīth* than ʿĀ'ishah: Abū Hurayrah, ʿAbdullāh bin ʿUmar, and Anas bin Mālik."

[31] *Ṣaḥīḥ al-Bukhārī* 6079

found in 'Ā'ishah, I do not say which one of them is better.[32]

'Ā'ishah ﵂ said that the Messenger of Allāh ﷺ said:

أُرِيتُكِ فِي الْمَنَامِ ثَلَاثَ لَيَالٍ جَاءَنِي بِكِ الْمَلَكُ فِي سَرَقَةٍ مِنْ حَرِيرٍ فَيَقُولُ هَذِهِ امْرَأَتُكَ . فَأَكْشِفُ عَنْ وَجْهِكِ فَإِذَا أَنْتِ هِيَ فَأَقُولُ إِنْ يَكُ هَذَا مِنْ عِنْدِ اللَّهِ يُمْضِهِ.

I saw you in a dream for three nights when an angel brought you to me in a silk cloth and he said, "Here is your wife," and when I removed (the cloth) from your face, there you were. So I said, "If this is from Allāh, let Him carry it out."[33]

'Ā'ishah ﵂ said:

لَقَدْ أُعْطِيتُ تِسْعًا مَا أُعْطِيَتْهَا امْرَأَةٌ بَعْدَ مَرْيَمَ بِنْتِ عِمْرَانَ: لَقَدْ نَزَلَ جِبْرِيلُ بِصُورَتِي فِي رَاحَتِهِ حَتَّى أُمِرَ رَسُولُ اللَّهِ صَلَّى اللَّهُ عَلَيْهِ وَسَلَّمَ أَنْ يَتَزَوَّجَنِي، وَلَقَدْ تَزَوَّجَنِي بِكْرًا، وَمَا تَزَوَّجَ بِكْرًا غَيْرِي، وَلَقَدْ قُبِضَ وَرَأْسُهُ فِي حِجْرِي، وَلَقَدْ قَبَرْتُهُ فِي بَيْتِي، وَلَقَدْ حَفَّتِ الْمَلَائِكَةُ بِبَيْتِي، وَإِنْ كَانَ الْوَحْيُ لَيَنْزِلُ عَلَيْهِ وَإِنِّي لَمَعَهُ فِي لِحَافِهِ، وَإِنِّي لَابْنَةُ خَلِيفَتِهِ وَصِدِّيقِهِ، وَلَقَدْ نَزَلَ عُذْرِي مِنَ السَّمَاءِ، وَلَقَدْ خُلِقْتُ طَيِّبَةً عِنْدَ طَيِّبٍ، وَلَقَدْ وُعِدْتُ مَغْفِرَةً وَرِزْقًا كَرِيمًا.

I have surely been given nine virtues which were not given to any woman after Maryam bint 'Imrān: Jibrīl descended with my image in his dream until the Prophet ﷺ was commanded to marry me. He married me when I was a virgin and he did not marry a virgin other

[32] **Translator's note:** Ibn Taymiyyah said, "Khadījah had a tremendous effect upon the early days of Islām. Her aid in establishing the religion is unrivaled; not even 'Ā'ishah compares to her in this regard, nor any of the Mothers of the Believers. 'Ā'ishah had a tremendous effect upon the later days of Islām. The manner in which she carried the religion, conveyed it, and the knowledge she acquired is unrivaled; not even Khadījah compares to her in this regard, nor any of the Mothers of the Believers." (*Collection of Fatāwā* 4/393)

[33] *Ṣaḥīḥ Muslim* 2438

than me. His soul was taken while his head was in my lap. He was buried in my home. The angels surrounded my home. Revelation descended while I was with him under his blanket. I am the daughter of his caliph and his friend. My name was cleared of the slander from the heavens. I was created pure for one who is pure. I have been promised forgiveness and a generous reward.[34]

This *ḥadīth* has been narrated by Abū Bakr al-Ājurrī from Aḥmad bin Yaḥyā. Its chain of narration is *ḥasan,* and it has other chains of narration as well.

After the death of Khadījah, the Prophet ﷺ married her and Sawdah at the same time. He consummated the marriage with Sawdah and he was only with her for three years before he consummated the marriage with 'Ā'ishah.

'Amr bin al-'Āṣ ﷺ asked the Messenger of Allāh ﷺ:

أَيُّ النَّاسِ أَحَبُّ إِلَيْكَ؟ قَالَ: عَائِشَةُ، فَقَالَ: مِنَ الرِّجَالِ؟ قَالَ: أَبُوهَا.

"Which of the people is most beloved to you?" He said, " 'Ā'ishah." He said, "Who from the men?" [The Prophet] said, "Her father."[35]

This narration is authentic, even if the Rāfiḍah hate it. The Prophet ﷺ only loved that which is good and wholesome.

The Messenger of Allāh ﷺ said:

لَوْ كُنْتُ مُتَّخِذًا مِنْ هَذِهِ الأُمَّةِ خَلِيلاً لاَتَّخَذْتُهُ، وَلَكِنْ خُلَّةُ الإِسْلاَمِ أَفْضَلُ.

If I were to take a *khalīl* from this nation, then I would have taken him (Abū Bakr), but the brotherhood of Islām is better.[36]

Thus, he loved the best man from this *ummah* and the best woman from this *ummah*. Whoever hates the beloved of the Messenger of

---

[34] Collected by al-Qāḍī Abū Ya'lā in *Aṣ-Ṣaḥīḥ*.

[35] *Ṣaḥīḥ al-Bukhārī* 3662; *Ṣaḥīḥ Muslim* 2384

[36] *Ṣaḥīḥ al-Bukhārī* 6738

Allāh ﷺ, then it is more befitting that he is hated by Allāh and His Messenger.

Abū Hishām said:

كَانَ النَّاسُ يَتَحَرَّوْنَ بِهَدَايَاهُمْ يَوْمَ عَائِشَةَ قَالَتْ عَائِشَةُ فَاجْتَمَعَ صَوَاحِبِي إِلَى أُمِّ سَلَمَةَ، فَقُلْنَ يَا أُمَّ سَلَمَةَ، وَاللَّهِ إِنَّ النَّاسَ يَتَحَرَّوْنَ بِهَدَايَاهُمْ يَوْمَ عَائِشَةَ، وَإِنَّا نُرِيدُ الْخَيْرَ كَمَا تُرِيدُهُ عَائِشَةُ، فَمُرِي رَسُولَ اللَّهِ صلى الله عليه وسلم أَنْ يَأْمُرَ النَّاسَ أَنْ يُهْدُوا إِلَيْهِ حَيْثُ مَا كَانَ أَوْ حَيْثُ مَا دَارَ، قَالَتْ فَذَكَرَتْ ذَلِكَ أُمُّ سَلَمَةَ لِلنَّبِيِّ صلى الله عليه وسلم قَالَتْ فَأَعْرَضَ عَنِّي، فَلَمَّا عَادَ إِلَيَّ ذَكَرْتُ لَهُ ذَاكَ فَأَعْرَضَ عَنِّي، فَلَمَّا كَانَ فِي الثَّالِثَةِ ذَكَرْتُ لَهُ فَقَالَ: يَا أُمَّ سَلَمَةَ لاَ تُؤْذِينِي فِي عَائِشَةَ، فَإِنَّهُ وَاللَّهِ مَا نَزَلَ عَلَيَّ الْوَحْىُ وَأَنَا فِي لِحَافِ امْرَأَةٍ مِنْكُنَّ غَيْرِهَا.

The people used to send presents to the Prophet ﷺ on the day of ʻĀ'ishah's turn. ʻĀ'ishah said, "My companions (the other wives of the Prophet) gathered in the house of Umm Salamah and said, 'O Umm Salamah! By Allāh, the people choose to send presents on the day of ʻĀ'ishah's turn, and we, too, love the good as ʻĀ'ishah does. You should tell Allāh's Messenger ﷺ to tell the people to send their presents to him wherever he may be, or wherever his turn may be.' Umm Salamah said that to the Prophet and he turned away from her, and when the Prophet ﷺ returned to her, she repeated the same, and the Prophet again turned away, and when she told him the same for the third time, the Prophet said, 'O Umm Salamah! Don't trouble me concerning ʻĀ'ishah, for by Allāh, the divine inspiration never came to me while I was under the blanket of any woman amongst you except her.' "[37]

The Messenger of Allāh ﷺ said:

فَضْلُ عَائِشَةَ عَلَى النِّسَاءِ كَفَضْلِ الثَّرِيدِ عَلَى سَائِرِ الطَّعَامِ.

The superiority of ʻĀ'ishah to other women is like the superiority of

[37] *Ṣaḥīḥ al-Bukhārī* 3775

***tharīd*[38] to other meals.[39]**

'Ā'ishah ﷺ said:

قَالَ رَسُولُ اللَّهِ صلى الله عليه وسلم "يَا عَائِشَ هَذَا جِبْرِيلُ يُقْرِئُكِ السَّلاَمَ". قُلْتُ وَعَلَيْهِ السَّلاَمُ وَرَحْمَةُ اللَّهِ. قَالَتْ وَهْوَ يَرَى مَا لاَ نَرَى.

The Messenger of Allāh ﷺ said, "O 'Ā'ishah, this is Jibrīl; he conveys the *salām* to you." I said, "Upon him be peace and the mercy of Allāh." He (the Messenger of Allāh) sees what we do not see.[40]

Allāh the Exalted cleared 'Ā'ishah from the slander against her. 'Ā'ishah said about the slander:

فَاضْطَجَعْتُ عَلَى فِرَاشِي، وَأَنَا حِينَئِذٍ أَعْلَمُ أَنِّي بَرِيئَةٌ وَأَنَّ اللَّهَ يُبَرِّئُنِي، وَلَكِنْ وَاللَّهِ مَا كُنْتُ أَظُنُّ أَنَّ اللَّهَ يُنْزِلُ فِي شَأْنِي وَحْيًا يُتْلَى، وَلَشَأْنِي فِي نَفْسِي كَانَ أَحْقَرَ مِنْ أَنْ يَتَكَلَّمَ اللَّهُ فِيَّ بِأَمْرٍ يُتْلَى، وَأَنْزَلَ اللَّهُ عَزَّ وَجَلَّ {إِنَّ الَّذِينَ جَاءُوا بِالإِفْكِ} الْعَشْرَ الآيَاتِ كُلَّهَا.

I went to my bed knowing at that time that I was innocent and that Allāh would reveal my innocence, but by Allāh, I never thought that Allāh would reveal in my favor a revelation which would be recited, for I considered myself too unimportant to be talked about by Allāh in the divine revelation that was to be recited. So Allāh revealed the 10 verses (of Sūrah an-Nūr): "Those who brought a false charge..." (24:11-20)[41]

'Ā'ishah said that the Messenger of Allāh ﷺ said:

إِنِّي لأَعْلَمُ إِذَا كُنْتِ عَنِّي رَاضِيَةً وَإِذَا كُنْتِ عَلَيَّ غَضْبَى. قَالَتْ: وَكَيْفَ

[38] **Translator's note:** Ibn al-Qayyim said, "*Tharīd* is composed of meat and bread. Meat is the best of those foods that are eaten with bread, and bread is the best of foodstuffs. If they are combined, there can be nothing better than that." (*Zād al-Ma'ād* 4/271).

[39] *Ṣaḥīḥ al-Bukhārī* 5428

[40] *Ṣaḥīḥ al-Bukhārī* 6201

[41] *Ṣaḥīḥ al-Bukhārī* 7545

يَا رَسُولَ اللَّهِ ؟ قَالَ: إِذَا كُنْتِ عَنِّي رَاضِيَةً، قُلْتِ: لَا وَرَبِّ مُحَمَّدٍ وَإِذَا كُنْتِ عَلَيَّ غَضْبَى، قُلْتِ: لَا وَرَبِّ إِبْرَاهِيمَ. قُلْتُ: أَجَلْ وَاللَّهِ، مَا أَهْجُرُ إِلَّا اسْمَكَ.

"Surely, I know when you are pleased with me or angry with me." I said, "How do you know that?" He said, "When you are pleased with me, you say, 'No, by the Lord of Muḥammad,' but when you are angry with me, then you say, 'No, by the Lord of Ibrāhīm.'" Thereupon I said, "Yes, (you are right), but by Allāh, I only boycott your name."[42]

Her Knowledge:

Abū Mūsā said:

مَا أَشْكَلَ عَلَيْنَا أَصْحَابَ رَسُولِ اللَّهِ صلى الله عليه وسلم حَدِيثٌ قَطُّ فَسَأَلْنَا عَائِشَةَ إِلاَّ وَجَدْنَا عِنْدَهَا مِنْهُ عِلْمًا.

There was never a *ḥadīth* that was problematic upon us—the Companions of the Messenger of Allāh ﷺ—except that when we asked 'Ā'ishah, we found that she had some knowledge concerning it.[43]

Masrūq said, "I saw the scholars from the major Companions of the Messenger of Allāh ﷺ asking her about the obligatory matters of the religion."[44]

'Aṭā' bin Abī Rabāḥ said, "'Ā'ishah was from the most knowledgeable people and generally had the best viewpoints."

Her Knowledge of Medicine:

'Urwah bin az-Zubayr, 'Ā'ishah's nephew, said to 'Ā'ishah, "O my aunt, I am not surprised by your knowledge of Islamic jurisprudence, because you are the wife of the Messenger of Allāh and the

[42] *Ṣaḥīḥ al-Bukhārī* 5228

[43] *Jāmi' at-Tirmidhī* 4257

[44] Collected by al-Ḥākim (11/4).

daughter of Abū Bakr. I am not surprised by your knowledge of poetry, because you are the daughter of Abū Bakr and he was from the most knowledgeable people in that field. But I am surprised that you know medicine!" ['Urwah said]: "She tapped me on my shoulder and said, 'The Messenger of Allāh ﷺ became sick during the end of his life and the delegation of Arabs would visit from every direction, and I would hear the doctors treating the sick and I memorized it.' "[45]

Her Generosity:

'Urwah bin az-Zubayr said, "Mu'āwiyah once sent 100,000 *dirham* to 'Ā'ishah. By Allāh, before the evening came, she had given it all away to the poor. When evening came, she said to her slave-girl, "Bring me food to break my fast with." The slave-girl brought her bread and oil and said, "O Mother of the Believers, were you not able to buy us meat with one *dirham*?" 'Ā'ishah ﵂ said, "Do not scold me; if you had reminded me, I would have done so."[46]

Her Death:

Ibn Abī Mulaykah narrated that Ibn 'Abbās asked permission to visit 'Ā'ishah before her death, and at that time, she was in a state of agony. She said, "I am afraid that he will praise me too much." And then it was said to her, "He is the cousin of the Messenger of Allāh ﷺ and one of the prominent Muslims." Then she said, "Allow him to enter." (When he entered) he said, "How are you?" She replied, "I am good if I fear Allāh." Ibn 'Abbās said, "Allāh willing, (you are good). You are the wife of the Messenger of Allāh, and he did not marry any virgin except you, and proof of your innocence was revealed from the heavens." Later on, Ibn az-Zubayr entered after him and 'Ā'ishah said to him, "Ibn 'Abbās came to me and praised me greatly, but I wish that I was a thing forgotten and out of sight."[47]

'Ā'ishah ﵂ died in Madīnah on the 17th of Ramaḍān in 58 AH, during the reign of Mu'āwiyah. She was 63 years old. She was

[45] *Siyar A'lām an-Nubalā'* by Imām adh-Dhahabī (182).

[46] *Siyar A'lām an-Nubalā'* by Imām adh-Dhahabī.

[47] *Ṣaḥīḥ al-Bukhārī* 4753

buried in al-Baqī' at night.[48] Abū Hurayrah prayed the funeral prayer over her.

Ḥafṣah bint 'Umar bin al-Khaṭṭāb

Ḥafṣah, the daughter of the leader of the believers Abū Ḥafṣ 'Umar bin al-Khaṭṭāb; the Prophet ﷺ married her after she completed her mourning period for Khunays bin Ḥudhāfah as-Sahmī, who was from those who migrated to Abyssinia and then to Madīnah. The Prophet ﷺ married her three years after the migration to Madīnah.

'Ā'ishah said, "She was the one among the wives of the Messenger of Allāh ﷺ who used to compete with me."

It has been narrated that Ḥafṣah was born five years before the Messenger of Allāh became a prophet. Based upon this, she was around 20 years old when he married her.

She narrated a number of *aḥādīth*. Her brother Ibn 'Umar narrated from her, and she was six years older than him.

Her father offered her to Abū Bakr for marriage, but Abū Bakr did not say anything to him in response. 'Umar then offered her to 'Uthmān for marriage, and 'Uthmān responded by saying, "I will not marry right now." This upset 'Umar, so he complained about this to the Prophet ﷺ. The Prophet ﷺ said to him, "Ḥafṣah will marry someone better than 'Uthmān, and 'Uthmān will marry someone better than Ḥafṣah." Then the Prophet ﷺ proposed to Ḥafṣah, and 'Umar married him to her. And the Prophet ﷺ married 'Uthmān to his daughter Umm Kulthūm, after her sister ('Uthmān's previous wife, Ruqayyah) had died.

'Umar bin al-Khaṭṭāb said, "I met 'Uthmān bin 'Affān and offered Ḥafṣah to him in marriage. I said, 'If you wish, I will marry Ḥafṣah bint 'Umar to you.' He said, 'I will think about it.' Several nights passed, then he said, 'I think that I do not want to get married at

---

[48] *Siyar A'lām an-Nubalā'* by Imām adh-Dhahabī.

this time.' Then I met Abū Bakr and I said, 'If you wish, I will marry Ḥafṣah bint 'Umar to you.' Abū Bakr kept quiet and did not give me any response. I was more upset about him than about 'Uthmān. Several nights passed, then the Messenger of Allāh ﷺ proposed to her and I married her to him. Then Abū Bakr met me and said, 'Perhaps you felt upset when you offered Ḥafṣah in marriage to me and I did not reply?' I said, 'Yes.' He said, 'Nothing prevented me from responding to your offer but the fact that I knew that the Messenger of Allāh ﷺ had mentioned her, and I did not want to disclose the secret of the Messenger of Allāh ﷺ. If he had decided not to marry her, I would have accepted your offer.' "[49]

It has been narrated that the Prophet ﷺ divorced her, but Jibrīl came to him with a command from Allāh. He said:

رَاجِعْ حَفْصَةَ فَإِنَّهَا صَوَّامَةٌ قَوَّامَةٌ وَهِيَ زَوْجَتُكَ فِي الْجَنَّةِ.

Go back to Ḥafṣah, for she fasts a lot and prays a lot at night, and she will be your wife in Paradise.[50]

Ḥafṣah and 'Ā'ishah were the two who cooperated against the Prophet ﷺ. Allāh sent down the verse concerning them:

﴿ إِن تَتُوبَا إِلَى اللَّهِ فَقَدْ صَغَتْ قُلُوبُكُمَا ۖ وَإِن تَظَاهَرَا عَلَيْهِ فَإِنَّ اللَّهَ هُوَ مَوْلَاهُ وَجِبْرِيلُ وَصَالِحُ الْمُؤْمِنِينَ ۖ وَالْمَلَائِكَةُ بَعْدَ ذَٰلِكَ ظَهِيرٌ ﴾

If you two turn in repentance to Allāh, (it will be better for you); your hearts are indeed so inclined (to oppose what the Prophet likes), but if you help one another against him (Muḥammad), then verily, Allāh is his protector, and Jibrīl, and the righteous among the believers; and furthermore, the angels are his helpers.

[Sūrah at-Taḥrīm 66:4]

[49] *Ṣaḥīḥ al-Bukhārī* 4005

[50] *Sunan Abī Dāwūd* 2283

And it has been narrated that when news reached 'Umar that the Prophet ﷺ had divorced Ḥafṣah, he threw dirt on his head and said, "Allāh will not be pleased with 'Umar and his daughter after this." So the next day, Jibrīl came to the Prophet ﷺ and said, "Verily, Allāh commands you to take Ḥafṣah back as a mercy to 'Umar." Thus, he took her back.[51]

Her Death:

Ḥafṣah bint 'Umar ﷺ died in 41 AH, and some say it was 45 AH, in Madīnah. Abū Hurayrah was from those who carried her casket. Marwān, who was the governor of Madīnah at that time, led the Janāzah prayer for her.

TRANSLATOR'S ADDENDUM

Ḥafṣah bint 'Umar ﷺ was entrusted with securing the *muṣ'ḥaf* after it had been written down in one collective book.

Imām al-Bukhārī narrated in his *Ṣaḥīḥ* that Zayd bin Thābit ﷺ said, "Abū Bakr aṣ-Ṣiddīq sent for me when the people of al-Yamāmah had been killed (the Companions who fought against the false prophet Musaylimah). (I went to him) and found 'Umar bin al-Khaṭṭāb sitting with him. Abū Bakr then said (to me), ''Umar has come to me and said, "Casualties were heavy among those who knew the Qur'ān by heart on the day of the Battle of al-Yamāmah, and I am afraid that more heavy casualties may take place among them on other battlefields, whereby a large part of the Qur'ān may be lost. Therefore, I suggest that you (Abū Bakr) order that the Qur'ān be collected." I said to 'Umar, "How can you do something that the Messenger of Allāh ﷺ did not do?" 'Umar said, "By Allāh, this is something good." 'Umar kept on urging me to accept his proposal until Allāh opened my heart to it and I began to realize the good in the idea which 'Umar had realized.'

"Then Abū Bakr said (to me), 'You are a wise young man and we do not have any suspicion about you, and you used to write the

[51] *The Prophet and His Ten Companions* by al-Ḥāfiẓ 'Abdul-Ghānī al-Maqdisī.

divine inspiration for the Messenger of Allāh ﷺ. So search for (the fragmentary scripts of) the Qur'ān and compile it in one book.' By Allāh, if they had ordered me to move one of the mountains, it would not have been heavier for me than this order to compile the Qur'ān. Then I said (to Abū Bakr), 'How can you do something that the Messenger of Allāh ﷺ did not do?' Abū Bakr replied, 'By Allāh, it is a good thing.' Abū Bakr kept on urging me to accept his idea until Allāh opened my heart to that which He had opened the hearts of Abū Bakr and 'Umar.

"So I started looking for the Qur'ān and collecting it from palm stalks and thin white stones (what it was written on), and also from the men who knew it by heart, until I found the last verse of Sūrah at-Tawbah with Abū Khuzaymah al-Anṣārī, and I did not find it with anybody other than him. The verse: 'Verily, there has come unto you a Messenger (Muḥammad) from amongst yourselves. It grieves him that you should receive any injury or difficulty...' (Sūrah at-Tawbah 9:128). Then the complete manuscript of the Qur'ān remained with Abū Bakr until he died, then with 'Umar until the end of his life, and then with Ḥafṣah bint 'Umar."[52]

Anas bin Mālik said that Ḥudhayfah bin al-Yamān came to 'Uthmān at the time when the people of Shām (Syria) and the people of Iraq were waging war to conquer Armenia and Azerbaijan. Ḥudhayfah was alarmed by their (the people of Shām and Iraq) differences in the recitation of the Qur'ān, so he said to 'Uthmān, "O Leader of the Believers! Save this nation before they dispute about the Book (Qur'ān) as the Jews and the Christians did before." So 'Uthmān sent a message to Ḥafṣah saying, "Send us the manuscript of the Qur'ān so that we may make copies of the *muṣ'ḥaf* and we will return the manuscript to you." Ḥafṣah sent it to 'Uthmān. Then 'Uthmān ordered Zayd bin Thābit, 'Abdullāh bin az-Zubayr, Sa'īd bin al-'Āṣ, and 'Abdur-Raḥmān bin Ḥārith bin Hishām to copy out the manuscripts. 'Uthmān said to the three men who were from Quraysh, "In case you disagree with Zayd bin Thābit on any point in the Qur'ān, then write it in the dialect of the Quraysh,

[52] *Ṣaḥīḥ al-Bukhārī* 4986

for the Qur'ān was revealed in their tongue." They did so, and when they had written many copies, 'Uthmān returned the original manuscripts to Ḥafṣah.[53]

ZAYNAB BINT KHUZAYMAH

Zaynab bint Khuzaymah bin al-Ḥārith bin 'Abdillāh al-Hilāliyyah.

She was called "the Mother of the Poor," even before Islām, due to her feeding the poor a great deal.

Her previous husband, 'Abdullāh bin Jaḥsh, was killed during the Battle of Uḥud[54]. The Prophet ﷺ married her in 3 AH during the month of Ramaḍān. She only remained with him for a short time—two or three months—before she died ﵂.

Her sister is the Mother of the Believers Maymūnah bint al-Ḥārith; they share the same mother.

She was buried in al-Baqī'. Other than Khadījah, she is the only wife of the Prophet ﷺ to die during his lifetime. And she benefited from this because the Prophet ﷺ led the Janāzah prayer over her and supplicated for her.

TRANSLATOR'S ADDENDUM

Her Siblings:

Zaynab's sisters who were the daughters of Hind bint 'Awf were: Maymūnah bint al-Ḥārith (the wife of the Prophet ﷺ), Asmā' bint 'Umays (the wife of Abū Bakr aṣ-Ṣiddīq), Salmā bint 'Umays (the wife of Ḥamzah bin 'Abdul-Muṭṭalib, the uncle of the Prophet ﷺ), Umm Faḍl Lubābah bint al-Ḥārith the Elder (the wife of 'Abbās bin 'Abdul-Muṭṭalib, the uncle of the Prophet ﷺ), and Lubābah bint al-Ḥārith the Younger (the mother of Khālid bin al-Walīd).

---

[53] *Ṣaḥīḥ al-Bukhārī* 4988

[54] *Siyar A'lām an-Nubalā'* by Imām adh-Dhahabī.

UMM SALAMAH HIND BINT ABĪ UMAYYAH BIN AL-MUGHĪRAH

She is the cousin of Khālid bin al-Walīd and the cousin of Abū Jahl bin Hishām.

She was from those who migrated to Abyssinia. Before she married the Prophet ﷺ, she was married to his brother through suckling, Abū Salamah 'Abdullāh bin 'Abdil-Asad al-Makhzūmī ﷺ. He was a righteous man. The Prophet ﷺ married her in 4 AH. She was from the most beautiful women and from the noblest of them regarding lineage.

She was from the last of the Mothers of the Believers to die. She lived to see Ḥusayn[55] killed as a martyr. That caused her tremendous sadness and grief. She only lived a short time after this before Allāh took her soul.

She had children who were also Companions: 'Umar, Salamah, and Zaynab.

She narrated a number of *aḥādīth*, and many of the great Tābi'īn narrated *aḥādīth* from her, such as Sa'īd bin al-Musayyib, 'Aṭā' bin Abī Rabāḥ, al-Aswad bin Yazīd, and many others.

She lived to be around 90 years old. Her father—nicknamed "provider for the traveler"—was an elite member of the tribe of Quraysh named Ḥudhayfah.

Her Knowledge:

She was considered one of the scholars from the Companions.

It was narrated from 'Abdul-Mālik bin Ḥārith bin Hishām, from his father, that:

أَنَّ النَّبِيَّ صلى الله عليه وسلم - تَزَوَّجَ أُمَّ سَلَمَةَ فِي شَوَّالٍ وَجَمَعَهَا إِلَيْهِ

[55] **Translator's note:** Ḥusayn was the grandson of the Prophet ﷺ, the son of 'Alī and Fāṭimah.

فِي شَوَّالٍ.

The Prophet ﷺ married Umm Salamah in Shawwāl and consummated the marriage with her in Shawwāl.[56]

He continued until he said, "And she died in 59 AH in the month of Dhul-Qa'dah."

Umm Salamah said to Abū Salamah, "It has reached me that if a woman's husband dies and he is from the inhabitants of Paradise and she does not remarry, Allāh will reunite them in Paradise. So come here; make a covenant that you will not marry after me, and I will make a covenant that I will not marry after you." He said, "Will you obey me?" She replied, "Yes." He said, "When I die, remarry. O Allāh, provide Umm Salamah with a man better than me after me, a man who will neither disgrace her nor harm her." When Abū Salamah died, she said, "Who is better than Abū Salamah?!" After her mourning period, it was not long before the Prophet ﷺ proposed to her through her nephew.

It was narrated from Umm Salamah that when her *'iddah* period had ended, Abū Bakr sent word to her proposing marriage to her, but she did not marry him. Then the Messenger of Allāh sent 'Umar bin al-Khaṭṭāb with a proposal of marriage. She said:

أَخْبِرْ رَسُولَ اللَّهِ صلى الله عليه وسلم أَنِّي امْرَأَةٌ غَيْرَى وَأَنِّي امْرَأَةٌ مُصْبِيَةٌ وَلَيْسَ أَحَدٌ مِنْ أَوْلِيَائِي شَاهِدٌ.

Tell the Messenger of Allāh that I am a jealous woman and that I have sons, and none of my guardians are present.

He went to the Messenger of Allāh and told him that. He said, "Go back to her and tell her:

أَمَّا قَوْلُكِ إِنِّي امْرَأَةٌ غَيْرَى فَسَأَدْعُو اللَّهَ لَكِ فَيُذْهِبُ غَيْرَتَكِ وَأَمَّا قَوْلُكِ إِنِّي امْرَأَةٌ مُصْبِيَةٌ فَسَتُكْفَيْنَ صِبْيَانَكِ وَأَمَّا قَوْلُكِ أَنْ لَيْسَ أَحَدٌ مِنْ أَوْلِيَائِي

[56] *Sunan Ibn Mājah*

شَاهِدٌ فَلَيْسَ أَحَدٌ مِنْ أَوْلِيَائِكِ شَاهِدٌ وَلاَ غَائِبٌ يَكْرَهُ ذَلِكَ.

"As for your saying that you are a jealous woman: I will pray to Allāh for you to take away your jealousy. As for your saying that you have sons: your sons will be taken care of. And as for your saying that none of your guardians are present: none of your guardians, present or absent, would object to that."

She said to her son 'Umar:

يَا عُمَرُ، قُمْ فَزَوِّجْ رَسُولَ اللَّهِ.

O 'Umar, stand and marry me to the Messenger of Allāh.

Thus, her son 'Umar[57] performed the marriage[58].

The Messenger of Allāh ﷺ said, "I will not shortchange you regarding what I have given my other wives."

Ḥabīb bin Thābit narrated, "When the Prophet ﷺ proposed to Umm Salamah, she said, 'I am an old woman, I have orphans, and I am jealous.' The Prophet ﷺ responded, 'As for your jealousy: Allāh will remove that. As for your age: I am older than you. And as for your orphans: Allāh and His Messenger will take care of them.' "[59]

From the virtue of the Mothers of the Believers is that Allāh sent down verses concerning them. Allāh the Exalted said:

﴿ إِنَّمَا يُرِيدُ اللَّهُ لِيُذْهِبَ عَنكُمُ الرِّجْسَ أَهْلَ الْبَيْتِ
وَيُطَهِّرَكُمْ تَطْهِيرًا ﴿٣٣﴾ وَاذْكُرْنَ مَا يُتْلَىٰ فِي بُيُوتِكُنَّ مِنْ
آيَاتِ اللَّهِ وَالْحِكْمَةِ ۚ إِنَّ اللَّهَ كَانَ لَطِيفًا خَبِيرًا ﴿٣٤﴾ ﴾

[57] **Translator's note:** Her son 'Umar is mentioned in the following famous narration: 'Umar bin Abī Salamah said, "I was a boy under the care of the Messenger of Allāh ﷺ, and as my hand used to wander around in the dish, he ﷺ said to me once, 'Mention the name of Allāh, eat with your right hand, and eat from what is in front of you.' " (Collected by al-Bukhārī and Muslim).

[58] *Sunan an-Nasā'ī* 3254

[59] *Aṭ-Ṭabaqāt* 8/90

Allāh intends only to remove from you the impurity [of sin], O members of the family, and to purify you with a thorough purification. And remember that which is recited in your houses of the verses of Allāh and wisdom. Verily, Allāh is Ever Most Courteous, Well-Acquainted with all things.

[Sūrah al-Aḥzāb 33:33-34]

These verses were an honor for the wives of the Prophet ﷺ. Ibn 'Abbās said, "The verse 'Allāh intends only to remove from you the impurity [of sin], O members of the family' was sent down concerning the wives of the Prophet ﷺ." 'Ikrimah said, "This verse was only sent down about the wives of the Prophet ﷺ."

Umm Salamah died in 61 AH ﵂.

The collection of *aḥādīth* narrated by her reached 378 in number.

TRANSLATOR'S ADDENDUM

Her mother was 'Ātikah bint 'Āmir bin Rabī'ah.

Umm Salamah ﵂ sat with the angel Jibrīl and the Messenger of Allāh ﵇.

Abū 'Uthmān said:

أُنْبِئْتُ أَنَّ جِبْرِيلَ، أَتَى النَّبِيَّ صلى الله عليه وسلم وَعِنْدَهُ أُمُّ سَلَمَةَ فَجَعَلَ يَتَحَدَّثُ فَقَالَ النَّبِيُّ صلى الله عليه وسلم لأُمِّ سَلَمَةَ "مَنْ هَذَا". أَوْ كَمَا قَالَ قَالَتْ هَذَا دِحْيَةُ. فَلَمَّا قَامَ قَالَتْ وَاللَّهِ مَا حَسِبْتُهُ إِلاَّ إِيَّاهُ حَتَّى سَمِعْتُ خُطْبَةَ النَّبِيِّ صلى الله عليه وسلم يُخْبِرُ خَبَرَ جِبْرِيلَ.

I was informed that Jibrīl came to the Prophet ﷺ while Umm Salamah was with him. Jibrīl started talking (to the Prophet). Then the Prophet ﷺ asked Umm Salamah, "Who is this?" She replied, "He is Diḥyah[60] (al-Kalbī)." When Jibrīl had left, Umm Salamah

[60] **Translator's note:** The angel Jibrīl used to take the form of the Companion Diḥyah

said, "By Allāh, I did not take him for anyone other than him (Diḥyah) until I heard the sermon of the Prophet ﷺ wherein he informed about the news of Jibrīl."[61]

ZAYNAB BINT JAḤSH BIN RIYĀB

She is the cousin of the Messenger of Allāh ﷺ. Her mother is Umaymah bint 'Abdul-Muṭṭalib bin Hāshim. She is the sister of Ḥamnah bint Jaḥsh, and Abū Aḥmad bin Jaḥsh, who were from those who partook in the first migration.

She was previously married to Zayd, the freed slave of the Prophet ﷺ. She is the one intended in the statement of Allāh the Exalted:

﴿ وَإِذْ تَقُولُ لِلَّذِي أَنْعَمَ اللَّهُ عَلَيْهِ وَأَنْعَمْتَ عَلَيْهِ أَمْسِكْ عَلَيْكَ زَوْجَكَ وَاتَّقِ اللَّهَ وَتُخْفِي فِي نَفْسِكَ مَا اللَّهُ مُبْدِيهِ وَتَخْشَى النَّاسَ وَاللَّهُ أَحَقُّ أَن تَخْشَاهُ ۖ فَلَمَّا قَضَىٰ زَيْدٌ مِّنْهَا وَطَرًا زَوَّجْنَاكَهَا لِكَيْ لَا يَكُونَ عَلَى الْمُؤْمِنِينَ حَرَجٌ فِي أَزْوَاجِ أَدْعِيَائِهِمْ إِذَا قَضَوْا مِنْهُنَّ وَطَرًا ﴾

And [remember, O Muḥammad], when you said to the one on whom Allāh bestowed favor and you bestowed favor, "Keep your wife and fear Allāh," while you concealed within yourself that which Allāh is to disclose. And you feared the people, while Allāh has more right that you fear Him. So when Zayd had no longer any need for her, We married her to you in order that there not be upon the believers any discomfort concerning the wives of their adopted sons when they no longer have need of them.

[Sūrah al-Aḥzāb 33:37]

al-Kalbī.

[61] *Ṣaḥīḥ al-Bukhārī* 4980

Thus, Allāh married her to His Prophet with this text from the Qur'ān, without a guardian or a witness.

Anas narrated:

كَانَتْ زَيْنَبُ تَفْخَرُ عَلَى أَزْوَاجِ النَّبِيِّ صلى الله عليه وسلم تَقُولُ زَوَّجَكُنَّ أَهَالِيكُنَّ، وَزَوَّجَنِي اللَّهُ تَعَالَى مِنْ فَوْقِ سَبْعِ سَمَوَاتٍ.

Zaynab used to boast to the wives of the Prophet ﷺ and say, "You were given in marriage by your families, while I was married (to the Prophet) by Allāh from over seven heavens."[62]

She was from the noblest women regarding her religiosity, piety, and knowledge. Her narrations are collected in the six books of *ḥadīth*. Some of those who narrated from her were: her nephew Muḥammad bin 'Abdillāh bin Jaḥsh, the Mother of the Believers Umm Ḥabībah, and Zaynab bint Abī Salamah.

She died in 21 AH during 'Umar's caliphate, and he led the Janāzah prayer over her.

Barazah bint Rāfi' narrated: " 'Umar sent a pension to Zaynab. She said, 'O Allāh, forgive 'Umar; others are more in need of this than I am.' It was said to her, 'All of this is for you.' She replied, '*SubḥānAllāh*! Cover this with a garment.' She took the money and divided it among the poor and orphans she knew and then said, 'Give me what is left.' They found 85 *dirham* remaining. She raised her hands to the heavens and said, 'O Allāh, don't allow me to reach 'Umar's pension next year.' "[63]

Ibn 'Umar said, "When Zaynab bint Jaḥsh died, 'Umar ordered a caller to announce that no one should carry her except a relative. Bint 'Umays said, 'O Leader of the Believers, shall I not show you how the Ethiopians shroud their women?' So she placed her in a coffin and shrouded the coffin with a garment. He said, 'How great is this covering!' He then ordered a caller to announce, 'Come out

---

[62] *Ṣaḥīḥ al-Bukhārī* 7420

[63] *Aṭ-Ṭabaqāt* 8/109

to pray over your Mother.' "[64]

The Generosity of Zaynab bint Jaḥsh:

'Ā'ishah ﷺ said:

أَنَّ بَعْضَ، أَزْوَاجِ النَّبِيِّ صلى الله عليه وسلم قُلْنَ لِلنَّبِيِّ صلى الله عليه وسلم أَيُّنَا أَسْرَعُ بِكَ لُحُوقًا قَالَ "أَطْوَلُكُنَّ يَدًا". فَأَخَذُوا قَصَبَةً يَذْرَعُونَهَا، فَكَانَتْ سَوْدَةُ أَطْوَلَهُنَّ يَدًا، فَعَلِمْنَا بَعْدُ أَنَّمَا كَانَتْ طُولَ يَدِهَا الصَّدَقَةُ، وَكَانَتْ أَسْرَعَنَا لُحُوقًا بِهِ وَكَانَتْ تُحِبُّ الصَّدَقَةَ.

Some of the wives of the Prophet ﷺ asked him, "Who amongst us will be the first to follow you (die after you)?" He said, "Whoever has the longest hand." So they started measuring their hands with a stick, and Sawdah had the longest hand. (When Zaynab bint Jaḥsh died first), we came to know that the long hand was a symbol of practicing charity, so she was the first to follow the Prophet ﷺ and she used to love to practice charity.[65]

The Piety of Zaynab bint Jaḥsh:

'Ā'ishah ﷺ said:

كَانَتْ زَيْنَبُ بِنْتُ جَحْشٍ تُسَامِينِي فِي الْمَنْزِلَةِ عِنْدَ رَسُولِ اللَّهِ صَلَّى اللَّهُ عَلَيْهِ وَسَلَّمَ؛ مَا رَأَيْتُ امْرَأَةً خَيْرًا فِي الدِّينِ مِنْ زَيْنَبَ، أَتْقَى لِلَّهِ، وَأَصْدَقَ حَدِيثًا، وَأَوْصَلَ لِلرَّحِمِ، وَأَعْظَمَ صَدَقَةً.

Zaynab bint Jaḥsh used to compete with me in the home with the Messenger of Allāh ﷺ. I have never seen a woman who was better in religious commitment than Zaynab, more fearing of Allāh, more truthful in speech, more keen to uphold family ties, more generous in giving charity.[66]

'Umar would give each of the Mothers of the Believers 12,000

[64] The chain of narration is authentic. Collected in *Aṭ-Ṭabaqāt* (8/111).

[65] *Ṣaḥīḥ al-Bukhārī* 1420

[66] *Ṣaḥīḥ al-Bukhārī* 2581; *Ṣaḥīḥ Muslim* 2442

dirham a year, except Juwayriyah and Ṣafiyyah—they received half of that.[67]

The Story of the Honey:

'Ā'ishah said, "The Prophet used to stay with Zaynab bint Jaḥsh and drink honey at her house. Ḥafṣah and I agreed that if the Prophet came to either of us, we would say, 'I detect the smell of *maghāfir* (a nasty-smelling gum) on you; have you eaten *maghāfir*?'" He came to one of them and she said that to him. He said, "No; rather, I drank honey at the house of Zaynab bint Jaḥsh, but I will never do it again." Then the following was revealed:

﴿ يَا أَيُّهَا النَّبِيُّ لِمَ تُحَرِّمُ مَا أَحَلَّ اللَّهُ لَكَ ۖ تَبْتَغِي مَرْضَاتَ أَزْوَاجِكَ ۚ وَاللَّهُ غَفُورٌ رَّحِيمٌ ﴾

O Prophet, why do you prohibit [yourself from] what Allāh has made lawful for you, seeking the approval of your wives? And Allāh is Forgiving and Merciful.

[Sūrah at-Taḥrīm 66:1]

The statement of Allāh:

﴿ إِن تَتُوبَا إِلَى اللَّهِ ﴾

If you two turn in repentance to Allāh, (it will be better for you).

[Sūrah at-Taḥrīm 66:4]

This statement is directed to 'Ā'ishah and Ḥafṣah.

The statement of Allāh:

﴿ وَإِذْ أَسَرَّ النَّبِيُّ إِلَىٰ بَعْضِ أَزْوَاجِهِ حَدِيثًا ﴾

And (remember) when the Prophet disclosed a

[67] Narrated by az-Zuhrī.

matter in confidence to one of his wives.

[Sūrah at-Taḥrīm 66:3]

This refers to the statement of the Prophet ﷺ, "No; rather, I drank honey."

The Honor Given to Zaynab bint Jaḥsh:

'Ā'ishah said, "May Allāh have mercy upon Zaynab; she achieved unattainable honor in this world. Verily, Allāh conducted her marriage and mentioned it in the Qur'ān. And the Messenger of Allāh informed us that the first of his wives to reunite with him would be the one with the longest hand; thus, he gave her glad tidings that she would reunite with him first. And she is his wife in Paradise."[68]

Her sister Ḥamnah bint Jaḥsh spoke during the slander of 'Ā'ishah, and she began to speak to Zaynab about it. But Allāh protected Zaynab from any involvement in this matter due to her piety[69]. Her sister Ḥamnah was married to Muṣ'ab bin 'Umayr, and he was killed in the Battle of Uḥud. Then she married Ṭalḥah bin 'Ubaydillāh and gave birth to Muḥammad and 'Imrān.

Zaynab's sister Ḥamnah is likewise mentioned in the *ḥadīth* concerning *istiḥāḍah* (non-menstrual vaginal bleeding).

Ḥamnah said, "I had a case of blood flow that was severe and excessive. So I went to the Prophet to inform him and ask him about it. I found him in the house of my sister, Zaynab bint Jaḥsh. I said, 'O Messenger of Allāh, I bleed a great deal all the time. What do you think—should I stop praying and fasting?' He said, 'I suggest you use a piece of cotton, for it will absorb the blood.' I said, 'It is more than that.' He said, 'That is a kick from the Shayṭān, so count your menses as six or seven days—which is something between you and Allāh—then wash yourself, and when you see that you have become pure and you are certain of it, then pray for 24 or 23 days,

---

[68] Narrated by 'Amrah; collected in *Genealogies of the Nobles* by Aḥmad bin Yaḥyā al-Balādhurī, *ḥadīth* 379.

[69] Collected in *Asad al-Ghābah* (7/69).

and fast.' "[70]

Their mother, Umaymah bint 'Abdul-Muṭṭalib, was the aunt of the Messenger of Allāh ﷺ.

Her Death:

Narrated from al-Qāsim: "Zaynab bint Jaḥsh said when death approached her, 'I have prepared my shroud; if 'Umar sends a shroud for me, give one of them away in charity. And if you are able to give my possessions away in charity, then do so.' "[71]

The Prophet ﷺ married Zaynab in the month of Dhul-Qa'dah in 5 AH. She was 25 years old at the time. She was a righteous, pious woman dedicated to fasting and standing the night in prayer. She was known as "the Mother of the Poor" due to her love of giving charity.

Anas bin Mālik narrated:

لَمَّا انْقَضَتْ عِدَّةُ زَيْنَبَ قَالَ رَسُولُ اللَّهِ صلى الله عليه وسلم لِزَيْدٍ "اذْكُرْهَا عَلَىَّ". قَالَ زَيْدٌ فَانْطَلَقْتُ فَقُلْتُ يَا زَيْنَبُ أَبْشِرِي أَرْسَلَنِي إِلَيْكِ رَسُولُ اللَّهِ صلى الله عليه وسلم يَذْكُرُكِ . فَقَالَتْ مَا أَنَا بِصَانِعَةٍ شَيْئًا حَتَّى أَسْتَأْمِرَ رَبِّي فَقَامَتْ إِلَى مَسْجِدِهَا وَنَزَلَ الْقُرْآنُ وَجَاءَ رَسُولُ اللَّهِ صلى الله عليه وسلم فَدَخَلَ بِغَيْرِ أَمْرٍ.

When the *'iddah* of Zaynab was over, the Messenger of Allāh said to Zayd, "Propose marriage to her on my behalf." Zayd went and said, "O Zaynab, rejoice, for the Messenger of Allāh has sent me to you to propose marriage on his behalf." She said, "I will not do anything until I consult my Lord." She went to her prayer place and Qur'ān was revealed, then the Messenger of Allāh came and entered upon her without any formalities.[72]

[70] This *ḥadīth* was narrated by Aḥmad and Abū Dāwūd, and narrated by and classed as *ṣaḥīḥ* by at-Tirmidhī; al-Bukhārī classed it as *ḥasan*.

[71] *Aṭ-Ṭabaqāt* 8/109

[72] *Sunan an-Nasā'ī* 3251

The Messenger of Allāh ﷺ said to 'Umar, "Verily, Zaynab bint Jaḥsh is imploring." It was said, "O Messenger of Allāh, what is 'imploring?'" He said, "Humble and beseeching.

﴿ إِنَّ إِبْرَاهِيمَ لَحَلِيمٌ أَوَّاهٌ مُّنِيبٌ ﴾

"'Verily, Ibrāhīm was, without doubt, forbearing, used to invoke Allāh with humility, frequently.'"

[Sūrah Hūd 11:75]

Zaynab narrated 11 *aḥādīth.*

'Uthmān bin 'Abdillāh said, "They sold Zaynab bint Jaḥsh's home to Walīd for 50,000 *dirham* when the *masjid* was torn down."

JUWAYRIYAH BINT AL-ḤĀRITH

Juwayriyah bint al-Ḥārith bin Abī Ḍirār al-Muṣṭaliqiyyah.

Juwayriyah bint al-Ḥārith was previously known as Barrah before her name was changed when she became Muslim.

'Ā'ishah ﵂ said about Juwayriyah ﵂:

وَكَانَتْ امْرَأَةً حُلْوَةً مُلَّاحَةً، لَا يَرَاهَا أَحَدٌ إِلَّا أَخَذَتْ بِنَفْسِهِ.

She was a sweet woman with extreme beauty; no one would look at her except that he would be captivated.[73]

Juwayriyah belonged to the tribe of Banul-Muṣṭaliq, and her father al-Ḥārith was the leader of the tribe, a noble man obeyed by his people. At that time, the tribe of Banul-Muṣṭaliq was pagan. Al-Ḥārith intended to attack the Muslims in 5 AH; this became known as the Battle of al-Muraysī'. During this battle, the Muslims were victorious, only losing one man. The tribe of Banul-Muṣṭaliq was defeated and their women were taken captive.

---

[73] *Sīrah Ibn Hishām*

Abū Qilābah narrates[74]: "After their defeat, the leader of the tribe, Juwayriyah's father—al-Ḥārith—came to the Prophet ﷺ and said, 'The like of my daughter is not taken captive; I am too honorable for this to happen.' The Prophet ﷺ said to her father, 'What do you think if I were to choose her?' Her father went to her and said, 'This man has chosen you, so do not disgrace us' (meaning, do not marry him). She said to him, 'Verily, I choose Allāh and His Messenger.' Her father replied, 'By Allāh, you have disgraced us.' "

'Ā'ishah ﵂ said, "Juwayriyah bint al-Ḥārith al-Muṣṭaliqiyyah fell to the lot of Thābit bin Qays bin Shammās. She entered into an agreement to purchase her freedom. She was a very beautiful woman, most attractive to the eye. She then came to the Messenger of Allāh ﷺ asking him for the purchase of her freedom. When she was standing at the door, I looked at her with disapproval. I realized that the Messenger of Allāh ﷺ would look at her in the same way that I had looked.

"She said, 'Messenger of Allāh, I am Juwayriyah bint al-Ḥārith, and something has happened to me which is not hidden from you. I have fallen to the lot of Thābit bin Qays bin Shammās, and I have entered into an agreement to purchase my freedom. I have come to you to seek assistance for the purchase of my freedom.'

"The Messenger of Allāh ﷺ said, 'Are you inclined to that which is better?' She asked, 'What is that, Messenger of Allāh?' He replied, 'I shall pay the price of your freedom on your behalf, and I shall marry you.'

"She said, 'I shall do this.' The people then heard that the Messenger of Allāh ﷺ had married Juwayriyah. They released the captives in their possession and set them free, saying, 'They are the in-laws of the Messenger of Allāh ﷺ.' We did not see any woman greater than Juwayriyah who brought blessings to her people. One hundred families of Banul-Muṣṭaliq were set free on account of her."[75]

---

[74] *Aṭ-Ṭabaqāt* 8/118

[75] *Sunan Abī Dāwūd* 3931; declared *ḥasan* by al-Albānī.

Shu'bah said, "The Messenger of Allāh ﷺ freed Juwayriyah, sought her hand in marriage, and made her dowry the freedom of all the captives of her people from the tribe of Banul-Muṣṭaliq."[76]

Before Juwayriyah bint al-Ḥārith ؓ entered Islām, she was married to her cousin Musāfi' bin Ṣafwān bin Abish-Shufr.

Juwayriyah ؓ said, "The Messenger of Allāh ﷺ married me when I was 20 years old."

Her Father, al-Ḥārith bin Abī Ḍirār:

Ibn Is'ḥāq said in *Al-Maghāzī*: "The father of Juwayriyah ؓ came to Madīnah after she had married the Prophet ﷺ, attempting to purchase her release from him by giving him camels in exchange for her. Before reaching Madīnah, he looked at two of his camels and desired to keep those two for himself, so he hid them in the valley of 'Aqīq. When he reached the Prophet ﷺ he said, 'O Muḥammad, this is payment to release my daughter.' The Prophet ﷺ responded, 'Where are the other two camels you hid in 'Aqīq?' Al-Ḥārith said, 'I bear witness that nothing has the right to be worshiped except Allāh and you are the Messenger of Allāh! I swear by Allāh, no one saw me hide them except Allāh.' Thus, he entered Islām along with his two sons and a large contingent from among his people."[77]

The Mother of the Believers Juwayriyah bint al-Ḥārith ؓ died in 50 AH; this would put her age at 70 at the time of her death. Others say she died in 56 AH; this would put her age at 75 at the time of her death. She narrated seven *aḥādīth* and she was known as a devout worshiper; she prayed, fasted, and remembered Allāh much.

Some of Her Well-Known Narrations:

Juwayriyah ؓ narrated:

---

[76] Collected by Ibn Sa'd (8/118); all the men in the chain of narration are sound.

[77] *Prophetic Sīrah* by Ibn Hishām; narrated from Muḥammad bin Shu'ayb from 'Abdullāh bin Ziyād.

أَنَّ النَّبِيَّ صلى الله عليه وسلم دَخَلَ عَلَيْهَا يَوْمَ الْجُمُعَةِ وَهْىَ صَائِمَةٌ فَقَالَ "أَصُمْتِ أَمْسِ". قَالَتْ لاَ. قَالَ "تُرِيدِينَ أَنْ تَصُومِي غَدًا". قَالَتْ لاَ. قَالَ "فَأَفْطِرِي."

The Prophet ﷺ visited her (Juwayriyah) on a Friday and she was fasting. He asked her, "Did you fast yesterday?" She said, "No." He said, "Do you intend to fast tomorrow?" She said, "No." He said, "Then break your fast."[78]

Juwayriyah bint al-Ḥārith narrated:

أَنَّ النَّبِيَّ صلى الله عليه وسلم مَرَّ عَلَيْهَا وَهِيَ فِي الْمَسْجِدِ تَدْعُو ثُمَّ مَرَّ بِهَا قَرِيبًا مِنْ نِصْفِ النَّهَارِ فَقَالَ لَهَا "مَا زِلْتِ عَلَى حَالِكِ". قَالَتْ نَعَمْ. قَالَ لَقَدْ قُلْتُ بَعْدَكِ أَرْبَعَ كَلِمَاتٍ ثَلاَثَ مَرَّاتٍ لَوْ وُزِنَتْ بِمَا قُلْتِ مُنْذُ الْيَوْمِ لَوَزَنَتْهُنَّ: سُبْحَانَ اللَّهِ وَبِحَمْدِهِ، عَدَدَ خَلْقِهِ، وَرِضَا نَفْسِهِ، وَزِنَةَ عَرْشِهِ، وَمِدَادَ كَلِمَاتِ.

The Prophet ﷺ left her house one morning while she was in her prayer place, supplicating. He came back close to midday, and she was still sitting there. He said, "Are you still as you were when I left you?" She said, "Yes." The Prophet ﷺ said, "I said four sentences three times; if weighed against what you said today, they would outweigh it. 'Allāh is free from all imperfection as much as the number of His creation, as much as pleases Him, as much as the weight of His Throne, and as much as the ink of His words.' "[79]

Umm Ḥabībah Ramlah bint Abī Sufyān

She is the Mother of the Believers Umm Ḥabībah Ramlah bint Abī Sufyān Ṣakhr bin Ḥarb bin Umayyah bin 'Abd Shams bin 'Abd Manāf bin Quṣayy. Her parents were Abū Sufyān bin Ḥarb and

[78] *Ṣaḥīḥ al-Bukhārī* 1986

[79] *Sunan an-Nasā'ī* 1352

Ṣafiyyah bint Abil-'Āṣ. Her brother from her father was Mu'āwiyah bin Abī Sufyān ؓ.

She narrated 65 *aḥādīth*. Of all his wives, she was the closest to the Prophet in lineage, her dowry was the largest, and she was the farthest away from him when he married her.

Umm Ḥabībah was previously married to 'Ubaydullāh bin Jaḥsh; they were from the foremost to enter Islām. Umm Ḥabībah gave birth to her daughter Ḥabībah in Makkah; thereafter, they migrated to Abyssinia.

Umm Ḥabībah's first husband, 'Ubaydullāh bin Jaḥsh, was the brother of Zaynab bint Jaḥsh, the wife of the Prophet ﷺ. 'Uthmān bin 'Affān ؓ was Umm Ḥabībah's maternal first cousin.[80]

Ibn Sa'd said, "Umm Ḥabībah's husband who migrated with her to Abyssinia—'Ubaydullāh bin Jaḥsh bin Riyāb al-Asadī—apostated and converted to Christianity."

Ismā'īl bin 'Amr bin Sa'īd said, "Umm Ḥabībah said, 'I saw my husband 'Ubaydullāh in a dream in the worst distorted image, so I was frightened. I said to myself, "By Allāh, his condition has changed!" When the morning came, he said, "I looked into the religions and I did not see a better religion than Christianity. I used to practice Christianity and then I entered the religion of Muḥammad, but now I have reverted." So I informed him about my dream and he did not give it any concern. Then I heard someone say, "O Mother of the Believers," so I interpreted that the Messenger of Allāh ﷺ would marry me.' " This *ḥadīth* is weak.

Umm Ḥabībah ؓ narrated:

أَنَّهَا كَانَتْ تَحْتَ عُبَيْدِ اللَّهِ بْنِ جَحْشٍ فَمَاتَ بِأَرْضِ الْحَبَشَةِ فَزَوَّجَهَا النَّجَاشِيُّ النَّبِيَّ صلى الله عليه وسلم وَأَمْهَرَهَا عنه أَرْبَعَةَ آلاَفٍ وَبَعَثَ بِهَا إِلَى رَسُولِ اللَّهِ صلى الله عليه وسلم مَعَ شُرَحْبِيلَ ابْنِ حَسَنَةَ.

[80] Translator's addition.

She was previously married to 'Ubaydullāh bin Jaḥsh who died in Abyssinia, so an-Najāshī (the king of Abyssinia) married her to the Prophet ﷺ, giving her on his behalf a dower of 4,000 (*dirham*). He sent her to the Messenger of Allāh ﷺ with Shuraḥbīl bin Ḥasanah.[81]

Umm Ḥabībah ؓ was living in Abyssinia when her husband, 'Ubaydullāh bin Jaḥsh, died. After her mourning period, the Prophet ﷺ asked for her hand in marriage. An-Najāshī paid a dowry of 4,000 *dirham* on behalf of the Prophet ﷺ and he prepared a wedding feast for them. The marriage took place six years after the migration, and 'Uthmān bin 'Affān was her guardian. When she left Abyssinia and arrived in Madīnah, she was around 30 years old.

Those who narrated *aḥādīth* from her: her brother, the Caliph Mu'āwiyah bin Abī Sufyān; her nephew, 'Abdullāh bin 'Utbah bin Abī Sufyān; and 'Urwah bin az-Zubayr, Abū Ṣāliḥ as-Samān, Ṣafiyyah bint Shaybah, Zaynab bint Abī Salamah, and others.

She went to Damascus to visit her brother, and it is said that her grave is located in Damascus, but this has no validity. Rather, her grave is in Madīnah, and it is Umm Salamah Asmā' bint Yazīd al-Anṣārī who is buried at Bāb aṣ-Ṣaghīr in Damascus, Syria.

Umm Ḥabībah was a revered noblewoman, especially in the kingdom of her brother Mu'āwiyah. And due to the position he held with her, he is known as the Uncle of the Believers.

Abū 'Ubayd said, "Umm Ḥabībah died in 44 AH; al-Ghulābī said she died in 42 AH."

'Ā'ishah ؓ said:

دَعَتْنِي أُمُّ حَبِيبَةَ عِنْدَ مَوْتِهَا، فَقَالَتْ: قَدْ كَانَ يَكُونُ بَيْنَنَا مَا يَكُونُ بَيْنَ الضَّرَائِرِ، فَغَفَرَ اللَّهُ لِي وَلَكِ مَا كَانَ مِنْ ذَلِكَ، فَقُلْتُ: غَفَرَ اللَّهُ لَكِ ذَلِكَ كُلَّهُ وَحَلَّلَكِ مِنْ ذَلِكَ، فَقَالَتْ: سَرَرْتِنِي سَرَّكِ اللَّهُ، وَأَرْسَلَتْ إِلَى أُمِّ سَلَمَةَ، فَقَالَتْ لَهَا مِثْلَ ذَلِكَ.

[81] *Sunan Abī Dāwūd* 2107; declared authentic by al-Albānī.

Umm Ḥabībah called me when she was dying and said, "There has been between us what usually happens between co-wives; may Allāh forgive me and you for whatever happened of that." I said, "May Allāh forgive you and pardon you for all of that, and absolve you of that." She said, "You have made me happy; may Allāh make you happy." And she sent for Umm Salamah and said something similar to her.[82]

TRANSLATOR'S ADDENDUM

Umm Ḥabībah accepted Islām before her father, Abū Sufyān, and before her brother Mu'āwiyah. Abū Sufyān was initially the leader of the Quraysh tribe and a staunch opponent against the Prophet ﷺ, leading armies against the Muslims in the Battle of Uḥud and the Battle of the Trench. After the conquest of Makkah, he entered Islām and became one of the noble Companions رضي الله عنهم.

ṢAFIYYAH BINT ḤUYAYY

She is Ṣafiyyah bint Ḥuyayy bin Akhṭab bin Sa'yah from the tribe of Levi from the prophet of Allāh Isrā'īl (Ya'qūb) bin Is'ḥāq bin Ibrāhīm عليهم السلام. Then she is also from the offspring of the messenger of Allāh Hārūn عليه السلام.

Before she entered Islām, she had a truthful dream foretelling her marriage to the Messenger of Allāh ﷺ. Ṣafiyyah رضي الله عنها said, "I saw myself in a dream with that man who alleges to be a Messenger, and there was an angel covering us with his wings." Her people rebuffed her dream and spoke harsh words to her concerning it.[83]

She was previously married to Salām bin Abil-Ḥuqayq; then she was married to Kinānah Abul-Ḥuqayq. Both of them were from the Jewish poets. Kinānah was killed during the Battle of Khaybar, so Ṣafiyyah became a captive under the care of Diḥyah al-Kalbī.

[82] Narrated by Ibn Sa'd in *Aṭ-Ṭabaqāt* (8/79) and by Ibn 'Asākir in his *Tārīkh* (69/152) from 'Awf bin al-Ḥārith.

[83] Collected by Ibn Sa'd (8/122), narrated by Ḥumayd bin Hilāl.

Word was sent to the Prophet ﷺ that it was not befitting for her to be under the care of anyone except him. Consequently, he took her from Diḥyah and gave him seven captives in return. Then, after her menses, the Prophet ﷺ married her and freed her for her dowry.

Anas said, "Captives were gathered at Khaybar. Diḥyah came out and said, 'O Messenger of Allāh, give me a slave-girl from the captives.' He said, 'Go and take a slave-girl.' He took Ṣafiyyah bint Ḥuyayy. A man then came to the Prophet ﷺ and said, 'You gave Ṣafiyyah bint Ḥuyayy, chief lady of Qurayẓah and an-Naḍīr, to Diḥyah al-Kalbī? No one is worthy of her except you.' He said, 'Call him along with her.' When the Prophet ﷺ looked at her, he said to him, 'Take another slave-girl from the captives.' The Prophet ﷺ then set her free and married her."[84]

Ḥammād said, " 'Abdul-'Azīz said to Thābit, 'O Abū Muḥammad! Did you ask Anas what her dowry was?' He said, 'Her dowry was her freedom.' "[85]

Āminah bint Qays al-Ghifāriyyah said, "I was one of the women who beautified Ṣafiyyah for marriage on her wedding day, and I heard her say that she was 16 years old the day she married."

Anas bin Mālik said, "*Ḥays* (an Arabian dish) was prepared on a small leather mat. Then the Prophet ﷺ said to me, 'I invite the people around you.' So that was the marriage banquet of the Prophet ﷺ and Ṣafiyyah. Then we proceeded towards Madīnah, and I saw the Prophet making for her a kind of cushion with his cloak behind him (on his camel). He then sat beside his camel and put his knee for Ṣafiyyah to put her foot on, in order to ride (on the camel)."[86]

Ṣafiyyah bint Ḥuyayy entered Islām and perfected her Islām. The Prophet ﷺ returned from Khaybar with Ṣafiyyah and lodged her in a home. The women from the Anṣār heard of her beauty, so they

[84] *Sunan Abī Dāwūd* 2998; declared *ṣaḥīḥ* by al-Albānī.

[85] *Sunan Ibn Mājah* 2033

[86] *Ṣaḥīḥ al-Bukhārī* 4211

came to look at her. ʿĀ'ishah entered wearing a face veil, recognized Ṣafiyyah, and left. When she left, the Prophet ﷺ said, "What did you see?" She replied, "I saw a Jew." He said, "Don't say that, for surely, she has entered Islām."[87]

Ṣafiyyah bint Ḥuyayy was a woman of nobility, intellect, noble lineage, beauty, and religion ﵂.

She was a woman of forbearance and dignity. Abū ʿUmar bin ʿAbdil-Barr said, "It has been narrated to us that the slave-girl of Ṣafiyyah came to ʿUmar bin al-Khaṭṭāb and said, 'Verily, Ṣafiyyah loves Saturday, and she keeps communication with the Jews.' So ʿUmar mentioned this to her and she replied, 'As for Saturday: I have not loved it since Allāh exchanged it for me with Friday. And as for the Jews: I have relatives among them, so I keep the ties of kinship with them.' Then she said to her slave-girl, 'What made you say those things?' The slave-girl replied, 'The Shayṭān.' Ṣafiyyah said to her, 'Go; you are free.' "[88]

Ṣafiyyah bint Ḥuyayy said:

دَخَلَ عَلَيَّ رَسُولُ اللَّهِ صلى الله عليه وسلم وَقَدْ بَلَغَنِي عَنْ حَفْصَةَ وَعَائِشَةَ كَلاَمٌ فَذَكَرْتُ ذَلِكَ لَهُ فَقَالَ أَلاَ قُلْتِ فَكَيْفَ تَكُونَانِ خَيْرًا مِنِّي وَزَوْجِي مُحَمَّدٌ وَأَبِي هَارُونُ وَعَمِّي مُوسَى.

The Messenger of Allāh ﷺ entered upon me and some words had reached me from Ḥafṣah and ʿĀ'ishah. So I mentioned it to him. So he said, "Why did you not say, 'And how are you better than me, while my husband is Muḥammad and my father is Hārūn, and my uncle is Mūsā[89]?' "[90]

---

[87] Collected by Ibn Sa'd (8/126).

[88] *Al-Isti'āb* by Ibn 'Abdil-Barr (13/65).

[89] *Jāmi' at-Tirmidhī*

[90] **Translator's note:** This *ḥadīth* has weakness in the chain due to Hāshim bin Sa'īd al-Kūfī, but it is strengthened due to the authentic narration of Anas collected by at-Tirmidhī (3892): "It reached Ṣafiyyah that Ḥafṣah said, 'The daughter of a Jew,' so she wept. Then the Prophet ﷺ entered upon her while she was crying, so he said, 'What

The narrator said, "That which had reached her was that they had said, 'We are more honored to the Messenger of Allāh ﷺ than her,' and that they said, 'We are the wives of the Prophet ﷺ and his cousins.' "

Ṣafiyyah ﵂ was a woman of compassion. When the Prophet ﷺ was suffering from the illness which he eventually died from, Ṣafiyyah bint Ḥuyayy said:

وَاللَّهِ يَا نَبِيَّ اللَّهِ لَوَدِدْتُ أَنَّ الَّذِي بِكَ بِي.

I swear by Allāh, O Prophet of Allāh, I would love that the illness which is afflicting you was inflicting me instead.

Upon hearing this, his wives winked their eyes. The Prophet ﷺ said to them, "Go rinse your mouths." They replied, "From what?" He said:

مِنْ تَغَامُزِكُنَّ بِهَا، وَاللَّهِ إِنَّهَا لَصَادِقَةٌ.

From your winking to mock her, for I swear by Allāh, she is surely truthful.[91]

Ṣafiyyah ﵂ was known for her generosity. She entered upon Fāṭimah, removed the gold earrings she had, and gave them to Fāṭimah as a gift.[92] She was also known to give gold to her co-wives.

Some historians say that she died in 36 AH, but it is more correct that she died in 50 AH ﵂. Her grave is in al-Baqī'.

Ṣafiyyah ﵂ was a woman of knowledge, and she narrated 10 *aḥādīth*. 'Alī bin al-Ḥusayn, Is'ḥāq bin 'Abdillāh bin al-Ḥārith, and others narrated *aḥādīth* from her.

---

makes you cry?' She said, 'Ḥafṣah said to me that I am the daughter of a Jew.' So the Prophet ﷺ said, 'And you are the daughter of a prophet, and your uncle is a prophet, and you are married to a prophet, so what is she boasting to you about?' Then he said, 'Fear Allāh, O Ḥafṣah.' "

[91] Collected by Ibn Sa'd (8/122), narrated by Zayd bin Aslam.

[92] Collected by Ibn Sa'd (8/127).

TRANSLATOR'S ADDENDUM

One of the well-known *aḥādīth* mentioning the Mother of the Believers Ṣafiyyah ﵂ is the *ḥadīth* of *i'tikāf*. 'Alī bin Ḥusayn said, "Ṣafiyyah, the wife of the Prophet ﷺ, told me that she went to the Messenger of Allāh ﷺ to visit him in the *masjid* while he was in *i'tikāf* in the last 10 days of Ramaḍān. She talked with him for a while, then she got up to return home. The Prophet ﷺ accompanied her. When they reached the gate of the *masjid*, opposite the door of Umm Salamah, two Anṣārī men were passing by and they greeted the Messenger of Allāh. He told them:

عَلَى رِسْلِكُمَا إِنَّمَا هِيَ صَفِيَّةُ بِنْتُ حُيَيٍّ.

" 'Do not run away! She is (my wife), Ṣafiyyah bint Ḥuyayy.'

"Both of them said, '*SubḥānAllāh*, O Allāh's Messenger!' The Prophet said:

إِنَّ الشَّيْطَانَ يَبْلُغُ مِنَ الإِنْسَانِ مَبْلَغَ الدَّمِ، وَإِنِّي خَشِيتُ أَنْ يَقْذِفَ فِي قُلُوبِكُمَا شَيْئًا.

" 'Verily, Shayṭān reaches everywhere in the human body that blood reaches. I was afraid lest the Shayṭān might insert an evil thought in your minds.' "[93]

Shaykh Muḥammad 'Aqīl said, "Ṣafiyyah ﵂ said that the Prophet used to be the most hated man to her. This was because they killed her people during the Battle of Khaybar. The Muslims killed her husband, her father, and her uncle. They justly killed them in battle and they did not do so oppressively. She said, 'He was the most hated man to me, but he continued to treat me in a loving manner until he was the most beloved man to me.' Look at the tremendous effects of good manners. The Muslims killed her husband, her father, her uncle, and her brother in the Battle of Khaybar. But she forgot about all of that due to the kind treatment of the Messenger of Allāh ﷺ. This is proof of his great character. How else could a

[93] *Ṣaḥīḥ al-Bukhārī* 2035

woman love a man who was responsible for the death of her family except if he had great morals and character?! This also shows the wisdom behind him marrying from the different tribes, and even from among the Jews. By way of this, his great biography and character was spread among the people. Allāh said about him:

﴿ فَبِمَا رَحْمَةٍ مِّنَ اللَّهِ لِنتَ لَهُمْ ۖ وَلَوْ كُنتَ فَظًّا غَلِيظَ الْقَلْبِ لَانفَضُّوا مِنْ حَوْلِكَ ﴾

"'And by the mercy of Allāh, you dealt with them gently. And had you been severe and harsh-hearted, they would have broken away from about you.'

[Surah Āli 'Imrān 3:159]

"The affair of our Mother Ṣafiyyah is amazing. Animosity towards him had been placed in her heart since childhood. When the Prophet ﷺ entered Madīnah, her father and uncle went to visit him. When they returned home, their faces had changed due to the envy they harbored towards him. One of them said to the other, 'Is it him?' Meaning, is he the prophet we have been informed about in our Books? He responded in the affirmative. [The other] said, 'What is your position towards him?' He said, 'Hatred and animosity towards him until death.' Thus, the Jews knew the Prophet ﷺ completely, but they harbored envy towards him because prophecy had been removed from the Children of Israel."[94]

Ṣafiyyah رضي الله عنها had other dreams foretelling her marriage to the Prophet ﷺ while she was still a Jew. Ibn 'Umar رضي الله عنه said, "The Messenger of Allāh ﷺ saw some green discoloration in the eyes of Ṣafiyyah. He said, 'O Ṣafiyyah, what is this green discoloration?' She said, 'My head was in the lap of Ibn Abil-Ḥuqayq, and while I was sleeping, I saw in a dream that the moon fell into my lap. I told him about the dream and he slapped me and said, 'Do you want the king of Yathrib[95] (Madīnah)?' "

[94] *The Prophet and His Ten Companions*

[95] Collected by Ibn Ḥibbān (11/607); declared authentic by al-Albānī.

MAYMŪNAH BINT AL-ḤĀRITH AL-HILĀLIYYAH

Maymūnah bint al-Ḥārith bin Ḥazan bin Bujayr bin al-Huzm bin Rūbayyah bin 'Abdillāh bin Hilāl bin 'Āmir bin Ṣa'ṣa'ah al-Hilāliyyah.

Her Name:

Abū Hurayrah said, "Maymūnah's name was Barrah and then the Prophet ﷺ renamed her Maymūnah."[96]

Her Lineage:

She is the Mother of the Believers, the wife of the Prophet ﷺ, the sister of Umm al-Faḍl (the wife of al-'Abbās); she is the maternal aunt of Khālid bin al-Walīd and the maternal aunt of Ibn 'Abbās.

Previous Marriage:

She was previously married to Mas'ūd bin 'Amr ath-Thaqafī shortly before Islām, then he divorced her. Then she was married to Abū Ruhm bin 'Abdil-'Uzzā until he died.

Her Marriage to the Prophet ﷺ:

Then the Prophet ﷺ married her after he completed 'Umrah in 7 AH in the month of Dhul-Qa'dah. The marriage was in Sarif, about 10 miles from Makkah in a village known as Abū 'Urwah. She was the last woman he married from the Mothers of the Believers.

Ibn 'Abbās ﷺ said[97], "The Prophet ﷺ married Maymūnah during the 'Umrah al-Qaḍā'."[98]

Abū Rāfi', the freed slave of the Messenger of Allāh ﷺ, said:

أَنَّ رَسُولَ اللَّهِ صَلَّى اللَّهُ عَلَيْهِ وَسَلَّمَ تَزَوَّجَ مَيْمُونَةَ حَلاَلاً وَبَنَى بِهَا حَلاَلاً

---

[96] *Al-Adab al-Mufrad* 832

[97] *Ṣaḥīḥ al-Bukhārī* 4259

[98] 'Umrah performed in lieu of the 'Umrah which the Prophet ﷺ could not perform because the pagans prevented him.

وَكُنْتُ الرَّسُولَ بَيْنَهُمَا.

The Messenger of Allāh ﷺ married Maymūnah while he was not in a state of *iḥrām,* and he consummated the marriage with her while he was not in a state of *iḥrām*, and I was the messenger between the two of them.[99]

Her Piety:

'Ā'ishah ﵂ said, "Maymūnah was the most pious of us and the most diligent in keeping the ties of kinship."[100]

A relative of Maymūnah ﵂ visited her, and she could smell the scent of alcohol on him. She said to him:

لَئِنْ لَمْ تَخْرُجْ إِلَى الْمُسْلِمِينَ، فَيَجْلِدُوكَ، لَا تَدْخُلْ عَلَيَّ أَبَدًا.

If you don't go out to the Muslims so they can lash you, don't ever visit me again.[101]

The freed slave of Ibn 'Abbās, Kurayb, said, "Ibn 'Abbās sent me to drive Maymūnah's camel. I continued to hear her say, 'Nothing has the right to be worshiped except Allāh,' until she stoned the Jamarāt."[102]

Her Death:

Maymūnah ﵂ died in 51 AH. She was around 70 years old. She died in Sarif, the same location wherein she consummated her marriage with the Messenger of Allāh ﷺ.

'Aṭā' said, "We attended the funeral of Maymūnah, the wife of the Prophet, with Ibn 'Abbās in Sarif. Ibn 'Abbās said:

هَذِهِ مَيْمُونَةُ إِذَا رَفَعْتُمْ جَنَازَتَهَا فَلاَ تُزَعْزِعُوهَا وَلاَ تُزَلْزِلُوهَا.

[99] Collected by Aḥmad (26656); declared authentic by Ibn al-Qayyim.

[100] Collected by al-Ḥākim (4/32); the chain of narration is *ḥasan*.

[101] Collected by Ibn Sa'd (8/139); the chain of narration is *ḥasan*.

[102] Collected by Ibn Sa'd (8/138); the chain of narration is *ṣaḥīḥ*.

"'This is Maymūnah; when you lift up her bier, do not rock it or shake it.'"[103]

When she died, 'Ā'ishah ﵁ said, "Maymūnah is gone; she was the most pious of us and the most diligent in keeping the ties of kinship."[104]

She was from the noblest women and she narrated numerous *aḥādīth,* seven of which are collected in both al-Bukhārī and Muslim. Those who narrated from her were Ibn 'Abbās, her other nephew 'Abdullāh bin Shaddād bin al-Hād, 'Ubayd as-Sabq, 'Abdur-Raḥmān bin as-Sā'ib, her nephew Yazīd bin al-Aṣam, and others.

TRANSLATOR'S ADDENDUM

Some well-known *aḥādīth* narrated by Maymūnah ﵁:

Maymūnah ﵁ said:

كَانَ فِرَاشِي حِيَالَ مُصَلَّى النَّبِيِّ صلى الله عليه وسلم فَرُبَّمَا وَقَعَ ثَوْبُهُ عَلَيَّ وَأَنَا عَلَى فِرَاشِي.

My bed was beside the praying place of the Prophet ﷺ, and sometimes his garment fell on me while I used to lie in my bed.[105]

Ibn 'Abbās ﵁ said:

أَخْبَرَتْنِي خَالَتِي، مَيْمُونَةُ أَنَّهَا كَانَتْ تَغْتَسِلُ وَرَسُولُ اللَّهِ صلى الله عليه وسلم مِنْ إِنَاءٍ وَاحِدٍ.

My maternal aunt Maymūnah told me that she and the Messenger of Allāh ﷺ used to perform *ghusl* from one vessel.[106]

---

[103] *Sunan an-Nasā'ī* 3196

[104] *Al-Iṣābah* by Ibn Ḥajar

[105] Collected by al-Bukhārī under the heading "Prayer facing a bed occupied by a menstruating woman" (*Ṣaḥīḥ al-Bukhārī* 517).

[106] *Sunan an-Nasā'ī* 238

Maymūnah ﵂ said:

كَانَ رَسُولُ اللَّهِ صلى الله عليه وسلم يَضَعُ رَأْسَهُ فِي حِجْرِ إِحْدَانَا فَيَتْلُو الْقُرْآنَ وَهِيَ حَائِضٌ.

The Messenger of Allāh ﷺ used to lay his head in the lap of one of us and recite Qur'ān while she was menstruating.[107]

Maymūnah ﵂ said:

أَنَّ رَسُولَ اللَّهِ صلى الله عليه وسلم كَانَ يُصَلِّي عَلَى الْخُمْرَةِ.

The Messenger of Allāh ﷺ used to pray on a mat.[108]

Maymūnah ﵂ said:

أَنَّ النَّبِيَّ صلى الله عليه وسلم كَانَ إِذَا سَجَدَ جَافَى بَيْنَ يَدَيْهِ حَتَّى لَوْ أَنَّ بَهْمَةً أَرَادَتْ أَنْ تَمُرَّ تَحْتَ يَدَيْهِ مَرَّتْ.

When the Prophet ﷺ prostrated, he kept his arms so far away from his sides that if a lamb had wanted to pass under his arms, it could have done so.[109]

Maymūnah ﵂ said:

أَنَّ النَّاسَ، شَكُّوا فِي صِيَامِ النَّبِيِّ صلى الله عليه وسلم يَوْمَ عَرَفَةَ، فَأَرْسَلَتْ إِلَيْهِ بِحِلاَبٍ وَهْوَ وَاقِفٌ فِي الْمَوْقِفِ، فَشَرِبَ مِنْهُ، وَالنَّاسُ يَنْظُرُونَ.

The people doubted whether the Prophet ﷺ was fasting on the Day of ʻArafah or not, so I sent milk while he was standing at ʻArafah; he drank it, and the people were looking at him.[110]

---

[107] *Sunan an-Nasā'ī* 385

[108] *Sunan an-Nasā'ī* 738

[109] *Sunan Abī Dāwūd* 898; declared authentic by al-Albānī.

[110] *Ṣaḥīḥ al-Bukhārī* 1989

THE MAIDSERVANTS

OF THE PROPHET

1) Māriyah

2) Rayḥānah

3) A beautiful slave woman acquired as a prisoner of war

4) A slave woman given to him by Zaynab bint Jaḥsh

Ibn al-Qayyim said, "The Prophet ﷺ had four maidservants: Māriyah, who was the mother of his son Ibrāhīm; Rayḥānah; another beautiful slave woman whom he acquired as a prisoner of war; and a slave woman who was given to him by Zaynab bint Jaḥsh."[1]

TRANSLATOR'S ADDENDUM

UMM IBRĀHĪM MĀRIYAH THE COPTIC

The Messenger of Allāh ﷺ sent Ḥāṭib bin Abī Balta'ah to invite al-Muqawqis, the king of Alexandria and Egypt, to Islām. The king spoke kind words and considered the affair, but he did not enter Islām. He sent the Prophet ﷺ a gift: Māriyah the Coptic and

[1] *Zād al-Ma'ād* 1/114

her sister Sīrīn. The Prophet gave her sister as a gift to Ḥasan bin Thābit. She gave birth to his son 'Abdur-Raḥmān bin Ḥasan.

Māriyah, who was from Egypt, gave birth to Ibrāhīm, the son of the Prophet ﷺ. Thus, he advised that the people of Egypt should be treated well. He said:

إِنَّكُمْ سَتَفْتَحُونَ مِصْرَ وَهِيَ أَرْضٌ يُسَمَّى فِيهَا الْقِيرَاطُ فَإِذَا فَتَحْتُمُوهَا فَأَحْسِنُوا إِلَى أَهْلِهَا فَإِنَّ لَهُمْ ذِمَّةً وَرَحِمًا. أَوْ قَالَ ذِمَّةً وَصِهْرًا.

You would soon conquer Egypt, and that is a land known as the land of *al-qīrāṭ*. So when you conquer it, treat its inhabitants well. This responsibility lies upon you because of blood ties or relationship of marriage (with them).[2]

As for the blood ties, this is because the mother of the Arabs—Hājar, the mother of Ismā'īl ﷺ—was from Egypt. As for the relationship of marriage, this is because Māriyah the Coptic, the mother of Ibrāhīm—the son of the Prophet ﷺ—was from Egypt.

Ibn Sa'd said, "The Messenger of Allāh ﷺ housed Māriyah and her sister Sīrīn with Umm Sulaym bint Milḥān, and the Messenger of Allāh ﷺ entered upon them and invited them to Islām. Both of them became Muslim. He took Māriyah as a concubine and moved her to some property of his in al-'Awālī. And she became a good Muslim."[3]

Her Death:

Ibn 'Abdil-Barr said, "Māriyah ﷺ died during the caliphate of 'Umar bin al-Khaṭṭāb, in the month of Muḥarram in 16 AH. 'Umar gathered the people himself to attend her funeral, and he led the funeral prayer for her. She was buried in al-Baqī'."[4]

---

[2] *Ṣaḥīḥ Muslim* 2543

[3] *Aṭ-Ṭabaqāt al-Kubrā* 1/134-135

[4] *Al-Isti'āb* 4/ 1912

Rayḥānah bint Zayd

Rayḥānah was a member of the Jewish tribe Banū Naḍīr. She was taken captive during the war but refused any religion other than Judaism. One day, while the Messenger of Allāh ﷺ was with his Companions, he heard behind him the footsteps of Tha'labah bin Sa'yah. The Messenger of Allāh ﷺ said, "This is Tha'labah bin Sa'yah coming to bring the glad news that Rayḥānah has embraced Islām." Tha'labah gave the good news and the Prophet ﷺ offered to free her, marry her, and give her the *ḥijāb* to adorn. Rayḥānah responded by saying, "No, O Messenger of Allāh; rather, leaving me as a maidservant is easier for me and easier for you."

Rayḥānah bint Zayd ﵂ died 16 years before the Messenger of Allāh ﷺ.

THE CARETAKERS

OF THE PROPHET

1) Āminah bint Wahb

2) Thuwaybah

3) Ḥalīmah as-Sa'diyyah

4) Ash-Shaymā'

5) Umm Ayman Barakah

The Prophet ﷺ had five caretakers: his mother Āminah bint Wahb, Thuwaybah, Ḥalīmah as-Sa'diyyah, ash-Shaymā' (who was the daughter of Ḥalīmah as-Sa'diyyah, and thus the sister of the Prophet ﷺ through breastfeeding), and the noble Companion Umm Ayman Barakah from Ethiopia ﷺ.[1]

THUWAYBAH

Thuwaybah was the slave-girl of Abū Lahab, the uncle of the Prophet ﷺ. She breastfed the Prophet ﷺ, along with his uncle Ḥamzah and Abū Salamah 'Abdullāh bin 'Abdil-Asad al-Makhzūmī

[1] Ibn al-Qayyim mentioned this is *Zād al-Ma'ād* (1/83).

رضي الله عنها.

Thuwaybah was the first to breastfeed the Prophet ﷺ. She suckled him a few days before Ḥalīmah suckled him. She suckled him from the milk of her son Masrūḥ.

Umm Ḥabībah رضي الله عنها said:

يَا رَسُولَ اللَّهِ، انْكِحْ أُخْتِي بِنْتَ أَبِي سُفْيَانَ. قَالَ: أَوَ تُحِبِّينَ ذَلِكِ؟ قُلْتُ: لَسْتُ لَكَ بِمُخْلِيَةٍ وَأَحَبُّ إِلَيَّ مَنْ شَرَكَنِي فِي خَيْرٍ أُخْتِي. قَالَ: إِنَّ ذَلِكِ لَا يَحِلُّ لِي. فَقُلْتُ: يَا رَسُولَ اللَّهِ إِنَّا لَنَتَحَدَّثُ أَنَّكَ تُرِيدُ أَنْ تَنْكِحَ دُرَّةَ بِنْتَ أَبِي سَلَمَةَ. فَقَالَ: وَاللَّهِ لَوْ لَمْ تَكُنْ رَبِيبَتِي فِي حِجْرِي مَا حَلَّتْ لِي، إِنَّهَا ابْنَةُ أَخِي مِنَ الرَّضَاعَةِ، أَرْضَعَتْنِي وَأَبَا سَلَمَةَ ثُوَيْبَةُ، فَلَا تَعْرِضْنَ عَلَيَّ بَنَاتِكُنَّ وَلَا أَخَوَاتِكُنَّ.

"O Messenger of Allāh, marry my sister, the daughter of Abū Sufyān." The Prophet ﷺ said, "Would you like that?" I replied, "Yes, for even now I am not your only wife, and I like that my sister should share the good with me." The Prophet ﷺ said, "But that is not lawful for me." I said, "We have heard that you want to marry the daughter of Abū Salamah." He said, "(You mean) the daughter of Umm Salamah?" I said, "Yes." He said, "Even if she were not my step-daughter, she would be unlawful for me to marry as she is my foster niece. Abū Salamah and I were suckled by Thuwaybah. So you should not present to me your daughters or your sisters (in marriage)."[2]

'Urwah commented on this narration: "Thuwaybah was the freed slave-girl of Abū Lahab whom he had manumitted, and then she suckled the Prophet. When Abū Lahab died, one of his relatives saw him in a dream in a very bad state and asked him, 'What have you encountered?' Abū Lahab said, 'I have not found any rest since I left you, except that I have been given water to drink in this (the space between his thumb and other fingers), and that is because of my

[2] *Ṣaḥīḥ al-Bukhārī* 5101

manumitting Thuwaybah.' "[3]

Khadījah ﷺ would honor her, and she attempted to purchase her freedom from Abū Lahab but he refused. He eventually freed her during the year of migration. The Prophet ﷺ would keep ties with her while he was in Makkah, and once he migrated to Madīnah, he used to send her gifts until he was informed of her death. She died in 7 AH. Upon hearing this, the Prophet ﷺ said, "What happened to her son Masrūḥ?" They replied, "He died before her."

Ḥalīmah as-Sa'diyyah

The next woman to suckle the Prophet ﷺ was Ḥalīmah bint Abī Dhu'ayb as-Sa'diyyah. She took him to her village and kept him there for about four years; then she returned him to his mother.

'Abdullāh bin Ja'far narrated[4] from Ḥalīmah, the (foster) mother of the Messenger of Allāh ﷺ; she said, "I went to Makkah in the company of some women, hoping to find babies to nurse. I was riding a whitish donkey of mine, which was so slow that I was blamed for delaying the group. We went during a year of drought, and we didn't have anything. By Allāh, our camel could not produce even a drop of milk. My infant son was with me and he would not sleep at night due to his crying.

"When we arrived in Makkah, each one of us was offered the Prophet as a nursing son. We all refused because we depended on the generosity of the child's father for our services, and he was an orphan. Every woman in our group took a baby to nurse except me. I said to my husband, 'I will surely return and take him.' So I went back and took him. My husband said, 'Perhaps Allāh will place good within him.'

"I swear by Allāh, as soon as I put him in my lap, he turned to my breast and drank his fill of milk. Then his [foster] brother drank

[3] *Ṣaḥīḥ al-Bukhārī* 5101

[4] Collected by Ibn Hishām (1/162), narrated from Muḥammad bin Is'ḥāq.

until his thirst was quenched. When my husband went out that night to check our camel, its udder was full of milk. So he milked the camel and we drank until our thirst was quenched. We spent the night with full stomachs, replenished. And our boys likewise slept that night. My husband said, 'By Allāh, O Ḥalīmah, I believe you have acquired a blessed soul.'

"This time when we went out with our same old camel, it was in the lead and no one was able to keep up. We reached the outskirts of where our tribe, Banū Sa'd bin Bakr, was camped, and it was a very dry land. I swear by the One who has my soul in His Hand, our sheep would go out and graze and the sheep of the other people would go out and graze. Our sheep would return with full bellies and udders full of milk, while their sheep would return hungry without any milk. They would say to their shepherds, 'Why don't you graze where Ḥalīmah's shepherd is grazing?' So they sent their sheep to graze in the same pastures as our sheep, but their sheep returned hungry with dry udders, and our sheep returned again with full bellies and udders full of milk."

The Splitting of His Chest:

Ḥalīmah said, "The Prophet ﷺ matured in a way which no other child matured. The maturity the other children reached in a month, he achieved in one day. And the maturity they reached in one year, he reached in one month. When he completed two years, we returned to Makkah, his [foster] father and I. We said to his mother, 'We have not seen a child more blessed than him, and we fear he will be harmed by the diseases of Makkah if he stays here, so allow us to take him back with us until he gets older and develops immunity from these diseases.' We pleaded with her until she agreed. We kept him for about three or four months before the incident happened.

"One day, he and his brother were playing with some animals behind the houses when his brother came to us trembling. His father and I were inside the house when he came in and said, 'Two men wearing white garments took my Qurayshī brother, laid him down, and cut open his stomach!' His father and I ran out only to find him standing, and his color had changed. When he saw us, he was on the verge of tears. We hugged him and asked him what had happened. He said, 'Two men came to me, laid me down, and cut open my abdomen and did something, and then returned me back how I was.' His father said, 'This boy has been afflicted with something; let's take him back to his mother before more signs appear.' So we returned him to his mother.

"When his mother saw us, she knew something was wrong. She asked why we returned him so soon after having been persistent in taking him. We said, 'Nothing is wrong; we have completed the suckling period for him, so I thought it better for you to take him because we are concerned about him.' She did not accept our excuse, and she insisted we tell her the real story. After we told her what had occurred and why we feared for his wellbeing, she said, 'Nay, on the contrary, Allāh will never disgrace him; my son is special. Shall I tell you about him? When I was pregnant with him, I felt as though I never carried a lighter load or a greater blessing than him. When I delivered him, I saw a great light coming out of me, like a shooting star that illuminated the palaces in Basra. When he came out, he did not come out like other children. He came out supporting his hands on the ground, raising his head to the sky. So leave him; I will take care of him.' So we left him with her."[5]

The Prophet Honoring Ḥalīmah as-Sa'diyyah:

Abū Ṭufayl said:

رَأَيْتُ النَّبِيَّ صلى الله عليه وسلم يَقْسِمُ لَحْمًا بِالْجِعِرَّانَةِ - وَأَنَا يَوْمَئِذٍ غُلاَمٌ أَحْمِلُ عَظْمَ الْجَزُورِ- إِذْ أَقْبَلَتِ امْرَأَةٌ حَتَّى دَنَتْ إِلَى النَّبِيِّ صلى الله عليه وسلم فَبَسَطَ لَهَا رِدَاءَهُ فَجَلَسَتْ عَلَيْهِ فَقُلْتُ مَنْ هِيَ فَقَالُوا هَذِهِ أُمُّهُ الَّتِي أَرْضَعَتْهُ.

I saw the Prophet ﷺ distributing meat at al-Ji'irrānah.[6] I was a youth that day, and I was carrying the camel bones. I saw a woman

[5] Collected by Ibn Hishām (1/162); the chain of narration is *ḥasan.*

[6] **Translator's note:** Al-Ji'irrānah is a village in the province of Makkah.

turn towards him until she approached the Prophet ﷺ, and he spread out his cloak for her and she sat upon it. I said, "Who is she?" They said, "This is his mother who suckled him."[7]

ASH-SHAYMĀ', THE FOSTER SISTER OF THE PROPHET

Qatādah said, "On the day Hawāzin was conquered (at the Battle of Ḥunayn), a woman came to the Messenger of Allāh ﷺ. She said:

أَنَا أُخْتُكَ شَيْمَاءُ بِنْتُ الْحَارِثِ.

" 'I am your sister Shaymā', the daughter of al-Ḥārith.'

"He replied:

إِنْ تَكُونِي صَادِقَةً فَإِنَّ بِكِ مِنِّي أَثَرًا لَنْ يَبْلَى.

" 'If you are truthful, then you have a mark from me that will not fade away.'

"She said, 'Yes, O Messenger of Allāh. I held you when you were young, and you bit me, leaving this bite mark.' Thus, he laid down his cloak for her and said, 'Ask and you shall be given; request intercession and you will be interceded for.' "[8]

Ibn Ma'īn said that al-Ḥākim 'Abdul-Mālik, who is found in the chain of narration, is weak.

TRANSLATOR'S ADDENDUM

Ibn Is'ḥāq said, "Her name is Ḥudhāfah bint al-Ḥārith, and her nickname is ash-Shaymā'; and she became more known by her nickname than her given name. She is the sister of the Prophet ﷺ by way of suckling. She was likewise from the caretakers of the

[7] *Sunan Abī Dāwūd* 5144 (**Translator's note:** Shaykh al-Albānī said in *Ḍa'īf Abī Dāwūd* [1102] that the chain has weakness in it.)

[8] **Translator's note:** Collected in *The History of Islām* (2/610).

Prophet ﷺ along with her mother Ḥalīmah."

Ibn Ḥajar said, "Ash-Shaymā', the foster sister of the Prophet ﷺ, was taken captive during the Battle of Ḥunayn. She said to the Prophet's companion, 'I am the sister of your companion.' She went to the Prophet ﷺ and said, 'O Muḥammad, I am your sister.' And he recognized her by her mark. He laid his cloak down for her to sit on. He said to her, 'If you like, you can stay with me and you will be honored and loved. Or if you like, I can return you to your people and give you provisions.' She said, 'I want to return to my people.' So the Messenger of Allāh gave her three slaves and slave-girls, a camel, and a sheep."[9]

Umm Ayman Barakah

She is Umm Ayman the Abyssinian (Ethiopian), the freed slave of the Messenger of Allāh ﷺ. She was the caretaker of the Prophet ﷺ whom he inherited from his father. He freed her when he married Khadījah. She is from those who migrated to Ethiopia during the first migration.

Her first name is Barakah. She was from the first and foremost to embrace Islām after Khadījah رضي الله عنها. She was married to 'Ubayd bin al-Ḥārith al-Khazrajī. She gave birth to their son Ayman. Her son Ayman also migrated; he fought *jihād* and was martyred during the Battle of Ḥunayn. Then she married the noble Companion Zayd bin Ḥārithah[10] and gave birth to their son, the noble Companion Usāmah bin Zayd, who was known as "the beloved" of the Messenger of Allāh ﷺ.

Umm Ayman is considered to be from the family of the Prophet ﷺ.

---

[9] *Al-Iṣābah fī Tamyīz aṣ-Ṣaḥābah* by Ibn Ḥajar.

[10] **Translator's note:** Zayd is the noble Companion mentioned by name in the Qur'ān: "So when Zayd had accomplished his desire from her (divorced her), We gave her to you in marriage, so that (in future) there may be no difficulty to the believers regarding (the marriage of) the wives of their adopted sons when the latter have no desire to keep them." (Sūrah al-Aḥzāb 33:37)

The Prophet ﷺ used to say to Umm Ayman, "O mother." He used to say about Umm Ayman:

هَذِهِ بَقِيَّةُ أَهْلِ بَيْتِي.

This is the remainder of my household.[11]

Umm Ayman's Extraordinary Migration:

When Umm Ayman ﵂ migrated to Madīnah, she went out on foot without any riding beast, provisions, or water; in addition to this, she was fasting during the journey. When sunset arrived, she was severely thirsty, but she did not have any water to drink. She heard a noise above her, so she raised her head and saw a bucket suspended from a white well rope. She drank the water inside the bucket and quenched her thirst, and she never became thirsty again for the remainder of her life. She would say:

مَا أَصَابَنِي بَعْدَ ذَلِكَ عَطَشٌ، وَلَقَدْ تَعَرَّضْتُ لِلْعَطَشِ بِالصَّوْمِ فِي الْهَوَاجِرِ فَمَا عَطِشْتُ.

I was not afflicted with thirst after that, although I would expose myself to thirst by fasting during the severe heat of midday; but I never became thirsty.[12]

Umm Ayman used to honor and take care of the Prophet ﷺ.

Umm Ayman ﵂ was promised Paradise. The Prophet ﷺ said:

مَنْ سَرَّهُ أَنْ يَتَزَوَّجَ امْرَأَةً مِنْ أَهْلِ الْجَنَّةِ، فَلْيَتَزَوَّجْ أُمَّ أَيْمَنَ.

Whoever would be delighted to marry a woman from Paradise, then let him marry Umm Ayman.

---

[11] Collected by al-Ḥākim (4/63).

[12] Collected in *The Collection of Fatāwā* by Ibn Taymiyyah (11/276–280), and by Ibn Sa'd (8/224) from the narration of Jarīr bin Ḥāzim's narration from 'Uthmān bin al-Qāsim.

Therefore, Zayd married her.[13]

The Prophet ﷺ would joke with Umm Ayman ﷺ. Umm Ayman came to the Prophet ﷺ and said:

يَا رَسُولَ اللَّهِ، احْمِلْنِي. قَالَ: أَحْمِلُكِ عَلَى وَلَدِ النَّاقَةِ. قَالَتْ: إِنَّهُ لَا يُطِيقُنِي، وَلَا أُرِيدُهُ. قَالَ: لَا أَحْمِلُكِ إِلَّا عَلَيْهِ.

"O Messenger of Allāh, give me an animal to ride." He said, "I will give you the baby of a she-camel to ride." She responded, "It cannot hold me and I do not want it." The Prophet ﷺ said, "I will only give you a baby of a she-camel."[14]

He was joking with her, because every camel is the baby of its mother she-camel.[15]

The Messenger of Allāh ﷺ used to give Umm Ayman lots of gifts. Anas ﷺ said, "Some (of the Anṣār) used to present date palm trees to the Prophet ﷺ until Banū Qurayẓah and Banū Naḍīr were conquered (then he returned to the people their date palms). My people ordered me to ask the Prophet ﷺ to return some or all of the date palms they had given to him, but the Prophet ﷺ had given those trees to Umm Ayman as a gift. Umm Ayman came and put a garment around my neck and said, 'No, by Him besides Whom none has the right to be worshiped, he will not return those trees to you, as he (the Prophet) has given them to me.' The Prophet ﷺ said (to her), 'Return those trees and I will give you so much (instead of them).' But she kept on refusing, saying, 'No, by Allāh,' until he gave her 10 times the number of her date palms in lieu of the original gift."[16]

---

[13] Collected by Ibn Sa'd (8/244).

[14] Collected by Ibn Sa'd (8/224), narrated from Abū Na'īm from Abū Ma'shar from Muḥammad bin Qays.

[15] **Translator's note:** Another example of the Messenger of Allāh ﷺ joking with Umm Ayman is the narration collected in *Al-Iṣābah* (4/416). Umm Ayman said, "The Messenger of Allāh ﷺ said to me, 'Give me the *khimār* from the *masjid*.' I said to him, 'I am on my menses.' He responded, 'Your menses is not in your hand.' "

[16] *Ṣaḥīḥ al-Bukhārī* 4120

Her Grandson:

Ḥarmalah, the freed slave of Usāmah bin Zayd, said, "While we were in the company of 'Abdullāh bin 'Umar, al-Ḥajjāj bin Ayman came in, and he did not perform his bowing and prostrations properly while praying. So Ibn 'Umar told him to repeat his prayer. When he went away, Ibn 'Umar asked me:

مَنْ هَذَا؟

"'Who is he?'

"I said:

الْحَجَّاجُ بْنُ أَيْمَنَ بْنِ أُمِّ أَيْمَنَ.

"'Al-Ḥajjāj bin Ayman bin Umm Ayman.'

"Ibn 'Umar said:

لَوْ رَآهُ رَسُولُ اللَّهِ صَلَّى اللَّهُ عَلَيْهِ وَسَلَّمَ، لَأَحَبَّهُ.

"'If the Messenger of Allāh ﷺ had seen him, he would have surely loved him.'

"Then Ibn 'Umar mentioned the love the Prophet ﷺ had for the children of Umm Ayman."[17]

Umm Ayman's Love of the Revelation:

Anas said, "After the death of the Messenger of Allāh ﷺ, Abū Bakr said to 'Umar, 'Go with us to Umm Ayman so we can visit her just as the Messenger of Allāh ﷺ used to visit her.' When we reached her, she began to cry. Abū Bakr and 'Umar said to her:

مَا يُبْكِيكِ مَا عِنْدَ اللَّهِ خَيْرٌ لِرَسُولِهِ صلى الله عليه وسلم.

"'What makes you cry? What is in store with Allāh for His Messenger is better (than this worldly life).'

---

[17] *Ṣaḥīḥ al-Bukhārī* 3737

"Umm Ayman ﵂ said:

مَا أَبْكِي أَنْ لاَ أَكُونَ أَعْلَمُ أَنَّ مَا عِنْدَ اللَّهِ خَيْرٌ لِرَسُولِهِ صلى الله عليه وسلم وَلَكِنْ أَبْكِي أَنَّ الْوَحْىَ قَدِ انْقَطَعَ مِنَ السَّمَاءِ.

" 'I weep not because I am ignorant of the fact that what is in store with Allāh is better for His Messenger. Rather, I am crying because the revelation from the heavens has ceased.'

"Her statement moved them to tears, so they began to cry along with her."[18]

The Death of 'Umar ﵁:

When 'Umar was killed, Umm Ayman cried and said:

الْيَوْمَ وَهِيَ الإِسْلاَمُ.

Today, Islām has weakened.[19]

Umm Ayman's Death:

Umm Ayman ﵂ died during 'Uthmān bin 'Affān's caliphate ﵁. She narrated five *aḥādīth*.

TRANSLATOR'S ADDENDUM

Some *aḥādīth* narrated by Umm Ayman ﵂:

Umm Ayman ﵂ said, "The Prophet ﷺ said:

لاَ تُقْطَعُ الْيَدُ إِلاَّ فِي ثَمَنِ الْمِجَنِّ. وَثَمَنُهُ يَوْمَئِذٍ دِينَارٌ.

" 'The (hand of) a thief is not to be cut off except for the price of a shield.' And in those days, the price of a shield was a *dīnār*[20]."

It was narrated from Umm Ayman that she sifted some flour and

---

[18] *Ṣaḥīḥ Muslim* 2454

[19] Collected in *Aṭ-Ṭabaqāt* (8/226).

[20] *Sunan an-Nasā'ī* 4948

made a loaf of bread for the Prophet ﷺ. He said, "What is this?" She said, "It is food that we make in our land, and I wanted to make a loaf of it for you." He said, "Fold it onto itself and knead it."[21]

It was narrated that Ibn 'Abbās said, "When a young child of the Messenger of Allāh was dying, the Messenger of Allāh picked him up and held him to his chest, then he put his hand on him, and he died in front of the Messenger of Allāh. Umm Ayman wept, and the Messenger of Allāh said:

يَا أُمَّ أَيْمَنَ أَتَبْكِينَ وَرَسُولُ اللَّهِ صلى الله عليه وسلم عِنْدَكِ.

" 'O Umm Ayman, do you cry while the Messenger of Allāh is with you?'

"She said:

مَا لِي لاَ أَبْكِي وَرَسُولُ اللَّهِ صلى الله عليه وسلم يَبْكِي.

" 'Can I not cry while the Messenger of Allāh is crying?'

"The Messenger of Allāh ﷺ said:

إِنِّي لَسْتُ أَبْكِي وَلَكِنَّهَا رَحْمَةٌ.

" 'I am not crying; this is mercy.'

"Then he said:

الْمُؤْمِنُ بِخَيْرٍ عَلَى كُلِّ حَالٍ تُنْزَعُ نَفْسُهُ مِنْ بَيْنِ جَنْبَيْهِ وَهُوَ يَحْمَدُ اللَّهَ عَزَّ وَجَلَّ.

" 'The believer is fine whatever the situation; even when his soul is being pulled from his body and he praises Allāh, the Mighty and Sublime.' "[22]

---

[21] *Sunan Ibn Mājah* 3461

[22] *Sunan an-Nasā'ī* 1843

THE DAUGHTERS

OF THE PROPHET

1) Zaynab

2) Ruqayyah

3) Umm Kulthūm

4) Fāṭimah

ZAYNAB

Zaynab ﷺ was the oldest of her sisters.[1] She was from those who migrated, and she was from the noblest of women.

Her Husband:

She married her maternal cousin, Abul-'Āṣ,[2] while her mother was alive. She gave birth to their daughter Umāmah, who married 'Alī bin Abī Ṭālib after Fāṭimah's death. She also bore him a son named 'Alī bin Abil-'Āṣ. It has been said that 'Alī bin Abil-'Āṣ was riding with the Prophet on the day Makkah was conquered. And I believe

[1] **Translator's note:** She was born 23 years before migration.

[2] **Translator's note:** He is Abul-'Āṣ bin ar-Rabī'. His mother is Hālah bint Khuwaylid, the sister of Khadījah (the wife of the Prophet ﷺ).

he died as a child.[3]

Ibn Sa'd mentioned, "Abul-'Āṣ married Zaynab before the Messenger of Allāh became a prophet," but this is highly unlikely.

Zaynab accepted Islām and migrated six years before her husband.

'Ā'ishah narrated, "Abul-'Āṣ fought in the Battle of Badr as a pagan, and he was captured by 'Abdullāh bin Jubayr al-Anṣārī. When the people of Makkah came to seek ransom for their prisoners, Zaynab sent some property to ransom Abul-'Āṣ. She gave to 'Amr bin ar-Rabī' (her husband's brother) a necklace of hers which Khadījah had given to her as a wedding gift when she married Abul-'Āṣ. When the Messenger of Allāh ﷺ saw it, he recognized it and felt great sympathy for Zaynab, and he remembered Khadījah. He said, 'If you like, you can free her prisoner for her and return to her what belongs to her.' They said, 'Yes, we will do so.' The Messenger of Allāh ﷺ made an agreement with him that he should let Zaynab come to him (the Messenger ﷺ) in Madīnah. The Messenger of Allāh ﷺ sent Zayd bin Ḥārithah and a man of the Anṣār and said, 'Wait in the valley of Ya'jij (a place on the outskirts of Makkah) until Zaynab passes you, then you should accompany her and bring her back.' "[4]

It has been said that Zaynab migrated with her father, but this is not correct.

Abū Hurayrah said, "The Messenger of Allāh sent a military expedition and I was among them. He said, 'If you find Habbār bin al-Aswad and Nāfi' bin 'Abdul-'Amr, then burn both of them.' " In another narration, Abū Hurayrah said:

بَعَثَنَا رَسُولُ اللَّهِ صَلَّى اللهُ عَلَيْهِ وَسَلَّمَ فِي بَعْثٍ فَقَالَ: إِنْ وَجَدْتُمْ فُلاَنًا وَفُلاَنًا فَأَحْرِقُوهُمَا بِالنَّارِ، ثُمَّ قَالَ رَسُولُ اللَّهِ صَلَّى اللهُ عَلَيْهِ وَسَلَّمَ حِينَ أَرَدْنَا الخُرُوجَ: إِنِّي أَمَرْتُكُمْ أَنْ تُحْرِقُوا فُلاَنًا وَفُلاَنًا، وَإِنَّ النَّارَ لاَ يُعَذِّبُ

[3] *Asad al-Ghābah* 7/130

[4] *Sunan Abī Dāwūd* 2692; declared *ḥasan* by al-Albānī.

بِهَا إِلَّا اللَّهُ، فَإِنْ وَجَدْتُمُوهُمَا فَاقْتُلُوهُمَا.

The Messenger of Allāh ﷺ sent us on a mission and said, "If you find so-and-so and so-and-so, then burn them with fire." Then the Messenger of Allāh ﷺ said, when we were about to leave, "I had commanded you to burn so-and-so and so-and-so. But verily, no one punishes with fire except Allāh. So if you find them, execute them."[5]

These two men had prodded Zaynab's camel when she attempted to migrate to Madīnah, causing her and the camel to fall. She suffered a lingering illness from her injuries which she eventually died from.[6]

Zaynab رضي الله عنها Grants Asylum to Her Husband:

One morning, the Messenger of Allāh ﷺ led his Companions in the Fajr prayer. As they were praying, Zaynab called out:

إِنِّي قَدْ أَجَرْتُ أَبَا الْعَاصِ بْنَ الرَّبِيعِ.

Verily, I have granted asylum to Abul-'Āṣ bin ar-Rabī'.

After the Prophet ﷺ had completed the prayer, he said:

مَا عَلِمْتُ بِهَذَا؛ وَإِنَّهُ يُجِيرُ عَلَى النَّاسِ أَدْنَاهُمْ.

I was not previously aware of this. Protection given from the lowest

---

[5] *Ṣaḥīḥ al-Bukhārī* 3016

[6] **Translator's note:** Ibn Ḥajar said in his explanation of *Ṣaḥīḥ al-Bukhārī*: "Habbār bin al-Aswad—one of the men responsible for prodding Zaynab's camel—accepted Islām. And he is mentioned in the *ḥadīth* from Sulaymān bin Yasār: Habbār bin al-Aswad came on the Day of Sacrifice when 'Umar bin al-Khaṭṭāb was offering his sacrifice, and said, 'O Leader of the Believers, we miscounted the days and we thought that today was the Day of 'Arafah.' 'Umar said, 'Go to Makkah and do *ṭawāf* and *sa'ī*—you and the people with you—and slaughter the sacrificial animal, if you have one; then shave your head or cut your hair, and go home. Then next year, do Ḥajj and offer the sacrifice; whoever cannot afford it, let him fast three days during Ḥajj and seven days after he has returned home.'" (*Muwaṭṭa' Mālik* 865) Ibn Ḥajar continued, saying, "Habbār bin al-Aswad lived until the caliphate of Mu'āwiyah. But I did not find any information concerning Nāfi' bin 'Abdul-'Amr; perhaps he died before accepting Islām."

of Muslims is binding upon the people.[7]

Abul-'Āṣ Accepts Islām:

Abul-'Āṣ went to Shām with a caravan from the Quraysh. Zayd bin Ḥārithah was assigned the mission of intercepting the caravan, and he had 170 riders with him. They intercepted the caravan and sieged it in 6 AH. They took the people as prisoners—and Abul-'Āṣ was among them—and the prisoners were returned to Madīnah. Abul-'Āṣ went to see Zaynab secretly and she granted him asylum. Then she asked her father to return his possessions, and he did so. The Prophet ﷺ told him to not approach Zaynab as long as he remained a pagan, so Abul-'Āṣ returned to Makkah. Later, he returned to Madīnah as a Muslim, migrating for the sake of Allāh in 7 AH in the month of Muḥarram. Thus, Zaynab was returned to him on the basis of the first marriage.[8]

Ash-Shu'bah said, "Zaynab accepted Islām and migrated, then her husband accepted Islām after her, and they were not separated."[9]

Qatādah said, "After this, Sūrah at-Tawbah was revealed, so from that point on, if a woman accepted Islām before her husband, he had to accept Islām and marry her anew."[10]

'Amr bin Shu'ayb narrated from his grandfather:

أَنَّ رَسُولَ اللَّهِ صلى الله عليه وسلم - رَدَّ ابْنَتَهُ زَيْنَبَ عَلَى أَبِي الْعَاصِ بْنِ الرَّبِيعِ بِنِكَاحٍ جَدِيدٍ.

The Messenger of Allāh ﷺ returned his daughter to Abul-'Āṣ with a new marriage and a new dowry.[11]

---

[7] Collected by al-Ḥākim (4/45): Abul-'Āṣ sent word to Zaynab requesting asylum from her father, the Prophet ﷺ. Thus, she granted him asylum, and this was respected by all the Muslims.

[8] Collected by Ibn Sa'd (8/33).

[9] *Aṭ-Ṭabaqāt* 8/32

[10] *Aṭ-Ṭabaqāt* 8/32

[11] *Sunan Ibn Mājah* 2088; this narration was declared weak by Imām Aḥmad.

This narration is weak.

It has been authentically reported from Ibn 'Abbās:

إِنَّ لِلَّهِ مَا أَخَذَ وَلَهُ مَا أَعْطَى وَكُلُّ شَيْءٍ عِنْدَ اللَّهِ بِأَجَلٍ مُسَمًّى فَلْتَصْبِرْ وَلْتَحْتَسِبْ.

The Messenger of Allāh ﷺ returned his daughter to Abul-'Āṣ after a number of years on the basis of the first marriage, and he did not give her a new dowry.[12]

Anas said, "I saw upon Zaynab, the daughter of the Messenger of Allāh ﷺ, a stitched garment made from silk."[13]

Her Death:

Zaynab ﵂ died in the beginning of 8 AH.

It was narrated that Umm 'Aṭiyyah al-Anṣāriyyah[14] ﵂ said, "The Messenger of Allāh ﷺ entered upon us when his daughter died, and said, 'Wash her three times, or five, or more than that, if you see fit. Wash her with water and lotus leaves, and put camphor in the last wash, or a little camphor. And when you have finished, let me know.' When we had finished, we let him know, and he gave us his waist wrapper and said, 'Shroud her in it.' "[15]

Zaynab was the oldest daughter of the Prophet ﷺ. She died in 8 AH. The Prophet ﷺ loved her a great deal and would praise her. She died at the age of 33. Her husband Abul-'Āṣ died in 12 AH in the month of Dhul-Ḥijjah, during Abū Bakr's caliphate, may Allāh be pleased with them all.

TRANSLATOR'S ADDENDUM

Zaynab's son 'Alī bin Abil-'Āṣ died before her.

---

[12] *Sunan Abī Dāwūd* 2240

[13] Collected by al-Ḥākim (4/45-46).

[14] **Translator's note:** Umm 'Aṭiyyah Nasībah bint al-Ḥārith.

[15] *Ṣaḥīḥ al-Bukhārī* 1195; *Ṣaḥīḥ Muslim* 939

Abū 'Uthmān said, "Usāmah bin Zayd told me, 'The daughter (Zaynab)[16] of the Prophet sent word to him telling him, "A son of mine is dying; come to us." He sent word to her, conveying his greeting of *salām* and saying:

إِنَّ لِلَّهِ مَا أَخَذَ وَلَهُ مَا أَعْطَى وَكُلُّ شَيْءٍ عِنْدَ اللَّهِ بِأَجَلٍ مُسَمًّى فَلْتَصْبِرْ وَلْتَحْتَسِبْ.

" ' "To Allāh belongs that which He takes and that which He gives. And everything has an appointed term with Allāh. Let her be patient and seek reward."

" 'She sent word to him adjuring him to go to her. So he got up and went, accompanied by Sa'd bin 'Ubādah, Mu'ādh bin Jabal, Ubayy bin Ka'b, Zayd bin Thābit, and some other men. The boy was lifted up to the Messenger of Allāh, with the death rattle sounding in him, and [the Prophet's] eyes filled with tears. Sa'd said, "O Messenger of Allāh, what is this?" He said, "This is compassion which Allāh has created in the hearts of His slaves. Allāh has mercy on His compassionate slaves." ' "[17]

The Prophet ﷺ Supplicated for Her:

The Prophet ﷺ went to Zaynab's grave while he was sad. He said, "I thought of Zaynab and her fragility, so I asked Allāh the Exalted to lighten the tightness of the grave and its distress upon her. And He did so. Therefore, it is easy upon her."[18]

Zaynab ﷺ is Considered a Martyr:

Ibn Kathīr said, " 'Urwah said, 'When Zaynab migrated, a man pushed her camel, causing it to fall on her, which caused her to have a miscarriage. The injury continued to trouble her until she eventually died from it. Thus, they used to view her death as the

---

[16] **Translator's note:** Ibn Abī Shaybah said that this was Zaynab (*Explanation of Mishkāh al-Maṣābiḥ*).

[17] *Sunan an-Nasā'ī* 1868

[18] *Asad al-Ghābah* 5/468

death of a martyr.' "[19]

RUQAYYAH

Ruqayyah accepted Islām along with her mother and her sisters.

Ibn Sa'd said that she married 'Utbah bin Abī Lahab before prophethood, but what is correct is that she married him before migration. While they were married, the following verse was revealed:

﴿ تَبَّتْ يَدَا أَبِي لَهَبٍ وَتَبَّ ﴾

Perish the two hands of Abū Lahab, and perish he!

[Sūrah al-Masad 111:1]

When this verse was revealed, 'Utbah's father—Abū Lahab—said, "My head is impermissible for your head (meaning, I will not speak to you) if you do not divorce his daughter." Thus, 'Utbah divorced Ruqayyah before the marriage was consummated.

Her Second Marriage:

Then she married 'Uthmān bin 'Affān ﷺ and they migrated together to Abyssinia. It is mentioned in the narration:

إِنَّهُمَا لَأَوَّلُ مَنْ هَاجَرَ إِلَى اللَّهِ بَعْدَ لُوطٍ.

The two of them were the first people to migrate to Allāh after Lūṭ.[20]

Her Son:

Ruqayyah ﷺ gave birth to 'Uthmān's son 'Abdullāh. From this son, he took his *kunyah*. When 'Abdullāh reached the age of six, a rooster pecked him in the face. His face became infected and he died from his injury. (This occurred in 4 AH, so he died two years

[19] *Al-Bidāyah wan-Nihāyah* 5/234

[20] *Al-Iṣābah* 12/257

after his mother Ruqayyah).[21]

Her Migration:

Ruqayyah is from those who migrated to both Abyssinia and Madīnah.

Her Death:

After that, she migrated to Madīnah after 'Uthmān, while some say she migrated with 'Uthmān. She became sick shortly before the Battle of Badr, so the Prophet ﷺ ordered 'Uthmān bin 'Affān ؓ to remain behind and stay with her. Ruqayyah died while the Muslims were at the Battle of Badr.

The following *ḥadīth* attributed to Ibn 'Abbās concerning the death of Ruqayyah is weak and it opposes stronger narrations.

This narration states that Ibn 'Abbās said, "When Ruqayyah, the daughter of the Messenger of Allāh ﷺ, died, we met 'Uthmān bin Maẓ'ūn and the women were crying due to her death. 'Umar began to strike them with his whip, so the Prophet ﷺ grabbed his hand and said, 'Leave them alone to cry.' Then he said, 'Beware of the howling of the Shayṭān. Whatever comes from the heart and the eye is from Allāh and mercy, and whatever comes from the hand and the tongue is from the Shayṭān.' Then Fāṭimah sat at the edge of her grave beside the Messenger of Allāh ﷺ and she began to cry. The Messenger of Allāh ﷺ wiped her tears away with the edge of his garment."[22]

This *ḥadīth* is weak.

Ibn Sa'd said, "It has been affirmed with every narration we have that Ruqayyah died while the Messenger of Allāh was at the Battle of Badr. Thus, perhaps this narration is pertaining to someone other than her."

---

[21] *Explanation of Ṣaḥīḥ al-Bukhārī* 7/67

[22] Collected by Ibn Sa'd (8/36); this *ḥadīth* is *munkar,* meaning it is weak and opposed by a strong *ḥadīth.*

TRANSLATOR'S ADDENDUM

Ruqayyah ﵂ was the first wife of 'Uthmān bin 'Affān ﵁. He married her in Makkah.

Ruqayyah ﵂ was the first daughter of the Prophet ﷺ to die during his life. She died in 2 AH while the Prophet ﷺ was at the Battle of Badr.

Ibn 'Umar ﵄ said, "'Uthmān did not join the Battle of Badr because he was married to one of the daughters of the Messenger of Allāh ﷺ and she was ill. So the Prophet ﷺ said to him:

إِنَّ لَكَ أَجْرَ رَجُلٍ مِمَّنْ شَهِدَ بَدْرًا وَسَهْمَهُ.

"'You will get a reward and a share (from the spoils of war) similar to the reward and the share of one who has taken part in the Battle of Badr.'"[23]

Ruqayyah ﵂ was 20 years old when she died.[24]

UMM KULTHŪM

Umm Kulthūm ﵂ was the fourth child of the Messenger of Allāh ﷺ after Qāsim, Zaynab, and Ruqayyah.

Her First Marriage:

She was married to 'Utaybah bin Abī Lahab, and then he divorced her without consummating the marriage.

Her Second Marriage:

After her sister Ruqayyah died, she married 'Uthmān bin 'Affān while she was still a virgin. This marriage took place during the month of Rabī' al-Awwal in 3 AH. She did not give birth to any children.

[23] *Ṣaḥīḥ al-Bukhārī* 3130

[24] *Explanation of Ṣaḥīḥ al-Bukhārī* 7/73, narrated by Ibn Is'ḥāq.

Her Death:

Umm Kulthūm ﵅ died during the month of Sha'bān in 9 AH. Upon her death, the Prophet ﷺ said:

لَوْ كُنَّ عَشْرًا لِزَوَّجْتُهُنَّ عُثْمَانَ.

If there were 10 of them, I would surely marry them to 'Uthmān.[25]

Anas bin Mālik ﵁ said:

شَهِدْنَا بِنْتَ رَسُولِ اللَّهِ صلى الله عليه وسلم وَرَسُولُ اللَّهِ صلى الله عليه وسلم جَالِسٌ عَلَى الْقَبْرِ، فَرَأَيْتُ عَيْنَيْهِ تَدْمَعَانِ فَقَالَ هَلْ فِيكُمْ مِنْ أَحَدٍ لَمْ يُقَارِفِ اللَّيْلَةَ. فَقَالَ أَبُو طَلْحَةَ أَنَا. قَالَ فَانْزِلْ فِي قَبْرِهَا.

We were in the funeral procession of the daughter of the Messenger of Allāh ﷺ, and he was sitting near the grave and I saw his eyes full of tears. He said, "Is there anyone amongst you who did not surrender last night?[26]" Abū Ṭalḥah replied in the affirmative. So the Messenger of Allāh ﷺ told him to descend into her grave (to bury her).[27]

TRANSLATOR'S ADDENDUM

'Uthmān bin 'Affān ﵁ was married to two daughters of the Prophet ﷺ (at different times): Ruqayyah and Umm Kulthūm. For this reason, he was called "the Possessor of Two Lights."

Umm Kulthūm ﵅ was around 28 years old according to the Islamic calendar when she died.

Her First Husband 'Utaybah & the Lion:

'Utaybah bin Abī Lahab used to revile the Prophet ﷺ, so the Prophet ﷺ supplicated against him, saying:

[25] Collected in *Aṭ-Ṭabaqāt* (8/38).

[26] **Translator's note:** Meaning: Is there anyone who did not have intimate relations with his spouse last night?

[27] *Ṣaḥīḥ al-Bukhārī* 1342

اللهم سلط عليه كلباً من كلابك.

O Allāh, send one of Your dogs against him.

'Utaybah went out with a caravan heading towards Syria. He halted at some place and said, "I fear the supplication of Muḥammad." They said to him, "No, don't worry." They surrounded him with their luggage and stood guard over him; then a lion came and snatched him and took him away.[28]

FĀṬIMAH

She is the best of all the women of her era. She is a part of the Prophet[29]; the link to Muṣṭafā[30]; the mother of her father[31]. She is the daughter of the best of creation, Abul-Qāsim Muḥammad bin 'Abdillāh bin 'Abdul-Muṭṭalib bin Hāshim bin 'Abd Manāf al-Qurashī al-Hāshimī. She is the mother of al-Ḥasan and al-Ḥusayn.

Her Birth:

She was born a little before the first revelation was revealed.

Her Marriage:

She married the noble Companion, the Imām, 'Alī bin Abī Ṭālib ﷺ in the month of Dhul-Qa'dah or slightly before 2 AH, after the Battle of Badr. The marriage was consummated after the Battle of Uḥud.

---

[28] It was narrated by al-Ḥākim (3984) and by al-Bayhaqī in *Ad-Dalā'il* (622). Al-Ḥākim said that its chain of narration is *ṣaḥīḥ*, and adh-Dhahabī agreed with him. It was declared *ḥasan* by al-Ḥāfiẓ Ibn Ḥajar in *Fat'ḥ al-Bārī* (4/39).

[29] **Translator's note:** The Messenger of Allāh ﷺ said, "Fāṭimah is a part of me, and he who makes her angry, makes me angry." (*Ṣaḥīḥ al-Bukhārī* 3714)

[30] **Translator's note:** She is called this because she is his only child who had surviving offspring that connect back to the Prophet ﷺ.

[31] **Translator's note:** She is called this because of the way she took care of her father.

Her Children:

Fāṭimah ﷺ gave birth to al-Ḥasan, al-Ḥusayn, Muḥsin[32], Umm Kulthūm (the wife of 'Umar bin al-Khaṭṭāb), and Zaynab (the wife of 'Abdullāh bin Ja'far bin Abī Ṭālib).

Her Aḥādīth:

She narrated *aḥādīth* from her father, and many of the Companions narrated *aḥādīth* from her, such as her husband 'Alī, her son al-Ḥusayn, 'Ā'ishah, Umm Salamah, Anas bin Mālik, and others ﷺ.

The Prophet ﷺ loved her, honored her, and was happy with her.

Her Resemblance to the Prophet ﷺ:

'Ā'ishah ﷺ said:

ما رأيت أحدا كان أشبه كلاما وحديثا برسول الله صلى الله عليه وسلم من فاطمة، وكانت إذا دخلت عليه قام إليها، فقبلها، ورحب بها، وكذلك كانت هي تصنع به.

I have not seen anyone who resembled the Prophet ﷺ in speech more than Fāṭimah. When she entered, he would stand to greet her and kiss her and welcome her. And she would do the same towards him.[33]

Her Virtues:

Her virtues are plentiful. She was patient and persevering, benevolent, content, and grateful to Allāh.

The Prophet ﷺ said:

إِنَّ هَذَا مَلَكٌ لَمْ يَنْزِلِ الأَرْضَ قَطُّ قَبْلَ هَذِهِ اللَّيْلَةِ اسْتَأْذَنَ رَبَّهُ أَنْ يُسَلِّمَ

[32] **Translator's note:** According to the majority of the scholars, none of the history books mention a son named Muḥsin; rather, they all mentioned that Fāṭimah only had four children: al-Ḥasan, al-Ḥusayn, Umm Kulthūm, and Zaynab. Ibn al-Jawzī attributes the mention of Muḥsin to Ibn Is'ḥāq.

[33] *Sunan Abī Dāwūd* 5217

عَلَيَّ وَيُبَشِّرَنِي بِأَنَّ فَاطِمَةَ سَيِّدَةُ نِسَاءِ أَهْلِ الْجَنَّةِ وَأَنَّ الْحَسَنَ وَالْحُسَيْنَ سَيِّدَا شَبَابِ أَهْلِ الْجَنَّةِ.

Indeed, this is an angel that had never descended to the earth before tonight. He sought permission from his Lord to greet me with *salām* and to give me the glad tidings that Fāṭimah is the best of the women of Paradise, and that al-Ḥasan and al-Ḥusayn are the best of the youths of the people of Paradise.[34]

The Prophet ﷺ said:

أفضل نساء أهل الجنة خديجة وفاطمة.

The best women of Paradise are Khadījah and Fāṭimah.[35]

It was said to 'Ā'ishah ﵂:

أَيُّ النَّاسِ كَانَ أَحَبَّ إِلَى رَسُولِ اللَّهِ صلى الله عليه وسلم قَالَتْ فَاطِمَةُ. فَقِيلَ مِنَ الرِّجَالِ قَالَتْ زَوْجُهَا إِنْ كَانَ مَا عَلِمْتُ صَوَّامًا قَوَّامًا.

"Who are the most beloved people to the Messenger of Allāh?" She said, "Fāṭimah." It was said to her, "Who from among the men?" She said, "Her husband; surely, I knew him to fast much and stand in prayer much."[36]

The Prophet ﷺ said:

فَاطِمَةُ سَيِّدَةُ نِسَاءِ أَهْلِ الْجَنَّةِ، إِلَّا مَرْيَمَ بِنْتَ عِمْرَانَ.

Fāṭimah is the best of the women of Paradise, with the exception of Maryam bint 'Imrān.[37]

The Prophet ﷺ said:

[34] *Jāmi' at-Tirmidhī* 3781; the chain has been declared *ḥasan*.

[35] Collected by Aḥmad (1/293).

[36] *Jāmi' at-Tirmidhī* 3874; al-Ḥākim declared it *ṣaḥīḥ* (3/157).

[37] Collected and authenticated by al-Ḥākim (2/154).

أَفْضَلُ نِسَاءِ أَهْلِ الْجَنَّةِ: خَدِيجَةُ بِنْتُ خُوَيْلِدٍ، وَفَاطِمَةُ بِنْتُ مُحَمَّدٍ، وَآسِيَةُ بِنْتُ مُزَاحِمٍ امْرَأَةُ فِرْعَوْنَ، وَمَرْيَمُ ابْنَةُ عِمْرَانَ.

The best women of Paradise are Khadījah bint Khuwaylid, Fāṭimah bint Muḥammad, Āsiyah bint Muzāḥim (the wife of Pharaoh), and Maryam bint 'Imrān.[38]

Thawbān, the freed slave of the Messenger of Allāh, said, "The Messenger of Allāh entered upon Fāṭimah and she had a gold chain around her neck. She said:

هَذِهِ أَهْدَاهَا إِلَيَّ أَبُو حَسَنٍ.

" 'This is a gift given to me from Abul-Ḥasan ('Alī).'

"The Messenger of Allāh ﷺ said:

يا فاطمة، أيسرك أن يقول الناس: هذه فاطمة بنت محمد وفي يدها سلسلة من نار.

" 'O Fāṭimah, would you like for the people to say, "This is Fāṭimah, the daughter of Muḥammad, and in her hand is a chain from the Fire?" '

"So she purchased a slave with the chain and set him free. The Prophet ﷺ said:

الْحَمْدُ لِلَّهِ الَّذِي أَنْجَى فَاطِمَةَ مِنَ النَّارِ.

" 'All praises belong to Allāh, the One who has saved Fāṭimah from the Fire.' "[39]

The Prophet ﷺ became angry for her sake when he was informed that 'Alī bin Abī Ṭālib intended to marry the daughter of Abū Lahab. He stood up and said the testimony of faith, and then he said:

---

[38] Collected by Aḥmad (1/293).

[39] *Sunan an-Nasā'ī* 5140

أَمَّا بَعْدُ فَإِنِّي قَدْ أَنْكَحْتُ أَبَا الْعَاصِ بْنَ الرَّبِيعِ فَحَدَّثَنِي فَصَدَقَنِي وَإِنَّ فَاطِمَةَ بِنْتَ مُحَمَّدٍ بَضْعَةٌ مِنِّي وَأَنَا أَكْرَهُ أَنْ تَفْتِنُوهَا وَإِنَّهَا وَاللَّهِ لاَ تَجْتَمِعُ بِنْتُ رَسُولِ اللَّهِ وَبِنْتُ عَدُوِّ اللَّهِ عِنْدَ رَجُلٍ وَاحِدٍ أَبَدًا. قَالَ فَنَزَلَ عَلِيٌّ عَنِ الْخِطْبَةِ.

"As to what follows: I married my daughter (Zaynab) to Abul-'Āṣ bin ar-Rabī', and he spoke to me and was speaking the truth. Fāṭimah bint Muḥammad is a part of me, and I hate to see her faced with troubles. By Allāh, the daughter of the Messenger of Allāh and the daughter of the enemy of Allāh will never be joined together in marriage to one man." So 'Alī retracted his proposal.[40]

Therefore, while 'Alī was married to Fāṭimah, he did not take another wife or a slave-girl. When she died, he remarried and took slave-girls.

The Virtue of Fāṭimah's Household ﵂*:*

The bloodline of the Prophet ﷺ was severed except by way of Fāṭimah. As for Umāmah, Zaynab's daughter—the child the Prophet ﷺ would carry during his prayer—she married 'Alī bin Abī Ṭālib. After him, she married al-Mughīrah bin Nawfal bin al-Ḥārith bin 'Abdul-Muṭṭalib al-Hāshimī, and she bore him children.

Az-Zubayr bin Bakkār said, "The bloodline of Zaynab came to an end."

Umm Salamah said:

أَنَّ النَّبِيَّ صلى الله عليه وسلم جَلَّلَ عَلَى الْحَسَنِ وَالْحُسَيْنِ وَعَلِيٍّ وَفَاطِمَةَ كِسَاءً ثُمَّ قَالَ: اللَّهُمَّ هَؤُلاَءِ أَهْلُ بَيْتِي فَأَذْهِبْ عَنْهُمُ الرِّجْسَ وَطَهِّرْهُمْ تَطْهِيرًا.

The Prophet ﷺ wrapped a cloak around al-Ḥasan, al-Ḥusayn, 'Alī, and Fāṭimah, and then he said, "O Allāh, these are the members of

[40] *Sunan Ibn Mājah* 2077

my household, so remove *ar-rijs* (evil deeds and sins) from them and purify them with a thorough purification."[41]

The Prophet ﷺ looked at 'Alī, Fāṭimah, al-Ḥasan, and al-Ḥusayn and said:

أَنَا حَرْبٌ لِمَنْ حَارَبْتُمْ وَسَلْمٌ لِمَنْ سَالَمْتُمْ.

I am at war with whoever makes war with you, and peace for whoever makes peace with you.[42]

The Death of Her Father ﷺ*:*

Anas ﷺ narrated:

فَلَمَّا مَاتَ قَالَتْ يَا أَبَتَاهْ، أَجَابَ رَبًّا دَعَاهُ، يَا أَبَتَاهْ مَنْ جَنَّةُ الْفِرْدَوْسِ مَأْوَاهُ، يَا أَبَتَاهْ إِلَى جِبْرِيلَ نَنْعَاهْ. فَلَمَّا دُفِنَ قَالَتْ فَاطِمَةُ ـ عَلَيْهَا السَّلاَمُ ـ يَا أَنَسُ، أَطَابَتْ أَنْفُسُكُمْ أَنْ تَحْثُوا عَلَى رَسُولِ اللَّهِ صلى الله عليه وسلم التُّرَابَ؟

When he died, she (Fāṭimah) said, "O my dear father, who answered the call of his Lord. O my dear father, whose abode is the highest level of Paradise! O my father, to Jibrīl we announce the news of his death!" When he was buried, Fāṭimah ﷺ said, "O Anas, how could you bear to throw dust over the Messenger of Allāh ﷺ?"[43]

'Ā'ishah ﷺ said, "We, the wives of the Messenger of Allāh, were with him (during his last illness), and none of us were absent. Then Fāṭimah, who walked in the same manner as the Messenger of Allāh ﷺ, came. When he saw her, he welcomed her, saying:

مَرْحَبًا بِابْنَتِي.

" 'Welcome to my daughter.'

"He then made her sit on his right side or on his left side. Then he

---

[41] *Jāmi' at-Tirmidhī* 3510

[42] *Musnad Imām Aḥmad* 2/442

[43] *Ṣaḥīḥ al-Bukhārī* 4462

said something secretly to her and she wept bitterly, and when he found her in grief, he said something secretly to her for the second time and she laughed. I ('Ā'ishah) said to her, 'The Messenger of Allāh has singled you out amongst the women of the family. He told you a secret and you wept.' When the Messenger of Allāh left, I said to her, 'What did the Messenger of Allāh say to you?' She said, 'I am not going to disclose the secret of the Messenger of Allāh.' When the Messenger of Allāh ﷺ died, I said to her, 'I adjure you by the right that I have upon you that you should narrate to me what the Messenger of Allāh ﷺ said to you.' She said, 'Yes, now I can inform you. When he talked to me secretly the first time, he said that:

أَنَّ جِبْرِيلَ كَانَ يُعَارِضُهُ الْقُرْآنَ فِي كُلِّ سَنَةٍ مَرَّةً أَوْ مَرَّتَيْنِ وَإِنَّهُ عَارَضَهُ الآنَ مَرَّتَيْنِ وَإِنِّي لاَ أُرَى الأَجَلَ إِلاَّ قَدِ اقْتَرَبَ فَاتَّقِي اللَّهَ وَاصْبِرِي فَإِنَّهُ نِعْمَ السَّلَفُ أَنَا لَكِ.

" 'Jibrīl used to recite the Qur'ān along with him once or twice every year, but this year it had been twice, and so he perceived his death to be quite near, so fear Allāh and be patient, for surely he is the best Salaf for you.

" 'Thus I wept as you saw. And when he saw me in grief, he talked to me secretly for the second time and said:

يَا فَاطِمَةُ أَمَا تَرْضَىْ أَنْ تَكُونِي سَيِّدَةَ نِسَاءِ الْمُؤْمِنِينَ أَوْ سَيِّدَةَ نِسَاءِ هَذِهِ الأُمَّةِ.

" ' "O Fāṭimah, are you not pleased that you should be the leader of the believing women or the best woman from this *ummah*?"

" 'So, I laughed, and it was that laughter which you saw.' "[44]

Her Illness & Death:

When Fāṭimah became sick, Abū Bakr came to visit her, and he sought permission to enter. 'Alī said, "O Fāṭimah, Abū Bakr is

[44] *Ṣaḥīḥ Muslim* 245

seeking permission to enter." She said, "Would you like him to enter?" 'Alī said, "Yes." Thus, Fāṭimah ﷺ followed the Sunnah by not allowing anyone into her home without the permission of her husband. So Abū Bakr entered to make her happy. He said, "By Allāh, I have not left any home or wealth, family or kin, except that I sought to please Allāh and His Messenger regarding them, and I seek to please you all, the household of the Prophet." He continued to make her happy until she was pleased.[45]

Fāṭimah ﷺ died five or six months after the death of the Prophet ﷺ. She died at the age of 24 or 25, while others say she died at the age of 29. But no one said that she was older than that. What is most correct is that she died at the age of 24. She was younger than her sister Zaynab (the wife of Abul-'Āṣ), and younger than her sister Ruqayyah (the wife of 'Uthmān bin 'Affān), and younger than her sister Umm Kulthūm (who was also the wife of 'Uthmān bin 'Affān).

Sa'īd bin 'Ufayr said, "She died on a Tuesday after three nights of Ramaḍān had passed in 11 AH, and she was buried at night."

She was washed by her husband 'Alī ﷺ.

The Shyness of Fāṭimah Even in Death:

Fāṭimah said to Asmā' bint 'Umays, "Indeed, I hate what they do with the women (when shrouding the deceased). They put a garment over the woman and the shape of her limbs is defined." Asmā' said, "O daughter of the Messenger of Allāh, shall I show you what I saw in Abyssinia?" Thus, she requested some wet leaves and laid them down, and then she placed a garment over them. Fāṭimah replied, "This is wonderful and beautiful!"

Ibn 'Abdil-Barr said, "She was the first person to have her shroud-cover in Islām in this manner."

There are 18 *aḥādīth* narrated by her, which are collected in the *Musnad.*

---

[45] Collected by al-Bayhaqī in *As-Sunan al-Kubrā.*

Unauthentic Narrations Attributed to Her:

The following poem which has been widely attributed to Fāṭimah is not authentic: "What will happen to the one who smells the sweet fragrance of Aḥmad's grave, then he would never smell any other fragrance of the world; such sorrows flowed upon me that if it had descended upon the days, they would have turned into nights."

The Granddaughters

of the Prophet

1) Umāmah bint Abil-'Āṣ

2) Zaynab bint 'Alī bin Abī Ṭālib

3) Umm Kulthūm bint 'Alī bin Abī Ṭālib

Umāmah bint Abil-'Āṣ

Umāmah is the child that the Messenger of Allāh ﷺ would carry during his prayer. She is the daughter of his daughter Zaynab ﵂.

Her Marriage:

She married 'Alī bin Abī Ṭālib during 'Umar's caliphate, and she remained with him for a period of time and bore a child for him.[1] After 'Alī was killed, she married al-Mughīrah bin Nawfal bin al-Ḥārith al-Hāshimī.

Her Death:

She died while married to him after she gave birth to their son Yaḥyā bin al-Mughīrah. She died during the caliphate of Mu'āwiyah bin

[1] **Translator's note:** His son's name was Muḥammad al-Awsaṭ bin 'Alī.

Abī Sufyān.

TRANSLATOR'S ADDENDUM

Abū Qatādah said:

أَنَّ رَسُولَ اللَّهِ صلى الله عليه وسلم كَانَ يُصَلِّي وَهُوَ حَامِلٌ أُمَامَةَ بِنْتَ زَيْنَبَ بِنْتِ رَسُولِ اللَّهِ صلى الله عليه وسلم وَلأَبِي الْعَاصِ بْنِ الرَّبِيعِ فَإِذَا قَامَ حَمَلَهَا وَإِذَا سَجَدَ وَضَعَهَا.

The Messenger of Allāh ﷺ was praying while he was holding Umāmah, the daughter of Zaynab (the daughter of the Messenger of Allāh ﷺ), and she (Umāmah) was the daughter of Abul-'Āṣ bin ar-Rabī'. When he stood, he would hold her, and when he prostrated, he would put her down.[2]

'Ā'ishah ﵂ said:

أن رسول الله صلى الله عليه وسلم أُهْدِيَتْ لَهُ هَدِيَّةٌ فِيهَا قِلادَةٌ مِنْ جَزْعٍ، فَقَالَ: لأَدْفَعَنَّهَا إِلَى أَحَبِّ أَهْلِي إِلَيَّ. فَقَالَ النِّسَاءُ: ذَهَبَتْ بِهَا ابْنَةُ أَبِي قُحَافَةَ. فَدَعَا رسول الله صلى الله عليه وسلم أمامة بِنْتُ زَيْنَبَ فَأَعْلَقَهَا فِي عُنُقِهَا.

The Messenger of Allāh ﷺ was given a gift which contained a necklace from onyx; he said, "I will surely give this to the most beloved family member to me." The women said, "It will go to the daughter of Abū Quḥāfah (Abū Bakr)." So the Messenger of Allāh ﷺ called Umāmah bint Zaynab and linked the necklace around her neck.[3]

ZAYNAB BINT 'ALĪ BIN ABĪ ṬĀLIB

Imām adh-Dhahabī did not mention anything concerning the

[2] *Ṣaḥīḥ Muslim* 543

[3] *Al-Istī'āb fī Ma'rifah al-Aṣ'ḥāb*

biography of Zaynab bint 'Alī ﷺ.

TRANSLATOR'S ADDENDUM

Zaynab was born in 5 AH and she died in 62 AH.

UMM KULTHŪM BINT 'ALĪ BIN ABĪ ṬĀLIB

She is the full sister of al-Ḥasan and al-Ḥusayn. She was born in 6 AH. She saw the Prophet ﷺ, but she did not narrate from him.

'Umar bin al-Khaṭṭāb ﷺ proposed to her while she was young. He was asked, "Why do you want to marry her?" He said, "I heard the Messenger of Allāh ﷺ say:

كل سبب ونسب منقطع يوم القيامة إلا سببي ونسبي.

"'Every means and every lineage will be severed on the Day of Judgment except my means and my lineage.'"[4]

'Umar said to 'Alī, "Marry me to her, O Abul-Ḥasan, for I will preserve her honor like no one else can." 'Alī said, "I will send for her; if she is pleased, I will marry you to her." 'Umar married her and gave her 40,000 as a dowry. She gave birth to their son Zayd. It was also said that she gave birth to a daughter named Ruqayyah.

'Umar bin al-Khaṭṭāb died while married to her. Her father 'Alī strongly encouraged her to marry 'Awn bin Ja'far bin Abī Ṭālib. She married him and loved him a great deal. She remained with him until he died.

Then her father 'Alī ﷺ married her to Muḥammad bin Ja'far and then he died. Then her father married her to 'Abdullāh bin Ja'far, and she died while married to him. She did not bear any children for her last three husbands.

'Ammār bin Abī 'Ammār said, "Umm Kulthūm and Zayd died at

[4] Collected by al-Ḥākim (3/142).

the same time. So we shrouded them, and Sa'īd bin al-'Āṣ led the prayer over them."

Ibn 'Umar participated in the Janāzah prayer over his brother Zayd bin 'Umar and Zayd's mother, Umm Kulthūm bint 'Alī. Her son Zayd was from the nobles of the Quraysh tribe and he died while still a youth.

TRANSLATOR'S ADDENDUM

Muḥammad bin Ḥabīb said about Zayd bin 'Umar al-Khaṭṭāb, "There is a man from the Quraysh whose father was martyred, as was his maternal grandfather, his mother's uncle, the uncle of his maternal grandfather, and his uncle. This man is Zayd bin 'Umar. His father was 'Umar bin al-Khaṭṭāb, his uncle was Zayd bin al-Khaṭṭāb, his maternal grandfather was 'Alī bin Abī Ṭālib, his mother's uncle was Ja'far bin Abī Ṭālib, the uncle of his maternal grandfather was Ḥamzah bin 'Abdul-Muṭṭalib, and his uncle was al-Ḥusayn bin Abī Ṭālib; may Allāh be pleased with them all."[5]

---

[5] *Al-Munammaq* 426

THE PATERNAL AUNTS

OF THE PROPHET

1) Ṣafiyyah bint 'Abdul-Muṭṭalib

2) Arwā bint 'Abdul-Muṭṭalib

3) 'Ātikah bint 'Abdul-Muṭṭalib

4) Al-Bayḍā' bint 'Abdul-Muṭṭalib

5) Barrah bint 'Abdul-Muṭṭalib

6) Umāmah bint 'Abdul-Muṭṭalib

ṢAFIYYAH BINT 'ABDUL-MUṬṬALIB

Ṣafiyyah bint 'Abdul-Muṭṭalib al-Hāshimī; she is the full sister of Ḥamzah. She is the mother of the disciple of the Messenger of Allāh, az-Zubayr. Her mother was from the tribe of Banū Zuhrah.

Her Marriage:

She married al-Ḥārith, the brother of Abū Sufyān bin Ḥarb, and he died while married to her. Then she married al-'Awām, the brother of the best of women—Khadījah bint Khuwaylid. While married to him, she gave birth to az-Zubayr, as-Sā'ib[1], and 'Abdul-Ka'bah. The tribe of Banul-'Awām is the tribe which defended the Messenger of Allāh ﷺ.

It is the viewpoint of some scholars that she was the only paternal aunt of the Prophet ﷺ to enter Islām.

She was deeply grieved by the death of her brother Ḥamzah, but she was patient and she sought the reward from Allāh through her patience.

She was from those who migrated during the first migration, and I don't know if she accepted Islām with her brother Ḥamzah or with her son az-Zubayr.

Her Courage:

During the Battle of the Trench, Ṣafiyyah was in the fortress of Ḥasan bin Thābit with the women and children, as the men were off in battle. She said, "Ḥasan was with us when a spy sent by the Jews passed by the fortress, and he began to circle the fortress while the Muslims were engaging their enemy." She said, "I was the first woman to kill a man. Ḥasan was with us when a spy from the Jews began to circle the fortress. I said to Ḥasan, 'I don't trust him; he is going to inform the enemy of our location, so stand up and go kill him.' Ḥasan replied, 'May Allāh forgive you. You know I am not able to do this[2].' So I fortified myself, grabbed a pole, and went down and struck him until I killed him."[3]

Ṣafiyyah رضي الله عنها died in 20 AH, and she was buried in al-Baqī'. She was in her 70s.

'Ā'ishah رضي الله عنها said:

---

[1] **Translator's note:** As-Sā'ib is from the noble Companions; he witnessed many battles, such as the Battle of Badr. He was martyred at the Battle of Yamāmah.

[2] **Translator's note:** The scholars of history mention that this was likely due to his age or a medical condition, not his lack of bravery, because his bravery is well documented.

[3] Collected and authenticated by al-Ḥākim (4/51).

لَمَّا نَزَلَتْ {وَأَنْذِرْ عَشِيرَتَكَ الأَقْرَبِينَ} قَامَ رَسُولُ اللَّهِ صلى الله عليه وسلم عَلَى الصَّفَا فَقَالَ يَا فَاطِمَةَ بِنْتَ مُحَمَّدٍ يَا صَفِيَّةُ بِنْتَ عَبْدِ الْمُطَّلِبِ يَا بَنِي عَبْدِ الْمُطَّلِبِ لاَ أَمْلِكُ لَكُمْ مِنَ اللَّهِ شَيْئًا سَلُونِي مِنْ مَالِي مَا شِئْتُمْ.

When the verse was revealed: "And warn thy nearest kindred," the Messenger of Allāh ﷺ stood up on Ṣafā and said, "O Fāṭimah, daughter of Muḥammad. O Ṣafiyyah, daughter of 'Abdul-Muṭṭalib; O sons of 'Abdul-Muṭṭalib. I have nothing which can avail you against Allāh; you may ask me what you want of my worldly belongings."[4]

ARWĀ BINT 'ABDUL-MUṬṬALIB

She married 'Umayr bin Wahb and gave birth to their son Ṭulayb. Then she married Arṭāh and gave birth to their daughter Fāṭimah. Then Arwā accepted Islām and migrated. Her son Ṭulayb accepted Islām in the house of al-Arqam.[5]

We did not find any *aḥādīth* narrated by her.

'ĀTIKAH BINT 'ABDUL-MUṬṬALIB

She accepted Islām and migrated. She is the one who had the dream of the pagans' destruction at the Battle of Badr. That dream discouraged her brother Abū Lahab from attending the Battle of Badr.

TRANSLATOR'S ADDENDUM

'Ātikah bint 'Abdul-Muṭṭalib said, "I saw a rider standing on Abū Qubays (a mountain in Makkah). He shouted, 'O people of treachery, O people of evil: you have three days to flee.' Then he grabbed

[4] *Ṣaḥīḥ Muslim* 205

[5] **Translator's note:** The house of Arqam was the home of al-Arqam bin Abī Arqam. His home was a safe haven in Makkah for the earliest Muslims who entered Islām.

a boulder and dropped it from Abū Qubays and it shattered into pieces, and parts of it entered every home of the Quraysh except Banū Zuhrah." Al-'Abbās told her not to inform anyone about her dream. Al-'Abbās encountered al-Walīd bin 'Utbah and informed him of the dream. Al-Walīd mentioned it to his father, and it spread among the people. When the news spread, Abū Jahl said, "O Banū 'Abdul-Muṭṭalib, are you pleased that your men pretend to be prophets and now your women pretend to be prophets?! 'Ātikah alleges she had a dream and that you have three days to flee, so we will lie in wait for three days. If what she says is true, then it will happen, and if three days pass and nothing happens, you all will be the greatest liars in Arabia."

Three days later, a messenger from Abū Sufyān arrived in the valley; he stood up on his camel and tore his shirt, shouting, "O Quraysh, the merchant-camels, the merchant-camels! Muḥammad and his Companions are lying in wait for your property, which is with Abū Sufyān. I do not think that you will overtake it. So come help!" The Quraysh armed themselves for the Battle of Badr. However, 'Ātikah's brother Abū Lahab did not join the army, saying he was afraid of 'Ātikah's dream.[6]

Al-Bayḍā' bint 'Abdul-Muṭṭalib

She is Umm Ḥakīm bint 'Abdul-Muṭṭalib. I believe she died before the first revelation was revealed. She married Kurayz bin Rabī'ah al-'Abshamī and gave birth to their son 'Āmir, who was the father of 'Abdullāh[7]. Likewise, she gave birth to Arwā bint Kurayz, the mother of the martyr 'Uthmān bin 'Affān; thus, al-Bayḍā' bint 'Abdul-Muṭṭalib was the maternal grandmother of 'Uthmān bin 'Affān ﷺ.

Then she married 'Uqbah bin Abī Mu'ayṭ and she gave birth to

[6] *Al-Mu'jam al-Kabīr* by aṭ-Ṭabarānī.

[7] **Translator's note:** 'Abdullāh bin 'Āmir is a Companion who was the governor of Basra and a cousin to 'Uthmān bin 'Affān ﷺ.

al-Walīd, Khālid, and Umm Kulthūm; all three of them were Companions.

TRANSLATOR'S ADDENDUM

In the book *The History of Damascus*, al-Bayḍā' bint 'Abdul-Muṭṭalib—the grandmother of 'Uthmān bin 'Affān—is listed as the twin sister of 'Abdullāh bin 'Abdul-Muṭṭalib, the father of the Messenger of Allāh ﷺ.

BARRAH BINT 'ABDUL-MUṬṬALIB

Barrah bint 'Abdul-Muṭṭalib is the mother of the noble Companion Abū Salamah 'Abdullāh bin 'Abdil-Asad al-Makhzūmī ﷺ. After she married Abū Salamah's father, she was married to Abū Ruhm bin 'Abdil-'Uzzā al-'Āmirī, and she gave birth to their son, the noble Companion Abū Sabrah. He is from those who fought in the Battle of Badr. She did not live to see the first revelation.

UMĀMAH BINT 'ABDUL-MUṬṬALIB

She was married to Jaḥsh bin Riyāb, and she was the mother of his children: 'Abdullāh, the Mother of the Believers Zaynab, 'Ubaydullāh, Abū Aḥmad 'Abd, and Ḥamnah.

It is said that she accepted Islām and migrated. Ibn Sa'd mentioned in his book that the Messenger of Allāh ﷺ would send her 40 shipments of dates from the dates of Khaybar.

It has also been mentioned that the one who accepted Islām and was sent the shipment of dates from the Messenger of Allāh ﷺ was not his aunt; rather, it was Umāmah bint Rabī'ah bin al-Ḥārith bin 'Abdul-Muṭṭalib.

From what is apparent, the elder Umāmah—the aunt of the Prophet ﷺ—did not migrate, nor did she live long enough to reach the first revelation. And Allāh knows best. The only one to mention her accepting Islām was al-Wāqidī. And Allāh knows best.

THE PATERNAL COUSINS

OF THE PROPHET

1) Ḍubā'ah bint az-Zubayr bin 'Abdul-Muṭṭalib

2) Durrah bint Abī Lahab

3) Umm Hāni' Fākhitah bint Abī Ṭālib

ḌUBĀ'AH BINT AZ-ZUBAYR BIN 'ABDUL-MUṬṬALIB

Ḍubā'ah is the daughter of the Prophet's uncle az-Zubayr bin 'Abdul-Muṭṭalib. She is from those who migrated ﷺ.

She was married to al-Miqdād bin al-Aswad, and she gave birth to their children 'Abdullāh and Karīmah.

She narrated a few *aḥādīth* from the Messenger of Allāh ﷺ. Those who narrated from her include her daughter Karīmah, Sa'īd bin al-Musayyib, 'Urwah bin az-Zubayr, 'Abdur-Raḥmān al-A'rij, and Anas bin Mālik.

Some of the senior Companions narrated *aḥādīth* which mention her, like Ibn 'Abbās and Jābir.

Her son 'Abdullāh bin al-Miqdād was killed during the Battle of the Camel, fighting on the side of 'Ā'ishah ﵂.

'Ā'ishah ﵂ said:

دَخَلَ رَسُولُ اللَّهِ صلى الله عليه وسلم عَلَى ضُبَاعَةَ بِنْتِ الزُّبَيْرِ فَقَالَ لَهَا أَرَدْتِ الْحَجَّ. قَالَتْ وَاللَّهِ مَا أَجِدُنِي إِلاَّ وَجِعَةً. فَقَالَ لَهَا حُجِّي وَاشْتَرِطِي وَقُولِي اللَّهُمَّ مَحِلِّي حَيْثُ حَبَسْتَنِي. وَكَانَتْ تَحْتَ الْمِقْدَادِ.

The Messenger of Allāh ﷺ went to Ḍubā'ah bint az-Zubayr and said to her, "Did you intend to perform Ḥajj?" She said, "By Allāh, (I intend to do so), but I often remain ill," whereupon he said to her, "Go for Ḥajj, but stipulate a condition and say, 'O Allāh, I will exit *iḥrām* from the point where You have prevented me (from continuing, if some problem should arise).'" And she (Ḍubā'ah) was the wife of Miqdād.[1]

Ḍubā'ah lived until 40 AH ﵂.

DURRAH BINT ABĪ LAHAB

Durrah is the daughter of the Prophet's uncle Abū Lahab. She is from those who migrated. She narrated one *ḥadīth*. It is said that she was married to Diḥyah al-Kalbī.

TRANSLATOR'S ADDENDUM

When Durrah bint Abī Lahab migrated to Madīnah, some people said to her, "You are the daughter of the firewood of the Hellfire!" When the Prophet ﷺ heard of this, he stood up angrily and said:

ما بال أقوام يؤذونني في نسبي وذوي رحمي؟ ألا ومن آذى نسبي وذوي رحمي فقد آذاني، ومن آذاني فقد آذى اللَّه.

What is the matter with some people that they should offend my

[1] *Ṣaḥīḥ Muslim* 1207

lineage and my kinfolk? Surely, whoever offends my lineage and my kinfolk has offended me, and whoever offends me has offended Allāh.[2]

The following narration is the one *ḥadīth* narrated by Durrah.

Durrah bint Abī Lahab ﵁ said:

قَامَ رَجُلٌ إِلَى النَّبِيِّ صَلَّى اللَّهُ عَلَيْهِ وَسَلَّمَ وَهُوَ عَلَى الْمِنْبَرِ، فَقَالَ: يَا رَسُولَ اللَّهِ، أَيُّ النَّاسِ خَيْرٌ؟ فَقَالَ: خَيْرُ النَّاسِ أَقْرَؤُهُمْ، وَأَتْقَاهُمْ، وَآمَرُهُمْ بِالْمَعْرُوفِ، وَأَنْهَاهُمْ عَنِ الْمُنْكَرِ، وَأَوْصَلُهُمْ لِلرَّحِمِ.

A man stood while the Prophet ﷺ was on the *minbar* and said, "O Messenger of Allāh, who are the best people?" He said, "The best people are those with the most knowledge of the Qur'ān, those with the most *taqwā*, those who enjoin the good and forbid the evil the most, and those who keep the ties of kinship the most."[3]

UMM HĀNI' FĀKHITAH BINT ABĪ ṬĀLIB

She is the noble Companion Umm Hāni', the daughter of the Prophet's uncle Abū Ṭālib. She is the sister of 'Alī bin Abī Ṭālib and Ja'far bin Abī Ṭālib. Her name is Fākhitah. She delayed entering Islām.

The Prophet ﷺ entered her home the day of the conquest of Makkah and prayed eight *raka'āt* for Ḍuḥā prayer.

She is from the scholars of Islām and she narrated 46 *aḥādīth*. Those who narrated from her include: her grandson Ja'dah, her freed slave Abū Ṣāliḥ Bādhām, Kurayb (the freed slave of Ibn 'Abbās), 'Abdur-Raḥmān bin Abī Laylā, Mujāhid bin Jabr, 'Aṭā' bin Abī Rabāḥ, 'Urwah bin az-Zubayr, and others.

[2] Collected by Ibn 'Adī in *Al-Kāmil* (7/2717)

[3] Collected by Aḥmad (6/432)

Her Family:

She was married to Hubayrah bin 'Amr. He fled to Najrān on the day Makkah was conquered. She gave birth to 'Amr bin Hubayrah, Ja'dah, Hāni'ā, and Yūsuf.

She accepted Islām the day Makkah was conquered. It is not mentioned by anyone that Hubayrah accepted Islām. Umm Hāni' ﵂ said:

ذَهَبْتُ إِلَى رَسُولِ اللَّهِ صلى الله عليه وسلم عَامَ الْفَتْحِ فَوَجَدْتُهُ يَغْتَسِلُ، وَفَاطِمَةُ ابْنَتُهُ تَسْتُرُهُ، فَسَلَّمْتُ عَلَيْهِ فَقَالَ مَنْ هَذِهِ. فَقُلْتُ أَنَا أُمُّ هَانِئٍ بِنْتُ أَبِي طَالِبٍ. فَقَالَ مَرْحَبًا بِأُمِّ هَانِئٍ. فَلَمَّا فَرَغَ مِنْ غُسْلِهِ قَامَ، فَصَلَّى ثَمَانَ رَكَعَاتٍ مُلْتَحِفًا فِي ثَوْبٍ وَاحِدٍ، فَقُلْتُ يَا رَسُولَ اللَّهِ، زَعَمَ ابْنُ أُمِّي عَلِيٌّ أَنَّهُ قَاتِلٌ رَجُلاً قَدْ أَجَرْتُهُ فُلاَنُ بْنُ هُبَيْرَةَ. فَقَالَ رَسُولُ اللَّهِ صلى الله عليه وسلم " قَدْ أَجَرْنَا مَنْ أَجَرْتِ يَا أُمَّ هَانِئٍ. قَالَتْ أُمُّ هَانِئٍ وَذَلِكَ ضُحًى.

"I went to the Messenger of Allāh ﷺ on the day of the conquest of Makkah and found him taking a bath, and his daughter Fāṭimah was screening him. I greeted him with *salām* and he asked, 'Who is that?' I said, 'I, Umm Hāni' bint Abī Ṭālib.' He said, 'Welcome, O Umm Hāni'.' When he had finished his bath, he stood up and offered eight *raka'āt* while dressed in one garment. I said, 'O Messenger of Allāh, my brother 'Alī alleges that he will kill a man to whom I have granted asylum. The man is so-and-so bin Hubayrah.' The Messenger of Allāh ﷺ said, 'O Umm Hāni', we will grant asylum to the one whom you have granted asylum.'" (Umm Hāni') said, "That (visit) took place during the forenoon."[4]

'Alī bin Abī Ṭālib placed his nephew Ja'dah bin Hubayrah—the son of Umm Hāni'—in charge of Khurāsān.

When Umm Hāni's marriage from Hubayrah was dissolved due

---

[4] *Ṣaḥīḥ al-Bukhārī* 3171

to her Islām and his remaining upon disbelief, the Messenger of Allāh ﷺ proposed to her. She responded to him by saying, "I am a woman with a lot of children and I hate that they should bring you any inconvenience." Thus, the Prophet ﷺ did not reply to her statement.

Umm Hāni' lived until 50 AH.

TRANSLATOR'S ADDENDUM

The Messenger of Allāh ﷺ has other female cousins not mentioned by Imām adh-Dhahabī رحمه الله.

- Umm Ḥakīm bint az-Zubayr bin 'Abdul-Muṭṭalib
- Umm Zubayr bint az-Zubayr bin 'Abdul-Muṭṭalib
- Ṣafiyyah bint az-Zubayr bin 'Abdul-Muṭṭalib
- Umm Ṭālib Rayṭah bint Abī Ṭālib bin 'Abdul-Muṭṭalib
- Jumānah bint Abī Ṭālib bin 'Abdul-Muṭṭalib
- Umāmah bint Ḥamzah bin 'Abdul-Muṭṭalib
- Khālidah bint Abī Lahab bin 'Abdul-Muṭṭalib
- 'Uzzā bint Abī Lahab bin 'Abdul-Muṭṭalib
- Umm Ḥabīb bin al-'Abbās bin 'Abdul-Muṭṭalib
- Hind bint al-Muqawwim bin 'Abdul-Muṭṭalib
- Arwā bint al-Muqawwim bin 'Abdul-Muṭṭalib
- Umm 'Amr bint al-Muqawwim bin 'Abdul-Muṭṭalib

THE MUHĀJIRŪN

FROM THE FEMALE COMPANIONS

1) Fāṭimah bint Asad
2) Asmā' bint 'Umays
3) Asmā' bint Abī Bakr
4) Umm Kulthūm bint 'Uqbah
5) Fāṭimah bint Qays
6) Zaynab bint Abī Salamah
7) Umm Khālid bint Khālid
8) Umm al-Faḍl

FĀṬIMAH BINT ASAD BIN HĀSHIM BIN 'ABD MANĀF BIN QUṢAYY AL-HĀSHIMĪ

She is the mother of 'Alī and Ja'far bin Abī Ṭālib, and the mother-in-law of Fāṭimah.

She was from the first to migrate during the first migration. She was the first Hāshimī born to the Hāshimī tribe.

Her Death:

Ibn 'Abbās said, "When Fāṭimah, the mother of 'Alī, died, the Prophet ﷺ dressed his shirt over her and lay down on his side with her in her grave. They said, 'O Messenger of Allāh, what did she do (to deserve this honor)?!' He said, 'There was no one other than Abū Ṭālib who was kinder to me than she was. I only dressed her in my shirt so she can be dressed in the garments of Paradise, and I lay down beside her so the grave would be easy upon her.' "[1]

ASMĀ' BINT 'UMAYS BIN MA'BAD BIN AL-ḤĀRITH AL-KHATH'AMIYYAH

She is Umm 'Abdillāh, from those first and foremost to migrate. It is said that she embraced Islām before the Messenger of Allāh ﷺ entered the house of Arqam[2]. She migrated to Abyssinia with her husband, Ja'far bin Abī Ṭālib. There, she gave birth to her children 'Abdullāh, Muḥammad, and 'Awn.

Then she migrated with her husband—Ja'far bin Abī Ṭālib—to Madīnah in 7 AH. Ja'far bin Abī Ṭālib was martyred at the Battle of Mu'tah.

Her Second Marriage:

Then she married Abū Bakr aṣ-Ṣiddīq and gave birth to their son Muḥammad while in a state of *iḥrām,* and she performed the Farewell Pilgrimage.

'Ā'ishah ﵂ said:

نُفست أسماء بنت عميس – زوجة أبي بكر - بمحمد بن أبي بكر

[1] *Al-Istī'ābah fī Ma'rifah al-Aṣ'ḥāb* 13/108

[2] **Translator's note:** The house of Arqam was the home of al-Arqam bin Abī Arqam. His home was a safe haven in Makkah for the earliest Muslims who entered Islām.

بالشجرة فأمر رسول الله صلى الله عليه وسلم أبا بكر يأمرها أن تغتسل وتهل.

Asmā' bint 'Umays—Abū Bakr's wife—experienced postpartum bleeding after giving birth to Muḥammad bin Abī Bakr in Shajarah[3], and the Messenger of Allāh ﷺ told Abū Bakr to tell her to make *ghusl* and enter *iḥrām*.[4]

Before Abū Bakr died, he stipulated that his wife Asmā' bint 'Umays should wash his body upon his death. And on the day he was dying, she was fasting, so he obligated her to break her fast because it would give her more strength.

'Abdullāh bin Abī Bakr said that Asmā' bint 'Umays washed Abū Bakr aṣ-Ṣiddīq when he died. Then she went out and asked some of the Muhājirūn who were there, "I am fasting and this is an extremely cold day. Do I have to make *ghusl*?" They said, "No."[5]

At the end of the day, right before sunset, Asmā' remembered her oath to her husband to break her fast, so she asked for water and said, "By Allāh, today I will not follow his death by disobeying him."

When 'Umar became the caliph, he gave her a stipend of 1,000 *dirham*[6].

Her Third Marriage:

'Alī bin Abī Ṭālib then married her. She gave birth to their children Yaḥyā and 'Awn.

Her Two Migrations:

The *ḥadīth* of Abū Mūsā has been collected in *Al-Bukhārī* and

---

[3] **Translator's note:** Shajarah refers to Dhul-Ḥulayfah, which is the *mīqāt* from which the people of Madīnah enter *iḥrām*.

[4] *Ṣaḥīḥ Muslim* 1209

[5] *Muwaṭṭa' Mālik* 525

[6] Collected by Ibn Sa'd (8/284).

Muslim. He said, "The news of the migration of the Prophet (from Makkah to Madīnah) reached us while we were in Yemen. So we set out as emigrants towards him. We were (three): I and my two brothers. I was the youngest of them, and one of the two was Abū Burdah, and the other was Abū Ruhm, and our total number was either 53 or 52 men from my people. We got on board a boat, and our boat took us to an-Najāshī in Abyssinia. There, we met Ja'far bin Abī Ṭālib and stayed with him. Then we all came (to Madīnah) and met the Prophet ﷺ at the time of the conquest of Khaybar.

"The Prophet ﷺ allocated a share to us from the Battle of Khaybar. And in most cases, a share would only be given to those present at the battle, not those who were absent, but he made an exception for us. Some of the people who were present at the battle used to say to us—meaning, the people of the ship—'We have migrated before you.'

"Asmā' bint 'Umays came with us from Abyssinia. When she arrived in Madīnah, she visited Ḥafṣah, the wife of the Prophet ﷺ and the daughter of 'Umar. 'Umar said to his daughter Ḥafṣah, 'Who is that? Is that the woman from Abyssinia, the woman from the sea[7]?' 'Umar ﷺ said to her, 'O woman from Abyssinia, we have migrated before you; we have more right to the Messenger of Allāh than you.' She said to 'Umar, 'You have surely spoken the truth. You were with the Messenger of Allāh ﷺ, feeding the hungry and teaching the ignorant, while we were distant and repelled. By Allāh, I will surely mention this to the Messenger of Allāh ﷺ.' The Messenger of Allāh ﷺ said:

لَيْسَ بِأَحَقَّ بِي مِنْكُمْ وَلَهُ وَلأَصْحَابِهِ هِجْرَةٌ وَاحِدَةٌ وَلَكُمْ أَنْتُمْ أَهْلَ السَّفِينَةِ هِجْرَتَانِ.

"'They do not have more right to me than you all. He and his Companions migrated once, while you—the people of the boat—migrated twice.'"[8]

---

[7] **Translator's note:** Meaning, the woman who migrated to Abyssinia by way of the sea.

[8] *Ṣaḥīḥ al-Bukhārī* 4230; *Ṣaḥīḥ Muslim* 2502

Asmā' bint 'Umays ﵂ said:

يَا رَسُولَ اللَّهِ، إِنَّ هَؤُلَاءِ يَزْعُمُونَ أَنَّا لَسْنَا مِنَ الْمُهَاجِرِينَ. قَالَ: كَذَبَ مَنْ يَقُولُ ذَلِكَ، لَكُمُ الْهِجْرَةُ مَرَّتَيْنِ: هَاجَرْتُمْ إِلَى النَّجَاشِيِّ، وَهَاجَرْتُمْ إِلَيَّ.

"O Messenger of Allāh, they alleged that we are not from the Muhājirūn (those who migrated)." He said, "Whoever says that is incorrect. There are two migrations for you all: you migrated to Abyssinia and you migrated to me."[9]

Ash-Sha'bī said, "The first person to cover a woman's shroud with a coffin was Asmā'; she learned this from what she saw the Christians doing in Abyssinia."

Her Cleverness:

While Asmā' was married to 'Alī bin Abī Ṭālib, her two sons—Muḥammad bin Abī Bakr and Muḥammad bin Ja'far—had a dispute, with each one saying, "I am nobler than you; my father was better than your father." 'Alī said to her, "Decide the matter between them." She said to them, "I have not seen a youth from the Arabs better than Ja'far. And I have not seen an elder better than Abū Bakr." 'Alī said, "If you would have given any other answer, I would have been upset with you; but you didn't say anything about me." Asmā' replied, "Of the three, you were the least to choose."[10]

Her Narrations:

Asmā' ﵂ has narrations which have been collected in the books of *ḥadīth*. Those who narrated from her include: her son 'Abdullāh bin Ja'far, her nephew 'Abdullāh bin Shaddād, Sa'īd bin al-Musayyib, 'Urwah, ash-Sha'bī, al-Qāsim bin Muḥammad, and others.

She lived on after her husband 'Alī bin Abī Ṭālib was killed.

[9] Collected by Ibn Sa'd (8/281).

[10] Collected by Ibn Sa'd (8/285).

TRANSLATOR'S ADDENDUM

Asmā' bint 'Umays was married to two martyrs: Ja'far bin Abī Ṭālib and 'Alī bin Abī Ṭālib ﵄. And she was married to two caliphs: Abū Bakr aṣ-Ṣiddīq and 'Alī bin Abī Ṭālib ﵄.

Asmā' bint 'Umays had three sisters who were also from the noble Companions:

1) Maymūnah bint al-Ḥārith was her sister by way of her mother. She was married to the Messenger of Allāh ﷺ.

2) Umm al-Faḍl Lubābah bint al-Ḥārith was her sister by way of her mother. She was married to al-'Abbās, the uncle of the Messenger of Allāh ﷺ.

3) Salmā bint 'Umays; she was married to the Lion of Allāh Ḥamzah bin 'Abdul-Muṭṭalib, the uncle of the Prophet ﷺ.

The Messenger of Allāh ﷺ said about them:

الأخوات الأربع: ميمونة و أم الفضل و سلمى و أسماء بنت عميس - أختهن لأمهن مؤمنات.

The four sisters—Maymūnah, Umm al-Faḍl, Salmā, and Asmā' bint 'Umays—are believing sisters of the same mother.[11]

ASMĀ' BINT ABĪ BAKR

She is Umm 'Abdillāh Asmā' bint Abī Bakr bin 'Abdillāh bin Abī Quḥāfah 'Uthmān. Her mother is Qutaylah bint 'Abdil-'Uzzā al-'Āmiriyyah. She is the mother of the caliph 'Abdullāh bin az-Zubayr and the sister of the Mother of the Believers 'Ā'ishah.

She was the last of the Muhājirūn from among the women to die. She lived to be 100 years old and none of her teeth had fallen out; rather, all her teeth remained healthy. She was older than 'Ā'ishah

[11] Declared authentic by Shaykh al-Albānī in *Silsilah aṣ-Ṣaḥīḥah* (4/363).

by about 10 years.

Her Narrations:

Those who narrated from her are: her sons 'Abdullāh and 'Urwah, her grandson 'Abdullāh bin 'Urwah, and her great-grandson 'Abbād bin 'Abdillāh. Likewise, those who narrated from her were Ibn 'Abbās, Abū Wāqid al-Laythī, Ṣafiyyah bint Shaybah, Muḥammad al-Munkadir, and many others.

Her Bravery:

She participated in the Battle of Yarmūk[12] with her husband az-Zubayr.

Her Noble Lineage:

Her grandfather, father, and son (Ibn az-Zubayr) were all Companions; four generations of Companions ﷺ. She migrated when she was pregnant with 'Abdullāh.

Muslim al-Qurrī said, "We entered upon the mother of az-Zubayr, and she was a bulky blind woman. We asked her concerning Ḥajj *tamattu'*[13]; she said:

قَدْ رَخَّصَ رَسُولُ اللَّهِ صلى الله عليه وسلم فِيهَا.

" 'Verily, the Messenger of Allāh ﷺ permitted it.' "[14]

She was known as "the Owner of the Two Belts." Asmā' ﷺ said, "I prepared the journey-food for the Messenger of Allāh ﷺ in Abū Bakr's house when he intended to migrate to Madīnah. I could not find anything to tie the food container and the waterskin with. So I said to Abū Bakr, 'By Allāh, I do not find anything to tie (these things) with except my waist belt.' He said, 'Cut it into two pieces and tie the waterskin with one piece and the food container with

---

[12] **Translator's note:** The Battle of Yarmūk was a major battle between the army of the Byzantine Empire and the Muslim army of the Rāshidūn Caliphate. The Muslims were victorious.

[13] **Translator's note:** *Tamattu'* involves a complete 'Umrah and a complete Ḥajj.

[14] *Ṣaḥīḥ Muslim* 1238

the other.' " She did so, and that was the reason for calling her the Owner of the Two Belts.[15]

Asmā' bint Abī Bakr ﵂ said, "When the Prophet ﷺ headed to Madīnah from Makkah, he took Abū Bakr and he gathered all his wealth, which was five or six thousand. My grandfather Abū Quḥāfah came to visit me, and at this time he had gone blind. He said, 'This man (Abū Bakr) put you in adversity. He deprived you of himself and property.' I ﵂ said, 'No, on the contrary.' I covered some stones, took my grandfather's hands, placed them on the stones, and said, 'He left this for us.' He said, 'If he left this for you, there is no blame upon him.' "[16]

Asmā' bint Abī Bakr ﵂ said, "Abū Jahl came to me with a group of men, so I went out to them. They said, 'Where is your father?' I said, 'By Allāh, I don't know where he is.' Abū Jahl raised his hand and slapped me once, making my earring fall off. Then they left. Three days passed, and I did not know in what direction the Messenger of Allāh had traveled. Then a man from among the *jinn* approached, and his voice could be heard at the top of Makkah. He began to recite lines of poetry, saying:

جَزَى اللَّهُ رَبُّ النَّاسِ خَيْرَ جَزَائِهِ رَفِيقَيْنِ قَالَا خَيْمَتَيْ أُمِّ مَعْبَدِ.

" 'May Allāh, the Lord of mankind, reward the two comrades with the best reward! They took a midday nap in the tent of Umm[17] Ma'bad[18].'

"When we heard this, we knew that the Messenger of Allāh ﷺ was heading towards Madīnah."

Asmā' would get headaches, so she would place her hand on her

---

[15] *Ṣaḥīḥ al-Bukhārī* 2979

[16] Collected by Ibn Is'ḥāq (1/488) with an authentic chain of narration.

[17] **Translator's note:** Umm Ma'bad; her name was 'Ātikah bint Khālid. The Prophet ﷺ passed by her tent along with Abū Bakr and the freed slave of Abū Bakr, 'Āmir bin Fuhayrah, when they migrated to Madīnah.

[18] Collected by Ibn Hishām (1/487).

head and say, "This is due to my sins, and what Allāh has forgiven is more."[19]

Asmā' Married az-Zubayr bin al-'Awām:

Asmā' bint Abī Bakr ﷺ said, "When az-Zubayr married me, he had no real property or any slaves or anything else except a camel which drew water from the well, and his horse. I used to feed his horse with fodder and draw water and patch the bucket for drawing it, and prepare the dough, but I did not know how to bake bread. So our Anṣārī neighbors used to bake bread for me, and they were honorable ladies. I used to carry the datestones on my head from Zubayr's land given to him by the Messenger of Allāh ﷺ, and this land was about two miles from my house. One day, while I was coming with the datestones on my head, I met the Messenger of Allāh along with some Anṣārī people. He called me and then, (directing his camel to kneel down) said, '*Ikh*! *Ikh*!' so as to make me ride behind him on his camel. I felt shy to travel with the men and remembered az-Zubayr and his sense of jealousy, as he was one of those people who had the greatest sense of jealousy. The Messenger of Allāh ﷺ noticed that I felt shy, so he proceeded.

"I came to az-Zubayr and said, 'I met the Messenger of Allāh ﷺ while I was carrying a load of datestones on my head, and he had some Companions with him. He made his camel kneel so that I might ride, but I felt shy in his presence and remembered your sense of jealousy.' Az-Zubayr said, 'By Allāh, your carrying of the datestones (and you being seen by the Prophet in such a state) is more shameful to me than your riding with him.' I continued serving in this way until Abū Bakr sent me a servant to look after the horse, whereupon I felt as if he had set me free."[20]

The Quranic Verse Sent Down Concerning Her Situation:

Ibn az-Zubayr said, "This verse was sent down concerning Asmā'. Her mother's name was Qutaylah. Her mother came to her with a gift, but she did not accept it until she asked the Messenger of Allāh

---

[19] Collected by Ibn Sa'd (8/251).

[20] *Ṣaḥīḥ al-Bukhārī* 5224

ﷺ. Thus, the verse was sent down:

﴿ لَّا يَنْهَاكُمُ اللَّهُ عَنِ الَّذِينَ لَمْ يُقَاتِلُوكُمْ فِي الدِّينِ وَلَمْ يُخْرِجُوكُم مِّن دِيَارِكُمْ أَن تَبَرُّوهُمْ وَتُقْسِطُوا إِلَيْهِمْ ۚ إِنَّ اللَّهَ يُحِبُّ الْمُقْسِطِينَ ﴾

" 'Allāh does not forbid you to deal justly and kindly with those who fought not against you on account of religion and did not drive you out of your homes. Verily, Allāh loves those who deal with equity.' "

[Sūrah al-Mumtaḥanah 60:8]

Asmā' رضي الله عنها said:

قَدِمَتْ عَلَيَّ أُمِّي وَهِيَ مُشْرِكَةٌ، فَاسْتَفْتَيْتُ رَسُولَ اللَّهِ صَلَّى اللَّهُ عَلَيْهِ وَسَلَّمَ، فَقُلْتُ: يَا رَسُولَ اللَّهِ، قَدِمَتْ عَلَيَّ أُمِّي، وَهِيَ رَاغِبَةٌ، أَفَأَصِلُ أُمِّي؟ قَالَ: نَعَمْ، صِلِي أُمَّكِ.

My mother came to me when she was a pagan. I consulted the Messenger of Allāh ﷺ and said, "O Messenger of Allāh, my mother has come to me, and she is expecting something; should I uphold the ties of kinship with my mother?" He said, "Yes, uphold the ties of kinship with your mother."[21]

Her Divorce:

'Urwah[22] said, "Az-Zubayr hit Asmā', so she yelled for her son 'Abdullāh. When 'Abdullāh approached, az-Zubayr said, 'If you enter, your mother is divorced.' 'Abdullāh said, 'Will you make my mother liable for your oath?!' So he rushed in and set her free. Thus, she separated from him."[23]

Hishām bin 'Urwah said, "Az-Zubayr divorced Asmā' and he took

[21] *Ṣaḥīḥ al-Bukhārī* 2620; *Ṣaḥīḥ Muslim* 1003

[22] **Translator's note:** 'Urwah is the son of az-Zubayr and Asmā'.

[23] Collected by Ibn al-Athīr in *Asad al-Ghābah*.

their son ‘Urwah with him, and ‘Urwah was young at the time.”[24]

Her Generosity:

Muḥammad bin al-Munkadir said, “Asmā' bint Abī Bakr was a generous soul.”

Ibn az-Zubayr said:

مَا رَأَيْتُ امْرَأَتَيْنِ أَجْوَدَ مِنْ عَائِشَةَ، وَأَسْمَاءَ، وَجُودُهُمَا مُخْتَلِفٌ، أَمَّا عَائِشَةُ فَكَانَتْ تَجْمَعُ الشَّيْءَ إِلَى الشَّيْءِ، حَتَّى إِذَا كَانَ اجْتَمَعَ عِنْدَهَا قَسَمَتْ، وَأَمَّا أَسْمَاءُ فَكَانَتْ لاَ تُمْسِكُ شَيْئًا لِغَدٍ.

I have never seen anyone more generous than ‘Ā'ishah and Asmā', yet their generosity was different. ‘Ā'ishah used to gather things, and after they had been collected together, she would share them. Asmā' would not keep anything for the next day.[25]

‘Umar ﷺ used to give the women who migrated 1,000 *dirham*, and from them was Umm ‘Abd[26] and Asmā'.

When Asmā' became sick, she freed every slave she had[27].

Her Knowledge of Dream Interpretation:

Sa’īd bin al-Musayyib was the most proficient at interpreting dreams, and he learned that from Asmā', and she learned it from her father[28].

Asmā' said to her son, “O my dear son: live honorably and die honorably, and don’t let anyone take you as a slave.”

Hishām bin ‘Urwah said, “When the thieves increased in Madīnah during the era of Sa’īd bin al-‘Āṣ, Asmā' procured a dagger and

[24] Collected by Ibn Sa’d (8/253).

[25] *Al-Adab al-Mufrad* 280; authenticated by Shaykh al-Albānī.

[26] **Translator’s note:** This is the mother of ‘Abdullāh bin Mas’ūd.

[27] Collected by Ibn Sa’d (8/251).

[28] Collected in *Aṭ-Ṭabaqāt* (6/124).

placed it under her pillow. When asked why she did so, she said, 'If a burglar enters upon me, I will split open his belly.' And by this time, she was blind."[29]

The Death of Her Son During the Fitnah of al-Ḥajjāj[30]*:*

'Urwah said, "My brother and I visited my mother days before he was killed, and she was in pain. 'Abdullāh said, 'How are you?' She replied, 'I am in pain.' He said, 'Verily, there is relief in death.' She said, 'Perhaps you are hoping for me to die; don't do that.' And then she laughed. She went on to say, 'I swear by Allāh, I do not want to die until one of two extremes occurs: either you are killed so I can seek the reward through patience, or you are victorious so I can be happy. And beware of compromising the truth due to your fear of death.' "[31]

'Abdullāh bin az-Zubayr was killed and crucified in 73 AH. It was said to Ibn 'Umar, "Asmā' is in the corner of the *masjid*," and this was when Ibn az-Zubayr had been crucified. He went to her and said, "These corpses are nothing; the souls are with Allāh, so have *taqwā* of Allāh and be patient." She said, "And what would prevent me from being patient when the head of the prophet Yaḥyā bin Zakariyyā Tārīkh was given as a gift to a prostitute from the Children of Israel[32]?"

When al-Ḥajjāj killed Ibn az-Zubayr, he visited Asmā' and said to her, "O mother, the leader has ordered me to take care of you, so do you have any needs?" She said, "I am not your mother. I am the mother of the one who was crucified. I don't have any needs, but I have some words for you. I heard the Messenger of Allāh ﷺ say, 'There will appear from (the town of) Thaqīf a liar and a destroyer.' As for the liar, we have seen him (meaning, al-Mukhtār

[29] Collected by al-Ḥākim (4/64).

[30] **Translator's note:** Al-Ḥajjāj bin Yūsuf ath-Thaqafī was the governor of Iraq known for his oppression and killing.

[31] *The History of Islām* by Imām adh-Dhahabī (3/135).

[32] **Translator's note:** *Stories of the Prophets* by Ibn Kathīr contains the story of the killing of Prophet Yaḥyā.

ath-Thaqafī[33]); as for the destroyer, then it is you." So he stood up and never returned to her.

In another narration, it mentions: Al-Ḥajjāj went to Asmā' and said, "Verily, your son deviated and Allāh caused him to taste a grievous punishment." She replied, "You are a liar. He was kind to his mother, and he was steadfast in fasting and prayer. But it is just as the Messenger of Allāh ﷺ informed us when he said, 'From Thaqīf there will appear two liars; the second will be worse than the first, and he will be a destroyer.' Thus, you spoiled his life and he spoiled your Hereafter."

Asmā' ﵂ supplicated to Allāh that He not allow her to die until she was able to shroud her son. Allāh answered her supplication, as her son was brought to her and she washed him with Zamzam water and shrouded him, and she was blind at this time. She prayed the funeral prayer for him, and less than a week passed by before Asmā' died ﵂. She was the last to die of the women who migrated.

Her Aḥādīth:

She narrated 58 *aḥādīth*. From those narrations is the well-known narration collected in *Al-Bukhārī*: Asmā' ﵂ said that the Messenger of Allāh ﷺ said:

إِنِّي عَلَى الْحَوْضِ حَتَّى أَنْظُرُ مَنْ يَرِدُ عَلَيَّ مِنْكُمْ.

I will be at the Pond waiting to see which of you will come to me.[34]

Umm Kulthūm bint 'Uqbah bin Abī Mu'ayṭ

Umm Kulthūm bint 'Uqbah was from those women who migrated. She accepted Islām in Makkah and gave her pledge of allegiance. It took her seven years to prepare to migrate. She migrated during the Treaty of Ḥudaybiyyah.

[33] **Translator's note:** From the *ḥadīth* of Ibn 'Umar; the Prophet ﷺ said, "In Thaqīf there is a liar and a destroyer." Collected in *Jāmi' at-Tirmidhī* (4324).

[34] *Ṣaḥīḥ al-Bukhārī* 6593

Quranic Verse Revealed About Her:

When Umm Kulthūm bint 'Uqbah migrated to Madīnah, she was pursued by her two brothers, Walīd and 'Imārah, who were pagans at the time. When her brothers arrived shortly after Umm Kulthūm, they went to the Messenger of Allāh and said, "O Muḥammad, fulfill the condition." This is because the condition of the Treaty of Ḥudaybiyyah was that whoever migrated to Madīnah without the permission of their guardian would be returned. Umm Kulthūm said, "O Messenger of Allāh, will you return me to the disbelievers so they may put me to trial regarding my religion, and I might not have the strength to endure? And the women are weak, as you know." Thus, Allāh the Exalted sent down the verse:

﴿ يَا أَيُّهَا الَّذِينَ آمَنُوا إِذَا جَاءَكُمُ الْمُؤْمِنَاتُ مُهَاجِرَاتٍ
فَامْتَحِنُوهُنَّ ۖ اللَّهُ أَعْلَمُ بِإِيمَانِهِنَّ ۖ فَإِنْ عَلِمْتُمُوهُنَّ
مُؤْمِنَاتٍ فَلَا تَرْجِعُوهُنَّ إِلَى الْكُفَّارِ ۖ لَا هُنَّ حِلٌّ لَّهُمْ وَلَا
هُمْ يَحِلُّونَ لَهُنَّ ۖ وَآتُوهُم مَّا أَنفَقُوا ۚ وَلَا جُنَاحَ عَلَيْكُمْ
أَن تَنكِحُوهُنَّ إِذَا آتَيْتُمُوهُنَّ أُجُورَهُنَّ ۚ وَلَا تُمْسِكُوا
بِعِصَمِ الْكَوَافِرِ وَاسْأَلُوا مَا أَنفَقْتُمْ وَلْيَسْأَلُوا مَا أَنفَقُوا ۚ
ذَٰلِكُمْ حُكْمُ اللَّهِ ۖ يَحْكُمُ بَيْنَكُمْ ۚ وَاللَّهُ عَلِيمٌ حَكِيمٌ ﴿١٠﴾
وَإِن فَاتَكُمْ شَيْءٌ مِّنْ أَزْوَاجِكُمْ إِلَى الْكُفَّارِ فَعَاقَبْتُمْ فَآتُوا
الَّذِينَ ذَهَبَتْ أَزْوَاجُهُم مِّثْلَ مَا أَنفَقُوا ۚ وَاتَّقُوا اللَّهَ الَّذِي
أَنتُم بِهِ مُؤْمِنُونَ ﴿١١﴾ ﴾

O you who believe! When believing women come to you as emigrants, examine them; Allāh knows best as to their faith. Then if you ascertain that they are true believers, send them not back to the disbelievers; they are not lawful (wives) for the disbelievers nor are the disbelievers lawful (husbands) for them. But give the disbelievers that (amount of money) which they have spent [as their *mahr*] to them. And

there will be no sin on you to marry them if you have paid their *mahr* to them. Likewise, hold not the disbelieving women as wives, and ask for (the return of) that which you have spent (as *mahr*) and let them (the disbelievers, etc.) ask back for that which they have spent. That is the judgment of Allāh. He judges between you. And Allāh is All-Knowing, All-Wise. And if any of your wives have gone from you to the disbelievers, and you have an accession (by the coming over of a woman from the other side), then pay to those whose wives have gone, the equivalent of what they had spent (on their *mahr*). And fear Allāh in Whom you believe.

[Sūrah al-Mumtaḥanah 60:10-11]

Thus, he would ask them, "By Allāh, did you only migrate due to love of Allāh, His Messenger, and Islām? And you did not migrate for a husband or wealth?" If they swore they only migrated due to love of Allāh, His Messenger, and Islām, then he would not return them to the disbelievers.

Her Marriage:

Umm Kulthūm did not have a husband in Makkah, so Zayd bin Ḥārithah married her. Then he divorced her, so 'Abdur-Raḥmān bin 'Awf married her. She gave birth to their children Ibrāhīm and Ḥumayd. 'Abdur-Raḥmān bin 'Awf died while married to her. Next, she married 'Amr bin al-'Āṣ, and she died while married to him.

She narrated 10 *aḥādīth*. Those who narrated from her include her sons Ḥumayd and Ibrāhīm, and Busrah bint Ṣafwān.

She died during the caliphate of 'Alī ﵁.

TRANSLATOR'S ADDENDUM

Umm Kulthūm bint 'Uqbah is the half-sister of 'Uthmān bin 'Affān; their mother was Arwā bint Kurayz.

From the well-known *aḥādīth* narrated by her is the narration collected in *Al-Bukhārī* and *Muslim*. Umm Kulthūm bint 'Uqbah said, "I heard the Messenger of Allāh ﷺ say:

ليس الكذاب الذي يصلح بين الناس فينمي خيراً أو يقول خيراً.

"'He is not a liar who brings about reconciliation among people, conveys good words, and says good things.'"[35]

FĀṬIMAH BINT QAYS

Fāṭimah bint Qays al-Fihriyyah was from those women who migrated, and she was the sister of the Companion aḍ-Ḍaḥḥāk bin Qays.

Her Marriage:

She was married to Abū 'Amr bin Ḥafṣ bin al-Mughīrah, then he divorced her. After her divorce, three men sought her hand in marriage. Fāṭimah bint Qays said, "The Messenger of Allāh ﷺ said to me, 'When your period of *'iddah* is over, inform me.' So I informed him." (By that time) Mu'āwiyah, Abū Jahm, and Usāmah bin Zayd had given her the proposal of marriage. The Messenger of Allāh ﷺ said, "As far as Mu'āwiyah is concerned, he is a poor man without any property. As far as Abū Jahm is concerned, he hits women; but Usāmah bin Zayd..." She indicated with her hand that she did not approve of the idea of marrying Usāmah. But the Messenger of Allāh ﷺ said:

طَاعَةُ اللَّهِ وَطَاعَةُ رَسُولِهِ خَيْرٌ لَكِ. قَالَتْ فَتَزَوَّجْتُهُ فَاغْتَبَطْتُ.

Obedience to Allāh and obedience to His Messenger is better for you.

She said, "So I married him, and I became an object of envy."[36]

---

35 *Ṣaḥīḥ al-Bukhārī* 2546; *Ṣaḥīḥ Muslim* 2605

36 *Ṣaḥīḥ Muslim* 1480

Her Aḥādīth:

She narrated the *ḥadīth* concerning the woman who has been divorced three times. She said that the Messenger of Allāh ﷺ said about the woman who had been given an irrevocable divorce:

لَيْسَ لَهَا سُكْنَى وَلاَ نَفَقَةٌ.

There is no lodging and maintenance allowance for her.[37]

Likewise, Fāṭimah bint Qays narrated the famous *ḥadīth* concerning the Dajjāl.[38]

Those who narrated from her include ash-Sha'bī, Abū Salamah bin 'Abdir-Raḥmān, Abū Bakr bin 'Abdir-Raḥmān bin al-Ḥārith bin Hishām, and others.

Fāṭimah bint Qays ﷺ died during Mu'āwiyah's caliphate.

ZAYNAB BINT ABĪ SALAMAH, THE STEPDAUGHTER OF THE PROPHET

She is Zaynab bint Abī Salamah bin 'Abdil-Asad al-Makhzūmī, the stepdaughter of the Messenger of Allāh ﷺ from his wife Umm Salamah. Her brother was 'Umar bin Abī Salamah. Their mother gave birth to both of them in Abyssinia.

Her Aḥādīth:

She narrated a number of *aḥādīth*, narrating from the likes of 'Ā'ishah, Zaynab bint Jaḥsh, Umm Ḥabībah, and others. Those who narrated from her include 'Urwah, 'Alī bin al-Ḥusayn, al-Qāsim bin Muḥammad, Abū Qilābah al-Jurmī, 'Aṭā', and many others.

Zaynab bint Abī Salamah said, "The Messenger of Allāh ﷺ was with Umm Salamah when he placed Ḥasan on one side, Ḥusayn

[37] *Ṣaḥīḥ Muslim* 1480

[38] *Ṣaḥīḥ Muslim* 2942

on the other side, and Fāṭimah in front of him and said, 'May the mercy of Allāh and His blessings be upon you, O household.'"

Zaynab bint Abī Salamah died in 74 AH ﵂.

Umm Khālid bint Khālid, the Last Female Companion to Die

She is Umm Khālid bint Khālid bin Abī Uḥayḥah Sa'īd bin al-'Āṣ bin Umayyah bin 'Abdush-Shams bin 'Abd Manāf al-Qurashiyyah. She was born in Abyssinia. Her name was Amah.

She narrated two *aḥādīth*[39]. Those who narrated from her include Sa'īd bin 'Amr bin Sa'īd bin al-'Āṣ, Mūsā bin 'Uqbah, and others.

Her Marriage:

She married az-Zubayr bin al-'Awām and gave birth to their children 'Umar and Khālid.

Her Death:

She was the last of the female Companions to die. She lived until the days of the Companion Sahl bin Sa'd. She died in 91 AH.

Umm Khālid bint Khālid ﵂ said, "The day we left Abyssinia on the two ships, I heard an-Najāshī saying, 'All of you convey my *salām* to the Messenger of Allāh from me.' Thus, I was from those who conveyed the *salām* to the Messenger of Allāh ﷺ from an-Najāshī."[40]

Umm Khālid's Gift & Du'ā' From the Prophet ﷺ:

Umm Khālid ﵂ said:

أُتِيَ رَسُولُ اللَّهِ صلى الله عليه وسلم بِثِيَابٍ فِيهَا خَمِيصَةٌ سَوْدَاءُ قَالَ مَنْ تَرَوْنَ نَكْسُوهَا هَذِهِ الْخَمِيصَةَ. فَأُسْكِتَ الْقَوْمُ. قَالَ ائْتُونِي بِأُمِّ خَالِدٍ.

---

[39] **Translator's note:** Other scholars say she narrated seven *aḥādīth*.

[40] Collected by Ibn Sa'd (8/1234).

فَأُتِيَ بِي النَّبِيُّ صلى الله عليه وسلم فَأَلْبَسَهَا بِيَدِهِ وَقَالَ أَبْلِي وَأَخْلِقِي. مَرَّتَيْنِ فَجَعَلَ يَنْظُرُ إِلَى عَلَمِ الْخَمِيصَةِ، وَيُشِيرُ بِيَدِهِ إِلَيَّ وَيَقُولُ يَا أُمَّ خَالِدٍ هَذَا سَنَا. وَالسَّنَا بِلِسَانِ الْحَبَشِيَّةِ الْحَسَنُ.

Some clothes were presented to the Messenger of Allāh ﷺ as a gift and there was a black *khamīṣ* with it. The Prophet asked (his companions), "To whom do you suggest we give this *khamīṣ*?" The people kept quiet. Then he said, "Bring me Umm Khālid." So I was carried to him (as I was a small girl at that time). And he dressed me with it with his own hands and said twice, "May you live so long that you will wear out many garments." He then started looking at the embroidery of that *khamīṣ* and said, "O Umm Khālid! This is *sanā*!" (*Sanā* in the Ethiopian language means "beautiful"[41].) Is'ḥāq, a sub-narrator, said, "A woman of my family told me that she had seen the *khamīṣ* worn by Umm Khālid."

TRANSLATOR'S ADDENDUM

Both parents of Umm Khālid were Companions. Her father was Khālid bin Sa'īd and her mother was Āminah bint Khalaf رضي الله عنهما.

Abū 'Abdillāh said, "No woman lived as long as she did."[42]

Umm Khālid رضي الله عنها said:

سَمِعْتُ النَّبِيَّ صلى الله عليه وسلم يَتَعَوَّذُ مِنْ عَذَابِ الْقَبْرِ.

I heard the Prophet ﷺ seeking refuge with Allāh from the punishment of the grave.[43]

UMM AL-FAḌL, THE MOTHER OF SIX NOBLE COMPANIONS

She is Umm al-Faḍl bint al-Ḥārith bin Ḥazn bin Bujayr, the wife of

[41] *Ṣaḥīḥ al-Bukhārī* 5845

[42] *Tahdhīb at-Tahdhīb* 12/401

[43] *Ṣaḥīḥ al-Bukhārī* 6364

al-'Abbās (the uncle of the Prophet ﷺ). She is the mother of six of his noble sons:

- Al-Faḍl bin al-'Abbās
- 'Abdullāh bin al-'Abbās
- 'Ubaydullāh bin al-'Abbās
- Quthum bin al-'Abbās
- 'Abdur-Raḥmān bin al-'Abbās
- Ma'bad bin al-'Abbās

Her name is Lubābah. She is the sister of the Prophet's wife Maymūnah, and she is the maternal aunt of Khālid bin al-Walīd. She is likewise the sister of Asmā' bint 'Umays, sharing the same mother with her.

She was from the first and foremost to embrace Islām. It is said that she was the first woman to accept Islām after Khadījah.

Her son 'Abdullāh bin al-'Abbās said:

كُنْتُ أَنَا وَأُمِّي، مِنَ الْمُسْتَضْعَفِينَ أَنَا مِنَ الْوِلْدَانِ، وَأُمِّي، مِنَ النِّسَاءِ.

My mother and I were among the weak and oppressed; I was from the children, and my mother was from the women.[44]

This indicates that both of them accepted Islām before al-'Abbās, and they were unable to migrate.

Umm al-Faḍl was from the prominent women. After the conquest of Makkah, al-'Abbās took her to Madīnah.

She narrated a number of *aḥādīth*. Those who narrated from her include her son 'Abdullāh bin al-'Abbās, Anas bin Mālik, 'Abdullāh bin al-Ḥārith, and others. Her narrations have been collected in the six books of *ḥadīth*.

[44] *Ṣaḥīḥ al-Bukhārī* 1357

Her Death:

She died during 'Uthmān bin 'Affān's caliphate.

TRANSLATOR'S ADDENDUM

Umm al-Faḍl & Abū Lahab:

Abū Rāfi', the freed slave of the Messenger of Allāh ﷺ, was under the care of al-'Abbās while in Makkah, and he concealed his Islām due to the oppression of the pagans. Abū Lahab stayed behind from the Battle of Badr. When Abū Sufyān returned from Badr, Abū Lahab asked him, "Which side was victorious?" Abū Sufyān replied, "They killed us however they wanted, and captured us however they wanted, but I don't blame our people." Abū Lahab said, "Why not?" Abū Sufyān said, "By Allāh, I saw men dressed in all white riding piebald horses, and nothing could harm them!"

Abū Rāfi' said, "Upon hearing this, I said, 'Those were angels!' So Abū Lahab slapped me across my face, threw me to the ground, and stood over me and began to beat me, until he was kneeling on my chest. Umm al-Faḍl stood up, grabbed a tent pole, and struck Abū Lahab in the head, fracturing his skull. She said, 'O enemy of Allāh, you think it's okay to attack him because his master is not here?!' " Abū Lahab's wound became septic and he died seven days later from an ulcer. His sons left his body inside his home for two or three nights until his body began to decay. A man from the Quraysh said, "Are you not ashamed to leave the decaying body of your father in his home?" They replied, "We are afraid of the ulcer." So they then sent in slaves to remove his body. It was hosed with water from a distance, and then pushed with poles into a grave outside Makkah, and stones were thrown over it.[45]

The mother of Umm al-Faḍl Lubābah is Hind bint 'Awf al-Ḥārith. She is known as "the noblest mother-in-law." This is because the Prophet ﷺ married her daughter Maymūnah; al-'Abbās married her daughter Lubābah the Elder; Ja'far bin Abī Ṭālib, Abū Bakr aṣ-Ṣid-dīq, and 'Alī bin Abī Ṭālib were all married to her daughter Asmā'

[45] Collected by al-Ḥākim (5415) and aṭ-Ṭabarānī (907).

bint 'Umays; Ḥamzah bin 'Abdul-Muṭṭalib married her daughter Salmā bint 'Umays; and al-Walīd bin al-Mughīrah married her daughter Lubābah the Younger.

The Anṣār

from the Female Companions

1) Umm 'Imārah Nusaybah bint Ka'b

2) Umm Sulaym Rumayṣā'

3) Umm Ḥarām bint Milḥān

4) Umm 'Aṭiyyah Nasībah bint al-Ḥārith

5) Asmā' bint Yazīd bin as-Sakn

6) Ar-Rubayyi' bint Mu'awwidh

7) Barīrah, the freed slave of 'Ā'ishah

Umm 'Imārah Nusaybah bint Ka'b bin 'Amr bin 'Awf bin Mabdhūl, the Warrior

She is Umm 'Imārah Nusaybah bint Ka'b bin Mabdhūl, the Warrior from the Anṣār of Madīnah. Her brothers are 'Abdullāh bin Ka'b al-Māzinī, who fought in the Battle of Badr, and 'Abdur-Raḥmān.

Her Marriages:

She married Zayd bin 'Āṣim and gave birth to their two sons Ḥabīb and 'Abdullāh. When he died, she married Ghaziyyah bin 'Amr and gave birth to their children Tamīm and Khawlah.

The Pledge:

Umm 'Imārah was one of two women who were physically present at the Pledge of 'Aqabah.[1]

Her Bravery:

Umm 'Imārah participated in the Battle of Uḥud; she witnessed the Treaty of Ḥudaybiyyah. She participated in the Battle of Ḥunayn and the Battle of Yamāmah. She fought in these battles and performed bravely.

The Battle of Uḥud:

Translator's note:

During the Battle of Uḥud, the Messenger of Allāh ﷺ placed the archers at the rear to guard the Muslims from attack. He commanded them to never leave their position, even if they saw the Muslims collecting the spoils of war, unless told to do so by him. The Muslims won the initial battle and the pagans fled. Upon seeing this, many of the archers left their position to collect the spoils of war. Khālid bin al-Walīd, who was a pagan at this time, noticed that most of the archers had left their position, so he attacked the rear flank, killing the remaining archers and inflicting heavy casualties upon the Muslims. The pagans surrounded the Prophet ﷺ and the Muslims while other Muslim fighters fled. Here is the account of Nusaybah bint Ka'b during the Battle of Uḥud.

End of translator's note

Nusaybah bint Ka'b fought in the Battle of Uḥud alongside her husband Ghaziyyah and her two sons from her previous marriage, Ḥabīb bin Zayd and 'Abdullāh bin Zayd. She would go out with a waterskin to retrieve water and she would fight, and she fought

[1] **Translator's note:** This was the pledge to listen to, obey, support, and defend the Prophet ﷺ in good times and difficult times.

capably. Her grandson Ḍamrah bin Sa'īd spoke about his grandmother, saying, "She said she heard the Messenger of Allāh ﷺ saying:

لَمُقَامُ نُسَيْبَةَ بِنْتِ كَعْبٍ الْيَوْمَ خَيْرٌ مِنْ مُقَامِ فُلَانٍ وَفُلَانٍ.

" 'Surely, the stance of Nusaybah bint Ka'b today was better than the stance of so-and-so.' "

She was seen that day fighting fiercely. She would hold her garment up by the middle as she fought, such that she suffered 12 significant injuries during the Battle of Uḥud. She fought Ibn Qami'ah and he stabbed her in her shoulder, causing her a severe injury which she treated for a year. The Prophet ﷺ said, "I did not look to my right or to my left except that I saw Umm 'Imārah fighting beside me."[2]

Nusaybah bint Ka'b رضي الله عنها said, "I saw the people dispersing from the Messenger of Allāh ﷺ, so there only remained 10 fighters to protect him. I was there with my two sons and my husband standing in front of the Prophet, defending him. I was fighting without a shield. As the people were fleeing, I saw a man fleeing the battlefield with a shield. I said to him, 'Throw your shield to someone who will fight!' He threw his shield and I caught it and began shielding the Prophet ﷺ with it. It was only the horsemen that gained the upper hand on us. If they had been on foot like us, we would have defeated them *inshāAllāh*. I engaged a horseman and he attempted to strike me, but I blocked him with the shield so he couldn't do anything; thus, he turned away. As he tried to ride away, I struck his horse on its hamstring, causing it to fall on its back. The Prophet ﷺ began yelling, 'O Ibn 'Imārah—your mother, your mother!' So my sons helped me finish the soldier."[3]

'Abdullāh bin Zayd said, "She (Nusaybah) was severely injured that day and her blood would not cease to flow. The Prophet ﷺ said, 'Bandage your wound.' My mother turned to me and began to bandage her wounds. The Prophet ﷺ was standing and he said,

---

[2] *Al-Iṣābah* 4/457

[3] *Aṭ-Ṭabaqāt* 8/413, 414

'Attack, my sons; strike them.' And he said, 'Who can endure what you can endure, O Umm 'Imārah?!' "

Nusaybah ﵂ said, "The man who injured my son came towards me. The Messenger of Allāh ﷺ said, 'That is the man who injured your son.' So I attacked him and hit him in his leg, causing him to kneel down. I saw the Prophet ﷺ smiling such that I saw his molar teeth. He said, 'Retaliate, O Umm 'Imārah.' Then we started striking him with the sword until he died. The Prophet ﷺ said, 'All praises belong to Allāh, Who has made you victorious.' "

'Abdullāh bin Zayd ﵁ said, "I fought in the Battle of Uḥud. When the people abandoned the Prophet ﷺ, my mother and I stood next to him, defending him. He said to me, '(Is that) Ibn Umm 'Imārah?' I said, 'Yes.' He said, 'Throw,' so I threw a rock at a horseman in front of me and it hit his horse in the eye, causing the horse to flip and land on top of its rider. So I struck the man with another rock while the Prophet ﷺ smiled. The Prophet ﷺ looked at my mother's injury to her shoulder and said, 'Your mother, your mother! Bandage her wound! O Allāh, make them my companions in Paradise!' I said, 'I don't care what happens to me in this world (due to his supplication).' "[4]

The Battle of Yamāmah:

Translator's note:

After the death of the Prophet ﷺ, some of the Arab tribes apostated from Islām. Some of them followed Musaylimah the Liar. Thus, Abū Bakr waged war against them.

End of translator's note

Muḥammad bin Yaḥyā bin Ḥibbān said, "Umm 'Imārah received 12 injuries during the Battle of Uḥud and her hand was cut off during the Battle of Yamāmah. Other than her hand, she suffered 11 injuries. When she arrived in Madīnah with her injuries, Abū Bakr would check on her; this was during his caliphate."

[4] Collected by Ibn Sa'd (8/414, 415).

Her Sons:

Her son Ḥabīb bin Zayd was cut into pieces by Musaylimah the Liar.

Her son 'Abdullāh, who narrated the *ḥadīth* concerning the *wuḍū'* of the Messenger of Allāh ﷺ,[5] is also the Companion who delivered the death blow to Musaylimah the Liar with his sword. He was killed in the Battle of al-Ḥarrah.

Her Aḥādīth:

Umm 'Imārah Nusaybah bint Ka'b ﷺ narrated a number of *aḥādīth*.

Umm 'Imārah ﷺ said:

فَقَرَّبْنَا إِلَيْهِ طَعَامًا، وَكَانَ بَعْضُ مَنْ عِنْدَهُ صَائِمًا، فَقَالَ النَّبِيُّ صَلَّى اللَّهُ عَلَيْهِ وَسَلَّمَ: إِذَا أُكِلَ عِنْدَ الصَّائِمِ الطَّعَامُ، صَلَّتْ عَلَيْهِ الْمَلَائِكَةُ.

We brought some food to him and some people with him were fasting. The Prophet ﷺ said, "If someone eats in the presence of the fasting person, the angels send salutations upon him."[6]

TRANSLATOR'S ADDENDUM

Musaylimah the Liar & Umm 'Imārah's Sons:

When Musaylimah the Liar claimed prophecy, the Prophet ﷺ authored a letter and sent it to him by way of Ḥabīb bin Zayd. Musaylimah did not respect the code of not harming the messengers. Thus, he captured Ḥabīb and punished him. Musaylimah said to Ḥabīb, "Do you bear witness that Muḥammad is the Messenger of Allāh?" Ḥabīb replied, "Yes." Musaylimah said, "Do you bear witness that I am the Messenger of Allāh?" Ḥabīb replied, "I'm deaf; I can't hear you." Musaylimah continued to question him in

[5] **Translator's note:** 'Abdullāh bin Zayd said, "He rinsed his mouth and snuffed up water from one hand, doing that three times." (*Sunan Abī Dāwūd* 119; declared authentic by al-Albānī.)

[6] *Sunan Ibn Mājah* 1820; graded *ḥasan*.

this manner, with Ḥabīb giving the same answer. Musaylimah the Liar would cut off one of Ḥabīb's limbs each time he answered, until Ḥabīb died as a martyr ﷺ.[7]

During the Battle of Yamāmah, the noble Companion Waḥshī bin Ḥarb from Ethiopia—who had previously killed Ḥamzah, the uncle of the Prophet, before he embraced Islām—threw a spear and fatally wounded Musaylimah the Liar. 'Abdullāh bin Zayd dealt the final blow to Musaylimah with his sword. When Umm 'Imārah learned that her son had dealt the final blow, she prostrated in gratitude towards Allāh.[8]

UMM SULAYM RUMAYṢĀ'

She is Umm Sulaym Rumayṣā' bint Milḥān bin Khālid bin Zayd bin Ḥarām. Others have said that her first name is Ghumayṣā', or Sahlah, or Unayfah, or Rumaythah.

She is the mother of Anas bin Mālik, the servant of the Messenger of Allāh ﷺ.

Umm Sulaym first married Mālik bin an-Naḍr and gave birth to their son Anas bin Mālik. After they separated and he died, she married Abū Ṭalḥah Zayd bin Sahl al-Anṣārī. She gave birth to their sons Abū 'Umayr and 'Abdullāh.

Umm Sulaym & Her Son Anas bin Mālik Embrace Islām:

Is'ḥāq bin 'Abdillāh said about his grandmother Umm Sulaym, "She believed in the Messenger of Allāh ﷺ. She narrated her story, saying: Abū Anas came, and he had been absent. He said to her, 'Did you turn[9]?' She replied, 'I did not turn; rather, I believed.' Then she said to her son Anas, 'Say: I testify that nothing has the

[7] *Al-Iṣābah* 3/329

[8] *Al-Bidāyah wan-Nihāyah* by Ibn Kathīr (6/323).

[9] **Translator's note:** This phrase is used when a person abandons their religion and adopts another religion.

right to be worshiped except Allāh, and I testify that Muḥammad is the Messenger of Allāh.' Anas did so and embraced Islām. His father Mālik said to Umm Sulaym, 'Don't corrupt my son against me!' She replied, 'I am not corrupting him!' Mālik left them in a state of anger, intending to go to Shām, when he encountered his enemy and his enemy killed him. Umm Sulaym said, 'Certainly, I will not wean Anas until he leaves breast milk on his own, and I will not marry until Anas tells me to.' "

A Wise Mother:

Anas ﷺ said, "Umm Sulaym took me to the Messenger of Allāh ﷺ and said, 'Here is Anas; he is going to serve you. Supplicate to Allāh on his behalf.' The Prophet ﷺ said:

اللَّهُمَّ أَكْثِرْ مَالَهُ وَوَلَدَهُ وَبَارِكْ لَهُ فِيمَا أَعْطَيْتَهُ.

" 'O Allāh, increase his wealth and his progeny, and confer blessings upon him in everything You have bestowed upon him.' "[10]

In another narration, he said:

اللهم أكثر ماله وولده وأدخله الجنة.

O Allāh, increase his wealth and his offspring and enter him into Paradise.[11]

Anas would say, "My daughter Amīnah informed me that there were more than 129 of my offspring buried when Ḥajjāj appeared. And I have a garden in Madīnah that bears fruit twice a year, and I am hoping for the third." (Meaning, entering Paradise.)

Anas bin Mālik lived to be 125 years old.

The Greatest Dowry:

Abū Ṭalḥah proposed to Umm Sulaym while he was still a pagan. She said, "By Allāh, a man like you is not rejected, but you are a

---

[10] *Ṣaḥīḥ Muslim* 2480

[11] Collected by al-Bayhaqī (6/194).

disbeliever and I am a Muslim. And it is not permissible for me to marry you. Don't you know, O Abū Ṭalḥah, that your gods were sculpted by 'Abd from the family of so-and-so, and if you were to ignite them with fire, they would surely burn?! If you embrace Islām, that will suffice as my dowry, and I will not ask you for anything else." So he left while that was in his heart. Then he returned and said, "I have accepted that which you presented to me." Thus, her dowry was nothing other than Islām.

The Prophet ﷺ Would Visit Umm Sulaym's Family[12]*:*

Anas bin Mālik said, "The Prophet ﷺ used to visit Umm Sulaym, and she would present something prepared specially for him. I had a younger brother called Abū 'Umayr. He had a sparrow with which he played, but it died. So one day, the Prophet ﷺ came to see him and saw him grieved. He asked, 'Why is he sorrowed?' The people replied, 'His sparrow has died.' He then said:

يَا أَبَا عُمَيْرٍ مَا فَعَلَ النُّغَيْرُ؟

" 'Abū 'Umayr! What has happened to the little sparrow (*an-nughayr*)[13]?' "

Anas said, "The Messenger of Allāh ﷺ would not enter anyone's home in Madīnah other than that of Umm Sulaym and those of his wives. He was asked about that and he replied:

إِنِّي أَرْحَمُهَا، قُتِلَ أَخُوهَا مَعِي.

" 'I take pity on her; her brother was killed alongside me.' "[14]

Her brother was Ḥarām bin Milḥān, the martyr who said during the Battle of the Well of Ma'ūnah when he was stabbed in the back, "I swear by the Lord of the Ka'bah, I have succeeded." And the

[12] **Translator's note:** Imām an-Nawawī said, "Umm Sulaym and her sister Umm Ḥarām were *maḥram* for the Prophet ﷺ. They were his maternal aunts through breastfeeding." (*Explanation of Ṣaḥīḥ Muslim*)

[13] *Sunan Abī Dāwūd* 4969

[14] *Ṣaḥīḥ al-Bukhārī* 2844

bayonet was seen protruding through his chest ﷺ.[15]

Umm Sulaym ﷺ said, "The Messenger of Allāh ﷺ would take the midday nap in my home, and I would lay out a leather mat for him. One day, he slept on it and he sweated profusely, and I collected his sweat and put it in a perfume bottle. The Messenger of Allāh ﷺ said, 'Umm Sulaym, what is this?' I said, 'It is your sweat, which I put in my perfume. And I am taking the blessings which come from you.' "[16]

Ibn Sīrīn said, "I requested some of this perfume from Umm Sulaym, so she gave me some as a gift." Ayyūb said, "I requested some of this perfume from Muḥammad bin Sīrīn and he gave me some as a gift, and I have it with me up until now. And when Muḥammad bin Sīrīn died, he was perfumed with this perfume."

Umm Sulaym Was Promised Paradise:

Anas said that the Prophet ﷺ said:

وَدَخَلْتُ الْجَنَّةَ، فَسَمِعْتُ خَشْفَةً بَيْنَ يَدَيَّ; فَإِذَا أَنَا بِالْغُمَيْصَاءِ بِنْتِ مِلْحَانَ.

I entered Paradise and I heard some footsteps in front of me, and there was Ghumayṣā' bint Milḥān.[17]

A Wise & Caring Wife:

Anas bin Mālik ﷺ said, "My mother (Umm Sulaym) gave birth to a son and sent me with him to the Messenger of Allāh ﷺ. I said, 'This is my brother,' so he took him and softened a date and rubbed it on his palate."[18]

---

[15] **Translator's note:** 'Āṣim said, "Never did I notice the Messenger of Allāh ﷺ so much grieved (at the loss of a) small army as I saw him grieved at those 70 men who were called 'the reciters' and were killed at the well of Ma'ūnah; and he invoked curses for a full month upon their murderers." (*Ṣaḥīḥ Muslim* 677)

[16] *Ṣaḥīḥ Muslim* 2332

[17] *Ṣaḥīḥ al-Bukhārī* 7/34

[18] *Ṣaḥīḥ Muslim* 2144

Anas said, "The son of Umm Sulaym (Abū 'Umayr) became sick[19]. When Abū Ṭalḥah went to the *masjid*, he died. Umm Sulaym said to her family, 'No one inform him of the death of his son until I inform him.'

فلما رجع أبو طلحة قال: ما فعل ابني؟ قالت أم سليم وهى أم الصبي: هو أسكن ما كان، فقربت إليه العشاء فتعشى.

"When Abū Ṭalḥah returned, he said, 'How is my son doing?' Umm Sulaym—who was the boy's mother—said, 'He is more peaceful now than he was before.' She brought him his dinner and he ate.

"After dinner, Abū Ṭalḥah lay down to sleep. Umm Sulaym perfumed herself and lay next to him and they were intimate. At the end of the night, Umm Sulaym said, 'O Abū Ṭalḥah, if some people borrow something from another family and then (the members of the family) ask for its return, would they refuse to give it back to them?' He said, 'No.' She said:

فَإِنَّ ابْنَكَ كَانَ عَارِيَةً مِنَ اللَّهِ، فَقَبَضَهُ. فَاسْتَرْجَعَ، وَحَمِدَ اللَّهَ.

" 'Verily, your son was a loan from Allāh, and He took his soul. Thus, say: "Verily, from Allāh we come and to Him we return" and praise Allāh.'

"Abū Ṭalḥah got angry and said, 'You left me uninformed until I stained myself, and then you told me about my son.' He went to the Messenger of Allāh ﷺ and informed him about the matter. Thereupon, the Messenger of Allāh ﷺ said:

بَارَكَ اللَّهُ لَكُمَا فِي لَيْلَتِكُمَا.

" 'May Allāh bless the night you spent together!'

"Umm Sulaym رضي الله عنها became pregnant that night. Thereafter, she gave birth to a boy. Abū Ṭalḥah said to me (Anas), 'Take the boy and carry him to the Prophet ﷺ,' and he sent some dates with me. The

[19] **Translator's note:** Imām adh-Dhahabī said her son who became sick was Abū 'Umayr, the owner of the bird mentioned previously.

Prophet ﷺ took a date, chewed it, and put it in the mouth of the baby and rubbed the chewed date around the baby's gum, and he named him 'Abdullāh."[20]

'Abāyah said, "I saw 'Abdullāh and he had seven sons; all of them had memorized the Qur'ān."[21]

Her Courage:

She participated in the Battles of Ḥunayn and Uḥud. She is from the virtuous women.

Muḥammad bin Sīrīn said, "Umm Sulaym was with the Messenger of Allāh during the Battle of Uḥud and she had a dagger with her."[22]

Her son Anas said, "Umm Sulaym carried a dagger during the Battle of Ḥunayn. Abū Ṭalḥah said, 'O Messenger of Allāh, Umm Sulaym has a dagger with her!' She said, 'O Messenger of Allāh, if any pagan gets close to me, I am going to rip his stomach open with it.' "[23]

Her Aḥādīth:

She narrated 14 *aḥādīth*.

Umm Ḥarām bint Milḥān, the Martyr

She is Umm Ḥarām bint Milḥān bin Khālid bin Zayd bin Ḥarām, the sister of Umm Sulaym and the maternal aunt of Anas bin Mālik. She is the wife of 'Ubādah bin aṣ-Ṣāmit.

She is from the noble Companions. Those who narrated from her include Anas bin Mālik and others.

---

[20] *Ṣaḥīḥ al-Bukhārī* 5470; *Ṣaḥīḥ Muslim* 2144

[21] Collected by Ibn Sa'd (8/434).

[22] Collected by Ibn Sa'd in *Aṭ-Ṭabaqāt* (8/425).

[23] Collected by Ibn Sa'd in *Aṭ-Ṭabaqāt* (8/425).

Anas bin Mālik said:

دَخَلَ النَّبِيُّ صلى الله عليه وسلم عَلَيْنَا وَمَا هُوَ إِلاَّ أَنَا وَأُمِّي وَأُمُّ حَرَامٍ خَالَتِي فَقَالَ قُومُوا فَلأُصَلِّيَ بِكُمْ فِي غَيْرِ وَقْتِ صَلاَةٍ.

The Prophet ﷺ visited us and it was only me, my mother, and Umm Ḥarām, my aunt. He said, "Stand so I may lead you in prayer." This was not at the time of a prescribed prayer.[24]

Umm Ḥarām is Promised Martyrdom:

Anas bin Mālik said, "Whenever the Messenger of Allāh ﷺ went to Qubā', he used to visit Umm Ḥarām bint Milḥān, who would offer him meals; and she was the wife of 'Ubādah bin aṣ-Ṣāmit. One day, he went to her house and she offered him a meal, and after that he slept, and then he woke up smiling. She (Umm Ḥarām) said, 'I asked him, "What makes you smile, O Messenger of Allāh?" He said, "Some people of my *ummah* were displayed before me as warriors fighting for Allāh's cause and sailing over this sea, like kings on thrones." I (Umm Ḥarām) said, "O Messenger of Allāh! Invoke Allāh that He may make me one of them." He invoked Allāh for me and then lay his head down and slept again, and then he woke up smiling. I asked, "What makes you smile, O Messenger of Allāh?" He said, "Some people of my followers were displayed before me as warriors fighting for Allāh's cause and sailing over this sea, like kings on thrones." I (Umm Ḥarām) said, "O Messenger of Allāh! Invoke Allāh that He may make me one of them." He said, "You will be among the first ones."' Umm Ḥarām and her husband 'Ubādah bin aṣ-Ṣāmit participated in a battle on the sea. Upon their return, her donkey was brought to her to ride. The donkey knocked her down, breaking her neck, and she died ﷺ.[25]

This was known as the Battle of Cyprus during 'Uthmān's caliphate.

Her *aḥādīth* have been collected in *Al-Bukhārī* and *Muslim*.

[24] *Ṣaḥīḥ Muslim* 660

[25] *Ṣaḥīḥ al-Bukhārī* 6282, 6283

The Europeans visit her grave site.[26]

Umm 'Aṭiyyah Nasībah bint al-Ḥārith

She is Nasībah bint al-Ḥārith; others have said her name is Nasībah bint Ka'b.

Her Knowledge:

She is considered from the scholars of the Companions. She narrated several *aḥādīth.*

She washed the body of Zaynab, the daughter of the Prophet ﷺ, after her death.

Those who narrated from her include: Muḥammad bin Sīrīn and his sister Ḥafṣah bint Sirīn, Umm Sharāḥīl, 'Abdul-Mālik bin 'Umayr, and others. Her *aḥādīth* are collected in the six books of *ḥadīth.*

She lived to be in her 70s.

She is the one who said:

نُهِينَا عَنِ اتِّبَاعِ الْجَنَائِزِ، وَلَمْ يُعْزَمْ عَلَيْنَا.

We were prevented from following the funeral, but that was not made binding on us.[27]

Translator's Addendum

Umm 'Aṭiyyah Nasībah witnessed seven battles with the Messenger of Allāh ﷺ. She would take food to the fighters and nurse the wounded.[28]

---

[26] **Translator's note:** This place is known as Hala Sultan Tekke. The people of innovation have made this site into a shrine.

[27] *Sunan Ibn Mājah* 1644

[28] *Asad al-Ghābah* 7/280

ASMĀ' BINT YAZĪD BIN AS-SAKN

She is Asmā' bint Yazīd bin as-Sakn, Umm 'Āmir and Umm Salamah al-Anṣārī. She is the paternal cousin of Mu'ādh bin Jabal ﷺ. She was 'Ā'ishah's maid. She was known for her intelligence and piety.

Asmā' bint Yazīd ﷺ is from those women who migrated and fought in battles.

She narrated several *aḥādīth* from the Messenger of Allāh ﷺ. Those who narrated from her include her freed slave Muhājir, Mujāhid, Is'ḥāq bin Rāshid, and others.

Asmā' bint Yazīd said, "Some food was brought to the Prophet ﷺ and it was offered to us. We said, 'We do not have any appetite for it.' He said:

لاَ تَجْمَعْنَ جُوعًا وَكَذِبًا.

"'Do not combine hunger and lies.'"[29]

She killed nine Romans with a pole from her tent during the Battle of Yarmūk.[30]

She attended the Pledge of Riḍwān, also known as the Pledge Under the Tree.[31] And she gave her pledge of allegiance.

She was nicknamed "the Female Orator" (Khaṭībah an-Nisā').

Asmā' bint Yazīd was the first divorced woman to observe a waiting period. 'Amr bin Muhājir narrated from his father that Asmā' bint Yazīd bin as-Sakn was divorced in the time of the Messenger of Allāh ﷺ. No waiting period was prescribed for a divorced woman at

---

[29] *Sunan Ibn Mājah* 3423

[30] Collected by Ibn Ḥajar in *Al-Iṣābah* (4/229).

[31] **Translator's note:** The Messenger of Allāh ﷺ said, "None of those who gave the pledge under the tree shall enter the Fire." (*Jāmi' at-Tirmidhī* 4233)

that time. When Asmā' was divorced, Allāh the Exalted sent down the injunction of the waiting period for divorce. She is the first of the divorced women about whom the verse relating to the waiting period was sent down.[32]

AR-RUBAYYI' BINT MU'AWWIDH

She is ar-Rubayyi' bint Mu'awwidh bin 'Afrā' al-Anṣāriyyah from Banun-Najār. She is the mother of Muḥammad bin Iyās bin al-Bukayr.

The Messenger of Allāh ﷺ visited her the morning of her wedding. Ar-Rubayyi' bint Mu'awwidh said:

جاء النبي صلى الله عليه وسلم فدخل حين بُني علي فجلس على فراشي كمجلسك مني فجعلت جويريات لنا يضربن بالدف ويندبن من قتل من آبائي يوم بدر إذ قالت إحداهن: وفينا نبي يعلم ما في غد فقال: دعي هذه وقولي بالذي كنت تقولين.

After the consummation of my marriage, the Prophet ﷺ came and sat on my bed as far from me as you are sitting now, and our little girls started beating the duff and reciting verses mourning our fathers, who had been killed in the Battle of Badr. One of them said, "Among us is a prophet who knows what will happen tomorrow." On that, the Prophet said, "Omit this (saying) and keep on saying the verses which you had been saying before."[33]

She lived a long life, dying during 'Abdul-Mālik's caliphate 70-some years after the migration ﵂.

She narrated 21 *aḥādīth* which are collected in the six books of *ḥadīth*. Those who narrated from her include Abū Salamah bin 'Abdur-Raḥmān, Sulaymān bin Yasār, and others.

---

[32] *Sunan Abī Dāwūd* 2281; declared *ḥasan* by al-Albānī.

[33] *Ṣaḥīḥ al-Bukhārī* 4852

Her father Mu'awwidh was from the major participants in the Battle of Badr. He killed Abū Jahl in this battle.

Ar-Rubayyi' ﵂ said, "I took some perfume from Asmā' bint Mukharribah, the mother of Abū Jahl. I said to her, 'Write a bill for me, and write it for ar-Rubayyi' bint Mu'awwidh.' She replied, 'You are the daughter of the one who killed his master.' I replied, 'No; rather, I am the daughter of the one who killed his slave.' She said, 'By Allāh, I will never sell you anything.' "[34]

Her Khula':

Ar-Rubayyi' ﵂ said, "Some words were exchanged between me and my cousin (who was her husband). So I said to him, 'You can have everything I own if you grant me separation.' He replied, 'These are your words which you have said.' By Allāh, he took everything I owned, even my bed. So I went to 'Uthmān ﵁ and mentioned this to him. And during these days, he was under siege. 'Uthmān ﵁ said, 'The condition has the most right to ownership, so take everything she has, even her hairband if you like.' "

TRANSLATOR'S ADDENDUM

The grandmother of ar-Rubayyi' bint Mu'awwidh was 'Afrā'. 'Afrā' ﵂ gave birth to seven sons who all fought in the Battle of Badr alongside the Messenger of Allāh ﷺ.[35]

BARĪRAH, THE FREED SLAVE OF 'Ā'ISHAH

She is Barīrah, the freed slave of the Mother of the Believers 'Ā'ishah ﵂.

She narrated a *ḥadīth* which has been collected in *An-Nasā'ī*. Those who narrated from her included 'Abdul-Mālik bin Marwān and others.

[34] Collected in *Aṭ-Ṭabaqāt* (8/447).

[35] *Al-Iṣābah* 13/48

ʿĀ'ishah ﷺ said, "Barīrah came to me and said, 'My people (masters) have written the contract for my emancipation for nine *awāq* of gold to be paid in yearly installments, one *ūqiyyah* per year, so help me.' " ʿĀ'ishah said (to her), "If your masters agree, I will pay them the whole sum, provided the right of inheritance will be for me." Barīrah went to her masters and told them about it, but they refused the offer, and she returned from them while the Messenger of Allāh ﷺ was sitting. She said, "I presented the offer to them, but they refused unless the right of inheritance would be for them." When the Prophet ﷺ heard that, he said to ʿĀ'ishah, "Buy Barīrah and then set her free, and let them stipulate whatever they like. The right of inheritance is for the one who frees the slave."

ʿĀ'ishah did so. After that, the Messenger of Allāh ﷺ got up amidst the people, glorified and praised Allāh, and said, "What is wrong with some people who stipulate things which are not in Allāh's laws? Any condition which is not in Allāh's laws is invalid, even if there were a hundred such conditions. Allāh's rules are the most valid, and Allāh's conditions are the most solid. The *walā'* is for the one who frees the slave."[36]

Her Divorce After Freedom:

When Barīrah was freed, she was given the choice to stay with her husband or leave him.

Ibn ʿAbbās ﷺ said:

كَانَ زَوْجُ بَرِيرَةَ عَبْدًا يُقَالُ لَهُ مُغِيثٌ كَأَنِّي أَنْظُرُ إِلَيْهِ يَطُوفُ خَلْفَهَا وَيَبْكِي وَدُمُوعُهُ تَسِيلُ عَلَى خَدِّهِ فَقَالَ النَّبِيُّ ـ صلى الله عليه وسلم ـ لِلْعَبَّاسِ يَا عَبَّاسُ أَلاَ تَعْجَبُ مِنْ حُبِّ مُغِيثٍ بَرِيرَةَ وَمِنْ بُغْضِ بَرِيرَةَ مُغِيثًا. فَقَالَ لَهَا النَّبِيُّ ـ صلى الله عليه وسلم ـ لَوْ رَاجَعْتِيهِ فَإِنَّهُ أَبُو وَلَدِكِ قَالَتْ يَا رَسُولَ اللَّهِ تَأْمُرُنِي قَالَ إِنَّمَا أَشْفَعُ. قَالَتْ لاَ حَاجَةَ لِي فِيهِ.

Barīrah's husband was a slave called Mughīth. It is as if I can see

[36] *Ṣaḥīḥ al-Bukhārī* 2729

him now, walking behind her and weeping, with tears running down his cheeks. The Prophet ﷺ said to 'Abbās, "O 'Abbās, are you not amazed by the love of Mughīth for Barīrah, and the hatred of Barīrah for Mughīth?" And the Prophet said to her, "Why don't you take him back, for he is the father of your child?" She said, "O Messenger of Allāh, are you commanding me (to do so)?" He said, "No; rather, I am interceding." She said, "I have no need of him."[37]

[37] *Sunan Ibn Mājah* 2153

ENCYCLOPEDIA
OF FEMALE COMPANIONS

Taken from Al-Iṣābah fī Tamyīz aṣ-Ṣaḥābah

ALPHABETICAL GLOSSARY

OF THE FEMALE COMPANIONS

ALIF – أ

❖ ĀSIYAH bint al-Ḥārith as-Sa'diyyah is the sister of the Messenger of Allāh ﷺ through breastfeeding.

❖ ĀMINAH bint 'Affān is the sister of 'Uthmān bin 'Affān. She was a hairdresser during the Pre-Islamic Days of Ignorance. She accepted Islām during the conquest of Makkah. She, along with Hind (the wife of Abū Sufyān), were among those women who gave the pledge to the Messenger of Allāh ﷺ to not associate any partners with Allāh, nor steal or fornicate. She was married to al-Ḥakam bin Kaysān.

❖ ABRAHAH al-Ḥabashiyyah was from the servants of an-Najāshī, the king of Abyssinia. She was with Umm Ḥabībah when an-Najāshī married her to the Prophet ﷺ.

❖ ARWĀ bint Abil-'Āṣ is the paternal aunt of 'Uthmān bin 'Affān. She was among the women who gave their pledge during the conquest of Makkah.

❖ ARWĀ bint Kurayz is the mother of 'Uthmān bin 'Affān. She accepted Islām, migrated to Madīnah, and gave her pledge to the Messenger of Allāh ﷺ. She remained there until she died at the age of 90.

❖ ARWĀ bint al-Muqawwim bin 'Abdul-Muṭṭalib is the first cousin of the Prophet ﷺ. She was married to Abū Sufyān bin al-Ḥārith.

❖ ASMĀ' bint Anas bin Mudrik is the wife of Khālid bin al-Walīd.

❖ ASMĀ' bint 'Amr, known as Umm Manī' and Umm Shubāth, is the paternal cousin of Mu'ādh bin Jabal. She participated in the Battle of Khaybar alongside her husband. She is one of only two women who were physically present at the Pledge of 'Aqabah, the other being Umm 'Imārah. Umm 'Imārah said, "The men were shaking the hand of the Messenger of Allāh ﷺ on the night of the Pledge of 'Aqabah while al-'Abbās was holding his hand. When it was only Umm Manī' and I remaining, my husband Ghaziyyah called out, saying:

يا رسول الله؛ هاتان امرأتان حضرتا معنا يبايعانك.

"'O Messenger of Allāh, these two women are present with us to give you the pledge.'

"The Messenger of Allāh ﷺ said:

قَدْ بَايَعْتَكُمَا، إِنِّي لَا أُصَافِحُ النِّسَاءَ.

"'I have accepted the pledge from both of them, and I do not shake the hands of women.'"[1]

❖ AMAH al-Fārisiyyah is the woman Salmān al-Fārisī met in Madīnah when he arrived there. Salmān al-Fārisī said, "When I arrived in Madīnah, I saw a woman from Isfahan who had embraced Islām before me. I asked her about the Messenger of Allāh ﷺ, and

[1] Collected by Ibn Sa'd from the narration of al-Wāqidī.

thus she is the one who directed me to him."

❖ UMAYMAH bint Ṣabīḥ is the mother of Abū Hurayrah. Abū Hurayrah said, "I used to call my mother to Islām when she was still a polytheist. One day while I was calling her, she mentioned something about the Prophet ﷺ that I detested. So I went to see the Prophet ﷺ while crying, and I told him, 'I used to call my mother to Islām and she would refuse. I called her today and she mentioned something about you that I detested. Please invoke the guidance of Allāh on her.' He said, 'O Allāh, guide Abū Hurayrah's mother.' So I left full of hope because of the Prophet's supplication for my mother. When I reached home, I found that the door was partially closed. My mother heard my footsteps and said, 'Stay still, Abū Hurayrah.' Then I heard the water running; my mother performed *ghusl*, put on her clothes, and hurriedly opened the door without her headcover and said, 'None has the right to be worshiped but Allāh, and Muḥammad is the Messenger of Allāh.'

"I went back to the Prophet ﷺ, crying out of joy, and told him, 'I am bringing you good news: Allāh answered your prayers and guided the mother of Abū Hurayrah.' The Prophet ﷺ praised and glorified Allāh and said, 'This is good.' I said, 'O Messenger of Allāh, pray to Allāh to make me and my mother beloved by Allāh's believing slaves and make us love them.' The Prophet ﷺ said, 'O Allāh, make this little slave of Yours and his mother become beloved by Your believing slaves and make the believers dear to them.' Ever since, there was not a believer who heard of me, even without seeing me, that did not love me."

BĀ' – ب

❖ BĀDIYAH bint Ghaylān; her father embraced Islām, then she embraced Islām, and she narrated *aḥādīth*. She is mentioned in the *ḥadīth* of Umm Salamah:

أَنَّ النَّبِيَّ صلى الله عليه وسلم كَانَ عِنْدَهَا وَفِي الْبَيْتِ مُخَنَّثٌ، فَقَالَ

لِعَبْدِ اللَّهِ أَخِي أُمِّ سَلَمَةَ يَا عَبْدَ اللَّهِ إِنْ فُتِحَ لَكُمْ غَدًا الطَّائِفُ، فَإِنِّي أَدُلُّكَ عَلَى بِنْتِ غَيْلاَنَ، فَإِنَّهَا تُقْبِلُ بِأَرْبَعٍ وَتُدْبِرُ بِثَمَانٍ. فَقَالَ النَّبِيُّ ﷺ صلى الله عليه وسلم لاَ يَدْخُلَنَّ هَؤُلاَءِ عَلَيْكُنَّ.

The Prophet ﷺ was in her house, and an effeminate man was there too. The effeminate man said to ʻAbdullāh (Umm Salamah's brother), "O ʻAbdullāh! If Ṭā'if should be conquered tomorrow, I recommend you the daughter of Ghaylān, for she has four curves in the front and eight at the back." So the Prophet ﷺ said (to his wives), "These effeminate (men) should not enter your houses."[2]

❖ BUSRAH bint Ghazwān was the wife of Abū Hurayrah. He used to work for her as her employee before he married her. He would ride with the travelers and serve them when they took shelter. After that, he married her.

❖ BARRAH bint Sufyān as-Sulamiyyah was the wife of al-Ḥārith bin Ṭalḥah until he was killed during the Battle of Uḥud as a disbeliever. Then she married ʻAbdullāh bin ʻUmar and gave birth to their children ʻAbdullāh, Ṣafiyyah, and more. She outlived him.

❖ BUSRAH bint Ṣafwān bin Nawfal is the niece of the monk Waraqah bin Nawfal, who was the uncle of Khadījah, the wife of the Prophet ﷺ. She was from the first and foremost to embrace Islām, migrate, and give the pledge of allegiance. She narrated 11 *aḥādīth*. She is the maternal aunt of the great scholar from the Tābi'īn, Sa'īd bin al-Musayyib. Sa'īd bin al-Musayyib said, "Busrah bint Ṣafwān is one of my maternal aunts, and she said, 'The Messenger of Allāh ﷺ said, "If any of you touches his penis, let him perform ablution."' "[3] She lived until Mu'āwiyah bin Abī Sufyān's caliphate. She was a hairdresser for the women of Makkah.

❖ BINT Abī Sabrah is among the five women who upheld the

[2] *Ṣaḥīḥ al-Bukhārī* 5887

[3] *Sunan Ibn Mājah* 517

pledge along with Umm 'Aṭiyyah. Umm 'Aṭiyyah said, "None of those women abided by her pledge except Umm Sulaym, Umm al-'Alā', Bint Abī Sabrah, the wife of Mu'ādh, and the mother of Mu'ādh.

TĀ' - ت

❖ TUMĀḌIR bint al-Aṣbagh bin 'Amr is the wife of 'Abdur-Raḥmān bin 'Awf, who was from the 10 promised Paradise. When the Prophet ﷺ sent 'Abdur-Raḥmān bin 'Awf to the tribe of Kalb to invite them to Islām, they said to him, "If we accept your invitation, then marry the daughter of our king." They accepted Islām, and 'Abdur-Raḥmān bin 'Awf married Tumāḍir. Then he took her to Madīnah and she gave birth to their son Abū Salamah. She was the first person from the tribe of Kalb to marry someone from the tribe of Quraysh.

THĀ' - ث

❖ THUBAYTAH bint Nu'mān bin 'Amr. She, along with her father and grandfather, were all Companions of the Messenger of Allāh ﷺ.

❖ THUBAYTAH bint aḍ-Ḍaḥḥāk is the woman intended in the *ḥadīth* of Muḥammad bin Maslamah, who said, "I proposed marriage to a woman, then I hid and waited to see her until I saw her among some date palm trees that belonged to her." It was said to him, "Do you do such a thing when you are a Companion of the Messenger of Allāh ﷺ?" He said, "I heard the Messenger of Allāh ﷺ saying:

إِذَا أَلْقَى اللَّهُ فِي قَلْبِ امْرِئٍ خِطْبَةَ امْرَأَةٍ فَلاَ بَأْسَ أَنْ يَنْظُرَ إِلَيْهَا.

" 'When Allāh causes a man to propose to a woman, there is nothing

wrong with him looking at her.' "[4]

JĪM - ج

❖ JUDĀMAH bint Wahb al-Asadiyyah was from the narrators of *ḥadīth*. The Mother of the Believers 'Ā'ishah narrated from her. 'Ā'ishah ﵂ said, "Judāmah bint Wahb informed me that the Messenger of Allāh ﷺ said:

لَقَدْ هَمَمْتُ أَنْ أَنْهَى عَنِ الْغِيلَةِ حَتَّى ذَكَرْتُ أَنَّ الرُّومَ وَفَارِسَ يَصْنَعُونَ ذَلِكَ فَلاَ يَضُرُّ أَوْلاَدَهُمْ.

" 'I intended to prohibit *ghīlah*, but I remembered that the Greeks and Persians do that without it causing any injury to their children.' "[5]

(Mālik explained, "*Ghīlah* is that a man has intercourse with his wife while she is suckling.")

❖ JUMĀNAH bint Abī Ṭālib bin 'Abdul-Muṭṭalib is the first cousin of the Prophet ﷺ.

❖ JUMAYL bint Yasār is from the Companions who had a verse sent down concerning their situation. Her brother Ma'qil bin Yasār said, "I married my sister to a man and he divorced her, and when her days of *'iddah* (three menstrual periods) were over, the man came again and asked for her hand, but I said to him, 'I married her to you and made her your bed (your wife) and favored you with her, but you divorced her. Now you come to ask for her hand again? No, by Allāh, she will never go back to you (again)!' And he was a good man and she wanted to go back to him. Thus, Allāh the Exalted sent down the verse:

---

[4] Classed as *ṣaḥīḥ* by al-Albānī in *Ṣaḥīḥ Ibn Mājah* (1937).

[5] *Muwaṭṭa' Mālik* 1291

﴿ وَإِذَا طَلَّقْتُمُ النِّسَاءَ فَبَلَغْنَ أَجَلَهُنَّ فَلَا تَعْضُلُوهُنَّ أَن يَنكِحْنَ أَزْوَاجَهُنَّ إِذَا تَرَاضَوْا بَيْنَهُم بِالْمَعْرُوفِ ۗ ذَٰلِكَ يُوعَظُ بِهِ مَن كَانَ مِنكُمْ يُؤْمِنُ بِاللَّهِ وَالْيَوْمِ الْآخِرِ ۗ ذَٰلِكُمْ أَزْكَىٰ لَكُمْ وَأَطْهَرُ ۗ وَاللَّهُ يَعْلَمُ وَأَنتُمْ لَا تَعْلَمُونَ ﴾

"'And when you have divorced women and they have fulfilled the term of their prescribed period, do not prevent them from marrying their (former) husbands, if they mutually agree on reasonable basis. This (instruction) is an admonition for him among you who believes in Allāh and the Last Day. That is more virtuous and purer for you. Allāh knows and you know not.'

[Sūrah al-Baqarah 2:232]

"So I said, 'Now I will do it, O Messenger of Allāh,' so I remarried her to him."[6]

❖ JAMĪLAH bint Ubayy was the sister of 'Abdullāh bin Ubayy, who was known as the leader of the hypocrites. She was married to Thābit bin Qays. Her request for a *khula'* is mentioned in the well-known narration. Ibn 'Abbās ﷺ said:

أَنَّ امْرَأَةَ، ثَابِتِ بْنِ قَيْسٍ أَتَتِ النَّبِيَّ صلى الله عليه وسلم فَقَالَتْ يَا رَسُولَ اللَّهِ ثَابِتُ بْنُ قَيْسٍ أَمَا إِنِّي مَا أَعِيبُ عَلَيْهِ فِي خُلُقٍ وَلاَ دِينٍ وَلَكِنِّي أَكْرَهُ الْكُفْرَ فِي الإِسْلاَمِ. فَقَالَ رَسُولُ اللَّهِ صلى الله عليه وسلم أَتَرُدِّينَ عَلَيْهِ حَدِيقَتَهُ. قَالَتْ نَعَمْ. قَالَ رَسُولُ اللَّهِ صلى الله عليه وسلم اقْبَلِ الْحَدِيقَةَ وَطَلِّقْهَا تَطْلِيقَةً.

Thābit bin Qays' wife came to the Prophet ﷺ and said, "O Messenger of Allāh, I do not find any fault with Thābit bin Qays regarding his attitude or religious commitment, but I hate *kufr*

[6] *Ṣaḥīḥ al-Bukhārī* 5130

after Islām." The Messenger of Allāh ﷺ said, "Will you give him back his garden?" She said, "Yes." The Messenger of Allāh ﷺ said, "Take back the garden and divorce her once."[7]

Ibn 'Abbās said:

أوّل خلع كان في الإسلام أخت عبد الله بن أبيّ.

The first *khula'* (marriage annulment) in Islām was that of the sister of 'Abdullāh bin Ubayy.[8]

Before she married Thābit, she was married to Ḥanẓalah bin Abī 'Āmir, who was known as "the one washed by the angels." Ḥanẓalah went to the battlefield on his wedding night and he didn't have time to take a shower. When he was killed in battle, the Prophet ﷺ said:

إن صاحبكم تغسله الملائكة.

Verily, your Companion is being washed by the angels.[9]

❖ JAMĪLAH bint Thābit was the sister of 'Āṣim bin Thābit and the wife of 'Umar bin al-Khaṭṭāb. 'Umar married her in 7 AH. Before she embraced Islām, her name was 'Āṣiyah, which means "disobedient". She went to 'Umar and said, "I hate my name, so give me a name." He said, "You are Jamīlah." She became upset and said, "Could you not find a name to call me other than a slave name?" So she went to the Prophet ﷺ and said, "O Messenger of Allāh, I hate my name." He said, "Your name is Jamīlah." She became upset that he said the same name which 'Umar had said. The Prophet ﷺ said, "Didn't you know that Allāh has placed the truth upon the tongue of 'Umar and within his heart?!"

❖ JUWAYRIYAH bint Abī Jahl is the woman 'Alī bin Abī Ṭālib proposed to while married to Fāṭimah, the daughter of the Messenger of Allāh ﷺ. The Messenger of Allāh ﷺ said:

---

[7] *Sunan an-Nasā'ī* 3463

[8] Collected in the *Muwaṭṭa'* of Imām Mālik.

[9] Collected by al-Ḥākim (3/204).

لاَ تَجْتَمِعُ بِنْتُ رَسُولِ اللَّهِ وَبِنْتُ عَدُوِّ اللَّهِ عِنْدَ رَجُلٍ وَاحِدٍ أَبَدًا.

The daughter of the Messenger of Allāh and the daughter of the enemy of Allāh will never be joined together in marriage by one man.[10]

ḤĀ' - ح

❖ ḤABĪBAH bint Khārijah bin Zayd was the wife of Abū Bakr aṣ-Ṣiddīq. He died while she was pregnant with their daughter Umm Kulthūm.

❖ ḤUMAYNAH bint Abī Ṭalḥah bin 'Abdil-'Uzzā is one of four women who were married to their stepsons before the revelation was sent down prohibiting that. Ḥumaynah was married to Khalaf bin Asad. When he died, she married his son al-Aswad bin Khalaf. Then Islām separated them with the verse:

﴿ وَلَا تَنكِحُوا مَا نَكَحَ آبَاؤُكُم مِّنَ النِّسَاءِ إِلَّا مَا قَدْ سَلَفَ ﴾

And marry not women whom your fathers married, except what has already passed.

[Sūrah an-Nisā' 4:22]

❖ ḤAWWĀ' bint Yazīd was married to Qays bin al-Khaṭīm, one of the notable poets from the pagans. She was from the foremost to accept Islām, but she concealed her Islām from her husband. One day, he found her praying, so he threw her garments over her head and said, "You are practicing a religion and no one knows what it is." From that day forward, he would harm her due to her Islām. When this news reached the Prophet ﷺ, he went to Qays and said, "O father of Yazīd—as for your wife Ḥawwā', it has reached me that

[10] *Sunan Ibn Mājah* 2077

you have mistreated her since she abandoned your religion, so fear Allāh and guarantee me that you will not harm her again." Qays agreed to only treat her kindly from that point on. Qays said to his wife Ḥawwā', "O Ḥawwā', I met your companion Muḥammad and he told me to treat you kindly. I will comply with this, so you are free and I will never harm you again." Thus, Ḥawwā' began to openly display her Islām from that day forward. She was from the narrators of *ḥadīth*. Her grandson 'Abdur-Raḥmān bin Bujayd reported that his grandmother Ḥawwā' bint Yazīd said that the Messenger of Allāh ﷺ said:

يَا نِسَاءَ الْمُؤْمِنَاتِ، لاَ تَحْقِرَنَّ امْرَأَةٌ مِنْكُنَّ لِجَارَتِهَا، وَلَوْ كُرَاعُ شَاةٍ مُحَرَّقٍ.

O Muslim women, none of you should consider even a burnt sheep's foot too insignificant to give to her neighbor.[11]

❖ AL-ḤAWLĀ' bint Tuwayt would stand in prayer all night. 'Ā'ishah ﵂ said:

مَرَّتْ بِهَا وَعِنْدَهَا رَسُولُ اللَّهِ صلى الله عليه وسلم فَقُلْتُ هَذِهِ الْحَوْلاَءُ بِنْتُ تُوَيْتٍ وَزَعَمُوا أَنَّهَا لاَ تَنَامُ اللَّيْلَ فَقَالَ رَسُولُ اللَّهِ صلى الله عليه وسلم لاَ تَنَامُ اللَّيْلَ خُذُوا مِنَ الْعَمَلِ مَا تُطِيقُونَ فَوَاللَّهِ لاَ يَسْأَمُ اللَّهُ حَتَّى تَسْأَمُوا.

Al-Ḥawlā' passed by her (at the time) when the Messenger of Allāh ﷺ was with her. I ('Ā'ishah) said, "This is al-Ḥawlā' bint Tuwayt, and they say that she does not sleep at night." The Messenger of Allāh ﷺ said, "She does not sleep at night?! Choose an act which you are capable of doing (continuously). By Allāh, Allāh will not

[11] *Ṣaḥīḥ Muslim* 1030

become bored[12] until you become bored."[13]

KHĀ' - خ

❖ KHĀLIDAH bint al-Ḥārith was the paternal aunt of 'Abdullāh bin Salām, the Jewish scholar who embraced Islām[14]. 'Abdullāh bin Salām said, "When I heard of the Messenger of Allāh, I recognized his attributes, his name, and the time he would appear, which all coincided with our books. When he arrived in Madīnah, a man informed me of his arrival while I was atop my date palm tree. I exclaimed, 'Allāh is the Greatest!' My aunt, who was sitting beneath me, said, 'By Allāh, if you had heard that Mūsā was coming, you would not have been more enthusiastic.' I said to her, 'O Auntie, I swear by Allāh, he is the brother of Mūsā who has been sent.' She said, 'Is he the Prophet that we were informed would appear during this time?' I said, 'Yes'. She said, 'So be it.' My aunt Khālidah bint al-Ḥārith embraced Islām, and I went to my household and they embraced Islām.

❖ KHARQĀ' Umm Maḥjan is the black woman who used to clean the *masjid* of the Prophet ﷺ. She is mentioned in the well-known *ḥadīth* of Ibn 'Abbās ﷺ. He said, "The Messenger of Allāh passed by a grave of one who had been buried at night. He said, 'When was this (deceased person) buried?' The people said, 'Yesterday.' He said, 'Why did you not inform me?' They said, 'We buried her when it was dark and we disliked to wake you up.' He stood up and we lined up behind him. I was one of them, and the Prophet ﷺ offered the funeral prayer."[15]

---

[12] **Translator's note:** The former Grand Mufti of Saudi Arabia, Muḥammad bin Ibrāhīm Āl ash-Shaykh, said, "This 'boredom' is in a manner which is befitting to the greatness and majesty of the Creator and it does not resemble the 'boredom' of the creation in any way."

[13] *Ṣaḥīḥ Muslim* 785

[14] **Translator's note:** His story can be found in *Ṣaḥīḥ al-Bukhārī* (3938).

[15] *Ṣaḥīḥ al-Bukhārī* 1321

❖ KHARQĀ' was a woman from the *jinn* and a Companion of the Prophet ﷺ. Rāshid narrated that 'Umar bin 'Abdil-'Azīz (the caliph from the Tābi'īn) asked him to accompany him on a journey. Upon their return, they passed by a valley where they noticed a dead black snake cast upon the road. 'Umar descended his mount, wrapped the snake in a cloth, and buried it. As they continued on their journey, a caller called out, "O Kharqā', O Kharqā'!" 'Umar and Rāshid looked left and right but did not see anyone. 'Umar said, "May Allāh guide you, O caller. If you are from those who are visible, then show yourself; if not, then inform us about Kharqā'." The caller said, "I was from the seven (*jinn*) who gave the pledge of allegiance to the Prophet ﷺ in this valley[16]. The snake you encountered at such-and-such place, I heard the Messenger of Allāh ﷺ say to her one day, 'O Kharqā', you are going to die at such-and-such place and you will be buried by the best person upon the earth of that era.' " 'Umar said, "You heard that from the Messenger of Allāh ﷺ?!" So 'Umar was astounded, and he continued his journey. He said to Rāshid, "O Rāshid, don't tell anyone about this until I die."[17]

❖ KHANSĀ' bint Khidhām was married to a man against her will by her father. Thus, she went to the Messenger of Allāh ﷺ to complain about the affair, and he declared her marriage invalid.[18]

❖ KHAWLAH bint Ja'far al-Ḥanafiyyah was a slave-girl. 'Alī bin Abī Ṭālib freed her and married her. She gave birth to 'Alī's third son, who was known as Muḥammad al-Ḥanafiyyah, the narrator of the well-known *ḥadīth* collected in *Sunan Abī Dāwūd*. Muḥammad al-Ḥanafiyyah said:

قُلْتُ لأَبِي أَيُّ النَّاسِ خَيْرٌ بَعْدَ رَسُولِ اللَّهِ صلى الله عليه وسلم قَالَ أَبُو

[16] **Translator's note:** Ibn Ḥazm رحمه الله said, "The Muslims did not differ concerning the fact that among the *jinn* were some who accompanied the Messenger of Allāh ﷺ and believed in him. Those *jinn* followed the truth and deserve respect from us, and they attained a similar level of knowledge and religious commitment as the rest of the Ṣaḥābah رضي الله عنهم." (*Al-Muḥallā* 9/4)

[17] Declared authentic by Ibn Ḥibbān (6671).

[18] *Ṣaḥīḥ al-Bukhārī* 5138

بَكْرٍ. قَالَ قُلْتُ ثُمَّ مَنْ قَالَ ثُمَّ عُمَرُ. قَالَ ثُمَّ خَشِيتُ أَنْ أَقُولَ ثُمَّ مَنْ
فَيَقُولَ عُثْمَانُ فَقُلْتُ ثُمَّ أَنْتَ يَا أَبَةِ قَالَ مَا أَنَا إِلاَّ رَجُلٌ مِنَ الْمُسْلِمِينَ.

I said to my father ('Alī bin Abī Ṭālib), "Which of the people after the Messenger of Allāh ﷺ is best?" He replied, "Abū Bakr." I then asked, "Who comes next?" He said, "'Umar." I was then afraid of asking him who came next, fearing he might mention 'Uthmān, so I said, "You come next, O my father?" He said, "I am only a man among the Muslims."[19]

❖ KHAWLAH bint Tha'labah; the first few verses of Sūrah al-Mujādilah were sent down concerning her situation. 'Ā'ishah رضي الله عنها said, "Blessed is the One Whose hearing encompasses all things. I heard some of the words of Khawlah bint Tha'labah—but some of her words were not clear to me—when she complained to the Messenger of Allāh ﷺ about her husband (Aws bin aṣ-Ṣāmit) and said, 'O Messenger of Allāh, he has consumed my youth and I split my belly for him (i.e., I bore him many children), but when I grew old and could no longer bear children, he declared me to be like his mother's back; O Allāh, I complain to You.' She continued to complain until Jibrīl brought down these verses:

﴿ قَدْ سَمِعَ اللَّهُ قَوْلَ الَّتِي تُجَادِلُكَ فِي زَوْجِهَا وَتَشْتَكِي
إِلَى اللَّهِ وَاللَّهُ يَسْمَعُ تَحَاوُرَكُمَا ۚ إِنَّ اللَّهَ سَمِيعٌ بَصِيرٌ
﴿١﴾ الَّذِينَ يُظَاهِرُونَ مِنكُم مِّن نِّسَائِهِم مَّا هُنَّ أُمَّهَاتِهِمْ ۖ
إِنْ أُمَّهَاتُهُمْ إِلَّا اللَّائِي وَلَدْنَهُمْ ۚ وَإِنَّهُمْ لَيَقُولُونَ مُنكَرًا مِّنَ
الْقَوْلِ وَزُورًا ۚ وَإِنَّ اللَّهَ لَعَفُوٌّ غَفُورٌ ﴿٢﴾ ﴾

"'Indeed, Allāh has heard the statement of her that disputes with you (O Muḥammad) concerning her husband, and complains to Allāh. And Allāh hears the argument between you both. Verily, Allāh is All-Hearer, All-Seer. Those among you who make

[19] *Sunan Abī Dāwūd* 4629

their wives unlawful to them by saying to them, "You are like my mother's back" (*aẓ-ẓihār*). They cannot be their mothers. None can be their mothers except those who gave birth to them. And verily, they utter an ill word and a lie. And verily, Allāh is Oft-Pardoning, Oft-Forgiving.' "[20]

[Sūrah al-Mujādilah 58:1-2]

❖ KHAYRAH bint Abī Ḥadrad is best known by her *kunyah* Umm ad-Dardā' the Elder. She was the wife of Abud-Dardā'. She was an intelligent woman of knowledge and worship. She died during 'Uthmān's caliphate. After her death, Abud-Dardā' married a woman with the same *kunyah,* and she was known as Umm ad-Dardā' the Younger. She was from the Tābi'īn.

DĀL – د

❖ DUBYAH bint Thābit bin Khālid was the wife of Yazīd bin Thābit bin aḍ-Ḍaḥḥāk and thus the sister-in-law of Zayd bin Thābit bin aḍ-Ḍaḥḥāk, the personal scribe of the Messenger of Allāh ﷺ. She accepted Islām and gave the pledge.

❖ DIJĀJAH bint Asmā' aṣ-Ṣalt was one of five wives married to 'Umayr at the same time. Thus, he was ordered to divorce one of them, and he divorced Dijājah. She then married 'Uthmān bin 'Affān's maternal uncle, 'Āmir bin Kurayz, who was the brother of 'Uthmān's mother Arwā bint Kurayz. She gave birth to 'Abdullāh bin 'Āmir, who would later become a distinguished military general.

❖ DURRAH bint Abī Sufyān is the sister of the Prophet's wife Umm Ḥabībah Ramlah bint Abī Sufyān. She is her sister intended in the *ḥadīth* collected in *Ṣaḥīḥ al-Bukhārī*. Umm Ḥabībah said:

يَا رَسُولَ اللَّهِ، انْكِحْ أُخْتِي بِنْتَ أَبِي سُفْيَانَ. قَالَ: أَوَ تُحِبِّينَ ذَلِكِ؟

[20] *Sunan Ibn Mājah* 2141

قُلْتُ: لَسْتُ لَكَ بِمُخَلِّيَةٍ وَأَحَبُّ إِلَيَّ مَنْ شَرَكَنِي فِي خَيْرٍ أُخْتِي. قَالَ: إِنَّ ذَلِكَ لَا يَحِلُّ لِي.

"O Messenger of Allāh, marry my sister, the daughter of Abū Sufyān." The Prophet ﷺ said, "Would you like that?" I replied, "Yes, for even now I am not your only wife, and I like that my sister should share the good with me." The Prophet ﷺ said, "But that is not lawful for me."[21]

❖ DURRAH bint Abī Salamah is the stepdaughter of the Messenger of Allāh ﷺ. She is the other woman referred to in the previous *ḥadīth* of Umm Ḥabībah.

Umm Ḥabībah said:

فَقُلْتُ: يَا رَسُولَ اللَّهِ إِنَّا لَنَتَحَدَّثُ أَنَّكَ تُرِيدُ أَنْ تَنْكِحَ دُرَّةَ بِنْتَ أَبِي سَلَمَةَ. فَقَالَ: وَاللَّهِ لَوْ لَمْ تَكُنْ رَبِيبَتِي فِي حِجْرِي مَا حَلَّتْ لِي، إِنَّهَا ابْنَةُ أَخِي مِنَ الرَّضَاعَةِ، أَرْضَعَتْنِي وَأَبَا سَلَمَةَ ثُوَيْبَةُ، فَلَا تَعْرِضْنَ عَلَيَّ بَنَاتِكُنَّ وَلَا أَخَوَاتِكُنَّ.

I said, "We have heard that you want to marry the daughter of Abū Salamah." He said, "(You mean) the daughter of Umm Salamah?" I said, "Yes." He said, "Even if she were not my stepdaughter, she would be unlawful for me to marry, as she is my foster niece. I and Abū Salamah were suckled by Thuwaybah. So you should not present to me your daughters or your sisters (in marriage)."[22]

DHĀL – ذ

There are no female Companions mentioned under this letter.

[21] *Ṣaḥīḥ al-Bukhārī* 5101

[22] *Ṣaḥīḥ al-Bukhārī* 5101

RĀ' – ر

❖ AR-RABĀB bint Ḥārithah is the mother of the well-known Companion Ḥudhayfah bin al-Yamān, the keeper of the secrets of the Messenger of Allāh ﷺ. He was called this because he is the only Companion whom the Prophet ﷺ told the names of the hypocrites. Some historians say her name was ar-Rabāb bint Ka'b.

❖ AR-RUBAYYI' bint Naḍr is the paternal aunt to Anas bin Mālik, the servant of the Messenger of Allāh ﷺ, and she is the sister of the Companion Anas bin Naḍr. Her story was narrated by Anas bin Mālik. Anas said, "Ar-Rubayyi', the paternal aunt of Anas, broke the tooth of a girl, and her family asked the girl's family to pardon her, but they refused. They offered to pay compensatory money, but they refused. So they came to the Prophet ﷺ, who ordered retaliation. Anas bin Naḍr said, 'O Messenger of Allāh, will the tooth of ar-Rubayyi' be broken? By the One Who sent you with the truth, it will not be broken!'[23] The Prophet ﷺ said, 'O Anas, the Book of Allāh has decreed retaliation.' After Anas made his oath, the people came to the Messenger of Allāh ﷺ, informing him that they had pardoned her. The Messenger of Allāh ﷺ said:

إِنَّ مِنْ عِبَادِ اللَّهِ مَنْ لَوْ أَقْسَمَ عَلَى اللَّهِ لأَبَرَّهُ.

"'There are among the slaves of Allāh those who, if they swear by Allāh, Allāh fulfills their oath.'"[24]

She is also known by her *kunyah* Umm Ḥārithah. Her nephew Anas bin Mālik said, "Ḥārithah was martyred in the Battle of Badr while he was young. His mother came to the Prophet ﷺ saying, 'O Messenger of Allāh, you know the relation of Ḥārithah to me and

---

[23] **Translator's note:** Shaykh 'Uthaymīn said in his explanation of this *ḥadīth*: "Anas bin Naḍr was not rejecting the legislation of Allāh regarding retaliation; rather, he was confident that Allāh would guide the hearts of the girl's family to pardon his sister." (*Riyāḍ aṣ-Ṣāliḥīn*)

[24] *Ṣaḥīḥ al-Bukhārī* 4500

how fond of him I was; so, if he is in Paradise, I will remain patient and hope for Allāh's reward, but if he is not there, then you will see what I will do.' The Prophet ﷺ replied, 'May Allāh be merciful upon you! You are bereaved. Do you think it is one Paradise? There are many Paradises and he is in the most superior Paradise of al-Firdaws.' "[25]

❖ RAJĀ' al-Ghanawiyyah was a narrator of *ḥadīth*. Ibn Sīrīn said, "A woman named Rajā' said:

كنت عند النبي صَلَّى الله عليه وسلم، فجاءته امرأة بابن لها فقالت: يا رسول الله، ادع الله لي فيه بالبركة، فإنه توفي لي ثلاثة. فقال لها رسول الله صَلَّى الله عليه وسلم: أَمُنْذُ أَسْلَمْتِ؟ قالت: نعم. فقال رسول الله صَلَّى الله عليه وسلم: جُنَّةٌ حَصِيْنَةٌ قالت: فقال لي رجل عند رسول الله صَلَّى الله عليه وسلم: اسمعي يا رجاءُ ما يقول رسول الله صَلَّى الله عليه وسلم.

" 'I was in the presence of the Messenger of Allāh ﷺ when a woman came with her son. She said, "O Messenger of Allāh, supplicate to Allāh for me that He bless my son, for surely three of my children have died." The Messenger of Allāh ﷺ said, "Since you have embraced Islām?" She replied in the affirmative. He said, "A fortified shield" (meaning, from the Hellfire). A man who was with the Messenger of Allāh ﷺ said, "Listen, O Rajā', to what the Messenger of Allāh has said ﷺ." ' "[26]

❖ RAZĪNAH was the servant of the Messenger of Allāh ﷺ, the freed slave of his wife Ṣafiyyah, and a narrator of *ḥadīth*. When the Prophet ﷺ married Ṣafiyyah, he included in her dowry a servant, and this servant was Razīnah. Amatullāh, Razīnah's daughter, said, "I asked my mother (Razīnah), 'What did the Messenger of Allāh ﷺ say concerning the fast of 'Āshūrā'?' She said, 'Surely, he used to

[25] *Ṣaḥīḥ al-Bukhārī* 6550

[26] *Musnad Imām Aḥmad* 20808

fast it, and he commanded us to fast it.' "[27]

❖ RUFAYDAH al-Aslamiyyah is known as the first nurse in Islām. When Sa'd bin Mu'ādh was injured in the Battle of the Trench and his median vein was cut, the Messenger of Allāh ﷺ said:

اجعلوه في خَيْمَة رفيدة التي في المسجد حتى أعودَه من قريب.

Place him in the tent of Rufaydah which is in the *masjid*, until I can visit him shortly.

When the Prophet ﷺ passed by him, he would inquire, "How are you this evening?" and in the morning, "How are you this morning?" and he would tell him.[28]

In addition to nursing the sick, Rufaydah took it upon herself to serve the needy and underprivileged Muslims.

❖ RUQAYQAH bint Ṣayfī is the niece of the Prophet's grandfather 'Abdul-Muṭṭalib. Ruqayqah was raised with 'Abdul-Muṭṭalib, and she was older than him. Her son Makhramah bin Nawfal said that his mother said, "It is as though I am looking at my uncle Shaybah—meaning 'Abdul-Muṭṭalib bin Hāshim—right now. The day he came to us, I was a young girl. I was the first person to go to him, and I clung close to him." She embraced Islām, met the Messenger of Allāh ﷺ, and she was severe upon her son Makhramah before he embraced Islām. Ruqayqah is the woman who warned the Prophet ﷺ that the Quraysh were planning to assassinate him. She said:

إنّ قريشًا قد اجتمعت تُرِيدُ بَياتَكَ الليلة.

Verily, the Quraysh have mobilized. They intend to attack you tonight.

Thus, 'Alī bin Abī Ṭālib took the place of the Prophet ﷺ in his place of sleeping.

---

[27] Collected by Ibn Abī 'Āṣim.

[28] *Al-Adab al-Mufrad* 1129

❖ RUQAYQAH ath-Thaqafiyyah was a believing woman amid the tribe of Thaqīf, who were pagans. She embraced Islām when the Prophet ﷺ left Makkah after the death of Abū Ṭālib. Ruqayqah said, "The Prophet ﷺ came seeking aid in Ṭā'if. He visited us and I brought him a drink from wheat flour and barley. He said:

يَا رُقَيْقَةُ، لاَ تَعْبُدِي طَاغِيَتَهُمْ وَلاَ تُصَلِّنَّ إِلَيْهَا.

"'O Ruqayqah, don't worship their false gods and do not pray towards them.'

"I said, 'In this case, they will kill me!' He said, 'If they ask you concerning this, then say:

رَبِّي رَبُّ هَذِهِ الطَّاغِيَةِ، فَإِذَا صَلَّيْتِ، فَوَلِّيْهَا ظَهْرَكِ.

"'"My Lord is the lord of these false gods." And when you pray, turn your back towards them.'

"And then the Prophet ﷺ left."

Ruqayqah's daughter said, "My brothers Sufyān and Wahb informed me that when the tribe of Thaqīf embraced Islām, they went to greet the Prophet ﷺ. He said to my brothers, 'What did your mother do?' They replied, 'She died just as you left her.' The Prophet ﷺ said, 'Surely, your mother was saved.'"

❖ RAWDAH was a maid for a woman living in Madīnah. She narrates her story, saying: "I was a maid for a woman from the people of Madīnah. When the Prophet ﷺ migrated from Makkah to Madīnah, my boss said to me, 'O Rawḍah, stand at the door. And if that man passes by, let me know.' I stood at the door of the house and he passed by with a group of his Companions. I grabbed the edge of his garment and smiled in his face. I said to my boss, 'That man has arrived.' My boss went out with her husband, and the Prophet ﷺ presented Islām to them and everyone embraced Islām."[29]

---

[29] Collected in *Asad al-Ghābah* (2252).

❖ RAYṬAH bint Abī Umayyah is the sister of Umm Salamah Hind bint Abī Umayyah, the wife of the Messenger of Allāh ﷺ.

❖ RAYṬAH bint Abī Ṭālib is the youngest sister of 'Alī bin Abī Ṭālib. Her *kunyah* is Umm Ṭālib.

ZĀY – ز

❖ ZINNĪRAH ar-Rūmiyyah was from Rome. She was from the first and foremost to embrace Islām. She was a slave of Banū Makhzūm, and Abū Jahl used to punish her. When she embraced Islām, she lost her eyesight. The pagans said to her, "Al-Lāt and al-'Uzzā blinded you because you disbelieved in them!" She replied, "Al-Lāt and al-'Uzzā don't even know who worships them, and my Lord has the ability to return my eyesight." The next day, Allāh returned her eyesight. The Quraysh said, "This is magic from Muḥammad." When Abū Bakr saw how she was punished, he purchased her and freed her. She is mentioned among the seven slaves freed by Abū Bakr.

❖ ZAYNAB bint al-Ḥārith bin Salām al-Isrā'īliyyah was the Jewish woman who poisoned the Messenger of Allāh ﷺ with a roasted sheep. Abū Hurayrah said:

أَهْدَتْ لَهُ يَهُودِيَّةٌ بِخَيْبَرَ شَاةً مَصْلِيَّةً سَمَّتْهَا فَأَكَلَ رَسُولُ اللَّهِ صلى الله عليه وسلم مِنْهَا وَأَكَلَ الْقَوْمُ فَقَالَ ارْفَعُوا أَيْدِيَكُمْ فَإِنَّهَا أَخْبَرَتْنِي أَنَّهَا مَسْمُومَةٌ. فَمَاتَ بِشْرُ بْنُ الْبَرَاءِ بْنِ مَعْرُورٍ الأَنْصَارِيُّ فَأَرْسَلَ إِلَى الْيَهُودِيَّةِ مَا حَمَلَكِ عَلَى الَّذِي صَنَعْتِ. قَالَتْ إِنْ كُنْتَ نَبِيًّا لَمْ يَضُرَّكَ الَّذِي صَنَعْتُ وَإِنْ كُنْتَ مَلِكًا أَرَحْتُ النَّاسَ مِنْكَ.

A Jewish woman presented him with a roasted sheep while at Khaybar. So the Messenger of Allāh ﷺ ate it, as did those with him. The Prophet ﷺ said, "Raise your hands away (from the food), for surely it (the food) has informed me it is poisonous." Bishr bin

al-Barā' bin Ma'rūr al-Anṣārī died. The Prophet sent for the Jewish woman and asked her what led her to do that. She replied, "If you were a prophet, what I did would not harm you, but if you were a king, I would relieve the people of you."[30]

Zaynab bint al-Ḥārith then embraced Islām, and the Prophet ﷺ did not punish her. Other reports say she was executed, but only as retaliation rights for the relatives of Bishr bin al-Barā'.

❖ ZAYNAB bint Ḥanẓalah, along with her father and her paternal aunt al-Jarbā' bint Qasāmah, went to the Prophet ﷺ. He married Zaynab to Usāmah bin Zayd. Then Usāmah divorced her. After her *'iddah* period, the Messenger of Allāh ﷺ said:

مَنْ يَتَزَوَّجُ زَيْنَبَ بِنْتَ حَنْظَلَةَ وَأَنَا أُمْهِرُهُ؟

Who will marry Zaynab bint Ḥanẓalah while I pay his dowry?

❖ ZAYNAB bint Zayd is the sister of Usāmah bin Zayd.

❖ ZAYNAB bint Abī Sufyān is the sister of the Prophet's wife Umm Ḥabībah Ramlah bint Abī Sufyān. She was married to 'Urwah bin Mas'ūd. 'Urwah had 10 wives when he embraced Islām, and he was instructed to keep only four. Zaynab was from the four he chose to keep.

❖ ZAYNAB bint 'Abdillāh bin Mu'āwiyah ath-Thaqafī, the wife of 'Abdullāh bin Mas'ūd, was a wealthy, skillful craftswoman. 'Abdullāh bin Mas'ūd did not have much wealth, so she would spend upon him, their son, and the orphans under her care from the money earned from her craft. Zaynab bint 'Abdillāh said, "The Messenger of Allāh ﷺ said, 'Give in charity, O women, even if it is from your jewelry.' I went back to 'Abdullāh and said, 'You are a man who has little, and the Messenger of Allāh ﷺ has commanded us to give in charity. Go and ask him if that is acceptable; otherwise, I will give my charity to someone else.' 'Abdullāh said to me,

[30] *Sunan Abī Dāwūd* 4512

'No; you go and ask him.' So I went, and there I saw a woman from among the Anṣār at the door of the Messenger of Allāh ﷺ, wanting to ask the same question. We felt too shy to speak to the Messenger of Allāh ﷺ.

"Bilāl came out to us and we said to him, 'Go to the Messenger of Allāh ﷺ and tell him that there are two women at the door asking whether it is acceptable for them to give charity (*zakāh*) to their husbands and the orphans who are in their care, but do not tell him who we are.' Bilāl went in to the Messenger of Allāh ﷺ and asked him, and the Messenger of Allāh ﷺ asked, 'Who are they?' He said, 'A woman from among the Anṣār and Zaynab.'[31] The Messenger of Allāh ﷺ asked, 'Which Zaynab?' He said, 'The wife of 'Abdullāh.' The Messenger of Allāh ﷺ said to him:

لَهُمَا أَجْرَانِ أَجْرُ الْقَرَابَةِ وَأَجْرُ الصَّدَقَةِ.

" 'They will have two rewards: the reward of (upholding ties of) kinship and the reward of giving charity.' "[32]

Some say her name was Rayṭah or Rā'iṭah, while some scholars say she was known by both of these names.

❖ ZAYNAB bint Qays is the sister of Thābit bin Qays, the *khaṭīb* of the Messenger of Allāh ﷺ.

SĪN – س

❖ SĀ'IBAH, the freed slave of the Messenger of Allāh ﷺ. She narrated *aḥādīth* from him concerning lost property.

❖ SUBAY'AH bint al-Ḥārith al-Aslamiyyah gave birth to her

[31] **Translator's note:** Shaykh 'Uthaymīn said in his explanation of this *ḥadīth*, "When the Prophet ﷺ asked Bilāl who the women were, it became binding on Bilāl to inform him."

[32] *Ṣaḥīḥ al-Bukhārī* 1466; *Ṣaḥīḥ Muslim* 1000

child a few days after her husband died. Her story is narrated in the *Muwaṭṭa'* of Imām Mālik. 'Abdullāh bin 'Abbās and Abū Salamah bin 'Abdur-Raḥmān bin 'Awf differed on the question of a woman who gave birth a few nights after the death of her husband. Abū Salamah said, "When she gives birth to the child she is carrying, she is free to marry." Ibn 'Abbās said, "At the end of two periods." Abū Hurayrah came and said, "I am with my nephew," meaning Abū Salamah. They sent Kurayb, a freed slave of 'Abdullāh bin 'Abbās, to Umm Salamah, the wife of the Prophet ﷺ, to ask her about it. He came back and told them that she had said that Subay'ah al-Aslamiyyah had given birth a few nights after the death of her husband, and she had brought the matter to the Messenger of Allāh ﷺ, and he had said:

You are free to marry, so marry whomever you wish.[33]

❖ SU'DĀ bint 'Amr al-Murriyyah narrated a *ḥadīth* on the virtue of saying "nothing has the right to be worshiped except Allāh" at the time of death. Yaḥyā bin Ṭalḥah said that his mother Su'dā al-Murriyyah said, "'Umar bin al-Khaṭṭāb passed by Ṭalḥah after the Messenger of Allāh ﷺ had died, and said, 'Why do you look so sad? Are you upset because your cousin has been appointed leader?' He said, 'No, but I heard the Messenger of Allāh ﷺ say, "I know a word which no one says at the time of death but it will be light in his record of deeds, and his body and soul will find comfort in it at the time of death," but I did not ask him about it before he died.' He ('Umar) said, 'I know what it is. It is what he wanted his uncle (Abū Ṭālib) to say, and if he had known anything that would be more effective in saving him, he would have told him to say it.'"[34]

❖ SU'DĀ bint Kurayz is the maternal aunt of 'Uthmān bin 'Affān. She embraced Islām and then invited 'Uthmān to embrace Islām. She was the first person to give 'Uthmān *da'wah*. Su'dā said to her

---

[33] *Muwaṭṭa' Mālik* 1249

[34] *Sunan Ibn Mājah* 3795

nephew 'Uthmān, "'Uthmān, O 'Uthmān, O 'Uthmān: you are handsome and you have status. This Prophet has with him proof and evidences, and he was sent with the true religion. He has brought revelation and a criterion. So follow him and do not allow those idols to destroy you. Surely, Muḥammad bin 'Abdillāh is the Messenger of Allāh. Jibrīl came to him and he invites to Allāh." The speech of Su'dā settled into 'Uthmān's heart. He went to Abū Bakr and informed him of what his aunt had told him. Abū Bakr said, "Woe to you, 'Uthmān; by Allāh, you are a perceptive man. You are able to distinguish truth from falsehood. Those idols that you worship are nothing more than inanimate. They cannot hear, see, cause harm, or bring benefit. Your aunt has spoken the truth."

Abū Bakr took 'Uthmān to see the Prophet ﷺ. He said to 'Uthmān, "O 'Uthmān, answer the call of Allāh to His Paradise. Verily, I am the Messenger of Allāh to you and to all the creation." 'Uthmān said, "By Allāh, once I heard that, I embraced Islām and I testified that nothing has the right to be worshiped except Allāh alone without partners and that Muḥammad is His slave and Messenger."

❖ SA'ĪDAH was from the Anṣār. She was married to a disbeliever named Abū Ṣayfī the Monk. Abū Ṣayfī left Madīnah, upset at his wife's family for embracing Islām. He took his family to Makkah and stayed there for a while. His wife Sa'īdah left him and migrated back to Madīnah during the truce. The people asked the Prophet ﷺ if she should be returned to her husband in Makkah based upon the conditions of the truce. He informed them that this condition only applied to the men and not the women.

❖ SU'AYRAH al-Asadiyyah is the Ethiopian woman who suffered from fits of epilepsy. Her *kunyah* is Umm Zufar. 'Aṭā' bin Abī Rabāḥ said, "Ibn 'Abbās said to me, 'Shall I not show you a woman from the inhabitants of Paradise?' So he showed me a tall, large, yellow Ethiopian woman. He said, 'This is Su'ayrah al-Asadiyyah; she went to the Messenger of Allāh ﷺ and said, "O Messenger of Allāh, I suffer from epilepsy, and during fits, my body is exposed; so supplicate to Allāh to cure me." He said, "If you want, I will supplicate to

Allāh to cure you, and your good deeds and evil deeds will remain as they are. Or if you like, you can be patient and Paradise is yours." Thus, she chose patience and Paradise.' "[35]

❖ SAKĪNAH bint Abī Waqqāṣ is the sister of Sa'd bin Abī Waqqāṣ, one of the 10 promised Paradise. Sakīnah bint Abī Waqqāṣ said, "O Messenger of Allāh, what is the *jihād* for the women?" He replied:

جِهَادُكُنَّ الحَجُّ.

Your *jihād* is Ḥajj.[36]

❖ SULĀFAH bint Sa'd is the mother of 'Uthmān bin Ṭalḥah. She was the keeper of the keys to the Ka'bah the day Makkah was conquered. The Prophet ﷺ entered Makkah the day of the conquest, prayed, and sat in the *masjid.* He then sent Bilāl to 'Uthmān bin Ṭalḥah to request the keys to the Ka'bah. 'Uthmān in turn went to his mother Sulāfah to request the keys to the Ka'bah. She argued with him for a long time about the matter before finally relinquishing the keys. Thus, the keys were given to the Prophet ﷺ, and Sulāfah embraced Islām after that.

❖ SALMĀ bint Ḥafṣah was the wife of Sa'd bin Abī Waqqāṣ. She participated with him in the Battle of al-Qādisiyyah, as well as other battles.

❖ SALMĀ bint Sa'diyyah is the sister of Ḥalīmah as-Sa'diyyah, the nursing mother of the Prophet ﷺ. Thus, she is the maternal aunt of the Prophet ﷺ through breastfeeding.

❖ SALMĀ bint Qays Umm Mundhir is a maternal aunt of the Messenger of Allāh ﷺ. She prayed with the Messenger of Allāh towards both prayer directions, and she gave the pledge of allegiance. The Messenger of Allāh ﷺ used to visit her and eat with her. Umm Mundhir said, "The Messenger of Allāh ﷺ entered upon

[35] *Musnad Imām Aḥmad* 1/347

[36] *Musnad Imām Aḥmad* 24303

us, and with him was 'Alī bin Abī Ṭālib, who had recently recovered from an illness. We had bunches of unripe dates hanging up, and the Prophet ﷺ was eating from them. 'Alī reached out to eat some, and the Prophet ﷺ said to 'Alī:

مَهْ يَا عَلِيُّ إِنَّكَ نَاقِهٌ.

" 'Stop, O 'Alī! You have just recovered from an illness.'

"I made some greens and barley for the Prophet ﷺ, and the Prophet ﷺ said to 'Alī, 'O 'Alī, eat some of this, for it is better for you.' "[37]

❖ SALMĀ Umm Rāfi' was the servant of the Messenger of Allāh ﷺ. She is the woman who incited Ḥamzah bin 'Abdul-Muṭṭalib, the uncle of the Prophet, to embrace Islām. She was married to Abū Rāfi', the freed slave of the Prophet ﷺ, and she was the freed slave of Ṣafiyyah bint 'Abdul-Muṭṭalib, the paternal aunt of the Prophet. Ḥamzah had not yet embraced Islām when he returned from a hunting trip one day. Upon his return, Salmā Umm Rāfi' said to him, "If you would have seen what Abū Jahl did to your nephew!" Ḥamzah went to find Abū Jahl in a fit of rage. He found him sitting at the Ka'bah with a group of elders. He struck Abū Jahl in the head with his bow and said:

أَتَشْتِمُهُ وَأَنَا عَلَى دِينِهِ أَقُولُ مَا يَقُولُ؟ فَرُدَّ ذَلِكَ عَلَيَّ إِنْ اسْتَطَعْتَ.

Do you insult him while I am upon his same religion, and I say what he says? Hit me back if you are able!

Abū Jahl's clan stood up to defend him, but he said to them, "Leave Ḥamzah be, for surely I insulted his nephew." Ḥamzah went to the house of al-Arqam and embraced Islām.[38]

'Ā'ishah ﷺ said, "Salmā, the wife of Abū Rāfi', came to the Prophet ﷺ to complain about Abū Rāfi'. She said, 'He hits me.' The Prophet ﷺ said to them, 'What is your complaint and what

---

[37] *Sunan Ibn Mājah* 3568

[38] *Sīrah Ibn Hishām*

is her complaint?' Abū Rāfi' said, 'She harms me, O Messenger of Allāh.' He said, 'How do you harm him, O Salmā?' She said, 'I do not harm him with anything, but he broke his *wuḍū'* while he was praying, so I said to him, "O Abū Rāfi', the Messenger of Allāh ﷺ commanded the Muslims to perform *wuḍū'* if they pass wind." Thus, he hit me.' The Prophet ﷺ smiled and said:

يَا أَبَا رَافِعٍ، لَمْ تَأْمُرْكَ إِلا بِخَيرٍ.

" 'O Abū Rāfi', she only commands you with good.' "[39]

❖ SUMAYYAH bint Khuyyāṭ was the first martyr in Islām. She was the freed slave of Abū Ḥudhayfah bin al-Mughīrah. She was the wife of Yāsir bin 'Āmir, and the mother of 'Ammār bin Yāsir. Sumayyah was the seventh person to embrace Islām. The tribe of al-Mughīrah used to punish her severely due to her Islām, but she refused to abandon it. The Prophet ﷺ used to pass by them as they were punished, and he would say:

صبرا يا آل ياسر، موعدكم الجنّة.

Patience, O family of Yāsir; your destination is Paradise.

Mujāhid said, "The first people to openly display their Islām in Makkah were seven: the Messenger of Allāh, Abū Bakr, Bilāl, Khabbāb[40], Ṣuhayb, 'Ammār, and Sumayyah. As for the Messenger of Allāh ﷺ and Abū Bakr, their tribes protected them. As for the others, they were dressed in iron sheets and laid in the sun. And Abū Jahl came to Sumayyah and killed her.[41]

One day, Abū Jahl began to verbally abuse her; then, he started beating her, until he took his spear and stabbed her in the heart, killing her. Thus, Sumayyah became the first martyr in Islām. Mujāhid said, "The first martyr in Islām was the mother of 'Ammār bin Yāsir. She was an elderly, fragile woman. When Abū Jahl was

---

[39] *Musnad Imām Aḥmad* 25134

[40] **Translator's note:** Khabbāb bin al-Aratt.

[41] Collected by Ibn Abī Shaybah.

killed at the Battle of Badr, the Prophet ﷺ said to 'Ammār:

قتل اللّٰه قاتل أمّك.

"'Allāh killed your mother's killer.'"[42]

❖ SANĀ' bint Asmā' aṣ-Ṣalt was from the wives of the Messenger of Allāh ﷺ. He married her, but she died before the marriage was consummated. Imām ar-Rashāṭī said that the cause of her death was that, upon hearing the news that she would be marrying the Messenger of Allāh, she became overcome with joy, and she died of happiness and excitement.

❖ SAJĀḤ bint al-Ḥārith at-Tamīmiyyah is the woman who claimed prophecy during the Wars of Apostasy and gained a following. Then she united with Musaylimah the Liar and he married her. After Musaylimah was killed, she returned to Islām and embraced it. She lived until Mu'āwiyah's caliphate.

SHĪN – ش

❖ ASH-SHIFĀ' bint 'Awf bin 'Abd bin al-Ḥārith is the mother of 'Abdur-Raḥmān bin 'Awf, one of the 10 promised Paradise. She migrated and died during the lifetime of the Prophet ﷺ.

ṢĀD – ص

❖ ṢAKHRAH bint Abī Lahab embraced Islām, and she was present during the conquest of Makkah.

❖ AṢ-ṢA'BAH bint al-Ḥaḍramī is the mother of Ṭalḥah bin 'Ubaydillāh, one of the 10 promised Paradise.

---

[42] Collected by Ibn Sa'd (8/193).

❖ ṢAFIYYAH bint al-Khaṭṭāb is the sister of 'Umar bin al-Khaṭṭāb. She married Sufyān bin 'Abdil-Asad and gave birth to their son al-Aswad.

❖ ṢAFIYYAH bint 'Umar bin al-Khaṭṭāb is the daughter of 'Umar. She was with the Messenger of Allāh ﷺ during the Battle of Khaybar.

❖ ṢUMAYTAH al-Laythiyyah was an orphan under the care of 'Ā'ishah.

❖ ṢAFIYYAH bint Abī 'Ubayd was the wife of 'Abdullāh bin 'Umar al-Khaṭṭāb.

ḌĀD - ض

❖ ḌUBAY'AH bint Ḥadhīm is the mother of 'Abdullāh bin Ḥudhāfah as-Sahmī, the courier of the Messenger of Allāh ﷺ. Whenever her son 'Abdullāh bin Ḥudhāfah would get into an argument, his adversary would slander him and attribute him to someone other than his father. Anas bin Mālik said, "The Messenger of Allāh ﷺ came out as the sun declined at midday and offered the Ẓuhr prayer. He then stood on the pulpit and spoke about the Day of Judgment, and he said that there would be tremendous things in it. He then said, 'Whoever likes to ask me about anything, he can do so, and I shall reply as long as I am at this place of mine.' Most of the people wept, and the Prophet ﷺ said repeatedly, 'Ask me.' 'Abdullāh bin Ḥudhāfah as-Sahmī stood up and said, 'Who is my father?' The Prophet ﷺ said, 'Your father is Ḥudhāfah.' The Prophet ﷺ repeatedly said, 'Ask me.' Then 'Umar knelt before him and said, 'We are pleased with Allāh as our Lord, Islām as our religion, and Muḥammad as our Prophet.' The Prophet then became quiet and said, 'Paradise and Hellfire were displayed in front of me on this wall just now, and I have never seen a better thing (than the former) and a worse thing (than the latter).' "[43]

Ḍubay'ah—'Abdullāh's mother—said to him, "I have never heard of a more disobedient child than you. Do you think your mother could have done the evil (adultery) of some women during the Pre-Islamic Days of Ignorance?! And then would you attempt to expose this in front of the eyes of the people? Your father is Ḥudhāfah, even if your mother had some other bad traits from pre-Islamic times."[44]

ṬĀ' – ط

❖ ṬĀHIRAH bint Khuwaylid is the sister of Khadījah bint Khuwaylid, the wife of the Prophet ﷺ.

ẒĀ' – ظ

❖ ẒABYAH bint Wahb is the mother of Abū Mūsā al-Ash'arī. She embraced Islām and migrated to Madīnah.

'AYN – ع

❖ 'ĀTIKAH bint 'Awf is the sister of 'Abdur-Raḥmān bin 'Awf, one of the 10 promised Paradise.

❖ 'ĀTIKAH bint Na'īm is the woman who came to the Prophet ﷺ after her son-in-law had died. Zaynab said, "I heard my mother, Umm Salamah, saying that a woman came to the Messenger of Allāh ﷺ and said, 'O Messenger of Allāh, the husband of my daughter has died and she is suffering from an eye disease; can she

[43] *Ṣaḥīḥ al-Bukhārī* 540

[44] *Explanation of Ṣaḥīḥ Muslim* by Imām an-Nawawī (2359).

apply *kuḥl* to her eye?' The Messenger of Allāh ﷺ replied, 'No,' two or three times. Every time she repeated her question, he said, 'No.' Then the Messenger of Allāh ﷺ said:

إِنَّمَا هِيَ أَرْبَعَةُ أَشْهُرٍ وَعَشْرٌ، وَقَدْ كَانَتْ إِحْدَاكُنَّ فِي الْجَاهِلِيَّةِ تَرْمِي بِالْبَعَرَةِ عَلَى رَأْسِ الْحَوْلِ.

" 'It (the mourning period) is only four months and ten days. In the Pre-Islamic Period of Ignorance, a widow among you should throw a globe of dung when one year had elapsed.' "[45]

❖ 'ĀTIKAH bint al-Walīd is the sister of Khālid bin al-Walīd.

❖ 'UZZAH bint Abī Lahab was the daughter of Abū Lahab.

❖ 'AFRĀ' bint 'Ubayd has a virtue no other woman has: she gave birth to seven sons who all fought in the Battle of Badr alongside the Messenger of Allāh ﷺ. Her sons from her first marriage are Mu'awwidh, Mu'ādh, and 'Awf. Her sons from her second marriage are Iyās, 'Āqil, Khālid, and 'Āmir.

❖ 'ULAYYAH bint Shurayḥ from Ḥaḍramawt in Yemen is the sister of as-Sā'ib bin Yazīd, as they share the same mother. And she is the sister of Makhramah bin Shurayḥ al-Ḥaḍramī, as they share the same father. Az-Zuhrī said, "As-Sā'ib bin Yazīd told me that Makhramah bin Shurayḥ al-Ḥaḍramī was mentioned in the presence of the Messenger of Allāh ﷺ, and the Messenger of Allāh ﷺ said:

ذَاكَ رَجُلٌ لاَ يَتَوَسَّدُ الْقُرْآنَ.

" 'He does not sleep on the Qur'ān.' "[46]

❖ 'AMRAH bint Mas'ūd bin Qays is the mother of Sa'd bin 'Ubādah. She died during the lifetime of the Messenger of Allāh ﷺ.

---

[45] *Ṣaḥīḥ al-Bukhārī* 5336

[46] *Sunan an-Nasā'ī* 1783

❖ 'AMRAH bint Rawāḥah is the mother of Nu'mān bin Bashīr and the sister of 'Abdullāh bin Rawāḥah. She was married to Bashīr bin Sa'd. She asked her husband to give a gift to their son Nu'mān but not to the other children. When he did so, she asked him to call the Messenger of Allāh ﷺ to witness it. Nu'mān bin Bashīr said that his father Bashīr brought him to the Messenger of Allāh ﷺ and said, "I have given this son of mine one of my slaves." The Messenger of Allāh ﷺ said:

أَكُلَّ وَلَدِكَ نَحَلْتَهُ مِثْلَ هَذَا. فَقَالَ لاَ. قَالَ رَسُولُ اللَّهِ صلى الله عليه وسلم فَارْتَجِعْهُ.

"Have you given each of your children the same as this?" He said, "No." The Messenger of Allāh ﷺ said, "Then take the slave back."[47]

❖ 'UMAYRAH bint Abil-Ḥakam was a young girl when her parents divorced. Her father Abul-Ḥakam was Muslim, but his wife had not embraced Islām. Abul-Ḥakam's wife went to the Messenger of Allāh ﷺ and said, "Abul-Ḥakam has taken my daughter and he is keeping her away from me." So he ordered Abul-Ḥakam to sit in one corner of the room and for his wife to sit in another corner of the room. He placed 'Umayrah between them and he told both of them to call her. They called her, and she began to incline towards her mother. The Messenger of Allāh ﷺ said, "O Allāh, guide her." So she inclined towards her father.[48]

GHAYN – غ

❖ GHUFAYRAH bint Rabāḥ is the sister of Bilāl bin Rabāḥ, the caller to prayer for the Prophet ﷺ. Their brother Khālid was also from the Companions.

---

[47] *Muwaṭṭa' Mālik* 1442

[48] Collected by Ibn Mājah.

FĀ' – ف

❖ FĀKHITAH bint 'Amr az-Zuhriyyah is the maternal aunt of the Messenger of Allāh ﷺ.

❖ FĀRI'AH al-Jinniyyah bint al-'Abduṣ-Ṣāliḥ was a woman from among the *jinn*. She used to come to the Prophet ﷺ on behalf of the women from her people. Ḥamzah bin Yūsuf al-Jurjānī mentioned her in *The History of Gorgon*.[49]

It has been narrated from Jābir that a woman from among the *jinn* used to come to the Prophet ﷺ on behalf of the women from her people. One day, she was late in arriving, so he said to her, "What delayed you?" She said, "One of our family members died in India, so I went to give condolences. While on the road, I saw Iblīs praying on a boulder. I said to him, 'What caused you to mislead Ādam?' He said, 'Leave me concerning this matter.' I said to him, 'You are praying despite who you are!' He said, 'Yes, O Fāri'ah bint al-'Abduṣ-Ṣāliḥ. Surely, I hope for forgiveness from my Lord if I fulfill His covenant.' "

Because there is someone within the chain of narration who is unknown, Ibn al-Jawzī graded this *ḥadīth* as fabricated.

❖ FĀṬIMAH bint Abil-Asad is the woman who stole during the conquest of Makkah, and thus the Prophet ﷺ ordered her hand to be amputated. 'Ā'ishah ﷺ said, "The Quraysh people became very worried about the Makhzūmī lady who had committed theft. They said, 'Who will speak in her favor to the Messenger of Allāh ﷺ, and who is brave enough to do so except Usāmah, who is the beloved of the Messenger of Allāh ﷺ?' When Usāmah spoke to the Messenger of Allāh ﷺ about that matter, the Messenger of Allāh ﷺ said:

أَتَشْفَعُ فِي حَدٍّ مِنْ حُدُودِ اللَّهِ.

[49] **Translator's note:** Gorgon is a province in Iran.

" 'Do you intercede concerning one of the *ḥadd* punishments set by Allāh?'

"Then he got up and addressed the people, saying:

يَا أَيُّهَا النَّاسُ إِنَّمَا ضَلَّ مَنْ قَبْلَكُمْ أَنَّهُمْ كَانُوا إِذَا سَرَقَ الشَّرِيفُ تَرَكُوهُ، وَإِذَا سَرَقَ الضَّعِيفُ فِيهِمْ أَقَامُوا عَلَيْهِ الْحَدَّ، وَايْمُ اللَّهِ لَوْ أَنَّ فَاطِمَةَ بِنْتَ مُحَمَّدٍ سَرَقَتْ لَقَطَعَ مُحَمَّدٌ يَدَهَا.

" 'O people! The nations before you went astray because, if a noble person committed theft, they used to leave him alone, but if a weak person among them committed theft, they used to inflict the legal punishment on him. By Allāh, if Fāṭimah, the daughter of Muḥammad committed theft, Muḥammad would surely cut off her hand!' "[50]

'Urwah bin az-Zubayr ﷺ said, "Usāmah said, 'O Messenger of Allāh, ask Allāh to forgive me.' The Messenger of Allāh ﷺ ordered her hand amputated. After her hand was amputated, she perfected her repentance and she married. 'Ā'ishah ﷺ said, 'She would visit me, and I would take her needs to the Messenger of Allāh ﷺ.' "[51]

❖ FĀṬIMAH bint Junayd was the wife of al-'Abbās bin 'Abdul-Muṭṭalib, the paternal uncle of the Messenger of Allāh ﷺ.

❖ FĀṬIMAH bint al-Khaṭṭāb is the sister of 'Umar bin al-Khaṭṭāb. She was married to Sa'īd bin Zayd, who is from the 10 promised Paradise. Fāṭimah and her husband Sa'īd were from the first and foremost to embrace Islām, doing so before her brother 'Umar bin al-Khaṭṭāb.[52]

❖ FĀṬIMAH bint 'Abdillāh witnessed the birth of the Messenger

---

[50] *Ṣaḥīḥ al-Bukhārī* 6788

[51] *Ṣaḥīḥ Muslim* 1688

[52] **Translator's note:** Fāṭimah bint al-Khaṭṭāb and her husband Sa'īd are the two mentioned in the famous narration concerning how 'Umar bin al-Khaṭṭāb embraced Islām. Shaykh Muqbil said that this narration is not authentic.

of Allāh ﷺ when his mother Āminah gave birth to him. She said about that night, "There was no house that I looked at except it was illuminated. And I looked at the stars, set such that I thought they would fall upon us." She is the mother of the Companion 'Uthmān bin Abil-'Āṣ ath-Thaqafī.

❖ FĀṬIMAH bint 'Amr bin Ḥarām is the sister of the Companion and martyr 'Abdullāh bin 'Amr bin Ḥarām, and the paternal aunt of Jābir bin 'Abdillāh. Jābir bin 'Abdillāh said, "My father fell as a martyr on the Day of Uḥud, and I attempted to uncover his face and weep, but they (the Companions) forbade me to do this, whereas the Messenger of Allāh ﷺ did not forbid me. Fāṭimah bint 'Amr, the sister of my father, was also crying. The Messenger of Allāh ﷺ said:

تَبْكِيهِ أَوْ لاَ تَبْكِيهِ مَا زَالَتِ الْمَلاَئِكَةُ تُظِلُّهُ بِأَجْنِحَتِهَا حَتَّى رَفَعْتُمُوهُ.

" 'Cry for him or do not cry for him; the angels continue to shade him with their wings until you lift him up (for burial).' "[53]

Ṭalḥah bin Khirāsh said, "I heard Jābir bin 'Abdillāh say, 'The Messenger of Allāh ﷺ met me and said to me, "O Jābir! Why do I see you upset?" I said, "O Messenger of Allāh! My father was martyred (on the Day of Uḥud), leaving my family and debt behind." He said, "Shall I give you news of what your father met Allāh with?" I said, "But of course, O Messenger of Allāh!" He said:

مَا كَلَّمَ اللَّهُ أَحَدًا قَطُّ إِلاَّ مِنْ وَرَاءِ حِجَابٍ وَأَحْيَا أَبَاكَ فَكَلَّمَهُ كِفَاحًا فَقَالَ يَا عَبْدِي تَمَنَّ عَلَىَّ أُعْطِكَ.

" ' "Allāh does not speak to anyone except from behind a veil, but He brought your father to life to speak to Him directly. He said, 'O My slave, ask of Me and it shall be given.'

" ' "He said, 'O Lord! Give me life so that I may be killed for You a second time.' So the Lord, Blessed and Most High, said, 'It has been decreed by Me that they shall not return.' " ' [Jābir] said, 'So

[53] *Ṣaḥīḥ Muslim* 2471

this verse was revealed:

﴿ وَلَا تَحْسَبَنَّ الَّذِينَ قُتِلُوا فِي سَبِيلِ اللَّهِ أَمْوَاتًا ۚ بَلْ أَحْيَاءٌ عِندَ رَبِّهِمْ يُرْزَقُونَ ﴾

"' "Think not of those who are killed in the way of Allāh as dead. Nay, they are alive, with their Lord, and they have provision."' "

[Sūrah Āli 'Imrān 3:169]

❖ FARAY'AH bint Wahb az-Zuhriyyah is the maternal aunt of the Messenger of Allāh ﷺ. The Messenger of Allāh ﷺ raised her up with his hand and said:

من أراد أن ينظر إلى خالة رسول الله صَلَّى الله عليه وسلم: فلينظر إلى هذه.

Whoever wants to see the aunt of the Messenger of Allāh, then look at her.[54]

❖ FIḌḌAH an-Nūbiyyah (the Nubian) was the slave girl of Fāṭimah, the daughter of the Messenger of Allāh ﷺ.

QĀF – ق

❖ QARĪBAH bint Abī Sufyān is the sister of Mu'āwiyah. Fourteen men who participated in the Battle of Badr asked for her hand in marriage. She refused them all and married 'Aqīl bin Abī Ṭālib, the brother of 'Alī bin Abī Ṭālib. She said, "He was with my loved ones." Meaning, her brothers and father, who were pagans at the time. 'Aqīl fought alongside them before they all embraced Islām.

❖ QARĪBAH bint Abī Quḥāfah is the sister of Abū Bakr aṣ-Ṣiddīq.

[54] *Asad al-Ghābah*

❖ QAYLAH bint Makhramah is from the noble Companions who migrated to Madīnah. The story of her migration is collected in *Adab al-Mufrad* by al-Bukhārī. She migrated to Madīnah when she first embraced Islām, seeking to become a Companion of the Messenger of Allāh ﷺ. She said, "We arrived in Madīnah while the Messenger of Allāh ﷺ was leading the people in the morning prayers. It was dark, such that one could not distinguish a man from a woman, so I stood in prayer beside a man. And I was a woman who was new to Islām. The man beside me in the row said to me, 'Are you a man or a woman?' I replied, 'I am a woman.' He said, 'You almost put me to temptation; go pray with the women.' I then noticed that the women were praying by the rooms and I had not noticed them when I entered the *masjid*.

"When the sun rose, I saw the Prophet ﷺ sitting, squatting with his arms wrapped around his legs. When I saw the Prophet ﷺ, humble in his form of sitting, I trembled from fear due to his awe-inspiring personality. A man sitting with him saw me and said, 'O Messenger of Allāh, this poor woman is trembling.' The Messenger of Allāh ﷺ said to me with his hand, without looking at me, 'O timid woman, be tranquil.' Once he said this, Allāh removed the fear from my heart and we gave him the pledge." [55]

KĀF – ك

❖ KABSHAH bint Ma'n bin 'Āṣim was married to Abū Qays bin al-Aslat. When he died, his son wanted to inherit her, as this was a practice they did before Islām. Thus, Allāh revealed the verse:

﴿ أَيُّهَا الَّذِينَ آمَنُوا لَا يَحِلُّ لَكُمْ أَن تَرِثُوا النِّسَاءَ كَرْهًا ﴾

O you who believe! You are forbidden to inherit women against their will.

[Sūrah an-Nisā' 4:19]

[55] *Al-Adab al-Mufrad* 1178; declared authentic by al-Albānī.

❖ KABĪRAH bint Sufyān said, "I said to the Prophet ﷺ, 'O Messenger of Allāh, during the Pre-Islamic Days of Ignorance, I buried four children alive.' He said to me, 'Free four slaves,' so I freed Abū Sa'īd, his son Maysarah, and Umm Maysarah." Al-Khaṭīb said, "The name of the fourth freed slave was not mentioned, so perhaps it was the narrator of the *ḥadīth*, Abū Waraqah."

❖ KANŪD Umm Sārah was the courier carrying the letter for Ḥāṭib bin Abī Balta'ah. 'Ubaydullāh bin Rāfi', the scribe of 'Alī, said, "I heard 'Alī ؓ saying, 'The Messenger of Allāh ﷺ sent me, Zubayr, and Miqdād, saying, "Go to the garden of Khākh. There you will find a woman riding a camel. She will be in possession of a letter; take the letter from her." So we rushed on horses, and when we met that woman, we asked her to hand over the letter to us. She said, "There is no letter with me." We said, "Either hand over the letter or we will take off your clothes." She brought out the letter from (the plaited hair of) her head. We delivered the letter to the Messenger of Allāh ﷺ, in which Ḥāṭib bin Abī Balta'ah had informed some people amongst the polytheists of Makkah about the plans of the Messenger of Allāh ﷺ.

" 'The Messenger of Allāh ﷺ said, "Ḥāṭib, what is this?" He said, "O Messenger of Allāh, do not be hasty in judging my intention. I was a person attached to the Quraysh. Those who are with you amongst the emigrants have blood relationships with them (the Quraysh), and thus they would protect their families. I wished that, when I had no blood relationship with them, I should find some supporters from (amongst them) who would help my family. I did not do this because of any disbelief or apostasy, and I have no liking for disbelief after I have accepted Islām." Thereupon, the Messenger of Allāh ﷺ said, "You have told the truth." 'Umar said, "O Messenger of Allāh, permit me to strike the neck of this hypocrite." The Prophet ﷺ said, "He was a participant in Badr, and did you know that Allāh said about the people of Badr, 'Do what you like, for I have forgiven you.' "' "[56]

[56] *Ṣaḥīḥ Muslim* 2494

About this incident, Allāh the Exalted revealed the verse:

﴿ يَا أَيُّهَا الَّذِينَ آمَنُوا لَا تَتَّخِذُوا عَدُوِّي وَعَدُوَّكُمْ أَوْلِيَاءَ تُلْقُونَ إِلَيْهِم بِالْمَوَدَّةِ ﴾

O you who believe, take not My enemies and your enemies as friends, showing affection towards them.

[Sūrah al-Mumtaḥanah 60:1]

It is said that the Prophet ﷺ permitted the execution of Kanūd, but then granted her safety during the conquest of Makkah.

❖ KUWAYSAH was an orphan girl raised in the home of the Messenger of Allāh ﷺ.

❖ KAYYISAH bint al-Ḥārith was married to Musaylimah the Liar, and then she married 'Abdullāh bin 'Āmir the Elder.

LĀM – ل

❖ LUBĀBAH bint al-Ḥārith the Younger is the mother of Khālid bin al-Walīd. She is the sister of Lubābah bint al-Ḥārith the Elder.

❖ LABĪBAH, the slave of Banul-Mu'ammal, was from the early Muslims tortured for their faith. She was one of the seven slaves purchased and freed by Abū Bakr.

❖ LUHAYYAH was the slave-girl of 'Umar bin al-Khaṭṭāb and the mother of his son 'Abdur-Raḥmān.

❖ LAYLĀ bint Abī Ḥathmah was from the first and foremost to embrace Islām. She migrated twice to Abyssinia and then to Madīnah. Her brother is Sulaymān, and she was married to 'Āmir bin Rabī'ah. She was the first woman to enter Madīnah migrating on camelback. Laylā said, " 'Umar bin al-Khaṭṭāb was from the harshest people against us due to our Islām. As I was preparing to migrate to Abyssinia, 'Umar bin al-Khaṭṭāb came to me while I was sitting on my camel. I wanted to turn away from him. He said to me, 'Where are you going, Umm 'Abdillāh?' I said, 'You all have harmed us because of our religion. Thus, we are going to the land of Allāh where the slaves of Allāh are not harmed.' 'Umar replied, 'May Allāh be with you'; then he left. When my husband, 'Āmir bin Rabī'ah, came home, I told him about the kindness I saw from 'Umar. He said, 'Do you want him to embrace Islām?!' I said, 'Yes.' He replied, 'By Allāh, 'Umar will not embrace Islām until their family donkey embraces Islām!' "[57]

Her son 'Abdullāh bin 'Āmir said:

دَعَتْنِي أُمِّي يَوْمًا وَرَسُولُ اللَّهِ صلى الله عليه وسلم قَاعِدٌ فِي بَيْتِنَا فَقَالَتْ هَا تَعَالَ أُعْطِيكَ. فَقَالَ لَهَا رَسُولُ اللَّهِ صلى الله عليه وسلم وَمَا أَرَدْتِ أَنْ تُعْطِيهِ. قَالَتْ أُعْطِيهِ تَمْرًا . فَقَالَ لَهَا رَسُولُ اللَّهِ صلى الله عليه وسلم أَمَا إِنَّكِ لَوْ لَمْ تُعْطِيهِ شَيْئًا كُتِبَتْ عَلَيْكِ كِذْبَةٌ.

My mother called me one day when the Messenger of Allāh ﷺ was sitting in our house. She said, "Come here and I shall give you something." The Messenger of Allāh ﷺ asked her, "What did you intend to give him?" She replied, "I intended to give him some dates." The Messenger of Allāh ﷺ said, "If you were not to give him anything, a lie would be recorded against you."[58]

❖ LAYLĀ al-Ghifāriyyah used to attend the battles with the Messenger of Allāh ﷺ and nurse the wounded.

❖ LAYLĀ Qānif assisted in washing the body of Umm Kulthūm, the daughter of the Prophet ﷺ, after her death.

❖ LĪNAH was the owner of the land at Qubā'; she would tie her mule there. Sa'd bin Khaythamah built a *masjid* there which became

[57] *Al-Mu'jam al-Kabīr* (*ḥadīth* 47).

[58] *Sunan Abī Dāwūd* 4991

Masjid Qubā'. The people of Masjid Ḍirār said, "Are we going to pray where Līnah tied her mule? No, we will build a *masjid* so we can pray there until Abū 'Āmir[59] arrives to lead us." Thus, Allāh the Exalted sent down the verse:

﴿ وَالَّذِينَ اتَّخَذُوا مَسْجِدًا ضِرَارًا وَكُفْرًا وَتَفْرِيقًا بَيْنَ الْمُؤْمِنِينَ وَإِرْصَادًا لِّمَنْ حَارَبَ اللَّهَ وَرَسُولَهُ مِن قَبْلُ ۚ وَلَيَحْلِفُنَّ إِنْ أَرَدْنَا إِلَّا الْحُسْنَىٰ ۖ وَاللَّهُ يَشْهَدُ إِنَّهُمْ لَكَاذِبُونَ ﴾

And as for those who put up a mosque by way of harming and disbelief, and to disunite the believers, and as an outpost for those who warred against Allāh and His Messenger aforetime, they will indeed swear that their intention is nothing but good. Allāh bears witness that they are certainly liars.

[Sūrah at-Tawbah 9:107]

MĪM – م

❖ MĀWIYYAH was the freed slave of Ḥujayr. Khubayb bin 'Adī was detained in her house as he awaited execution by the pagans of Makkah. After she embraced Islām, she spoke of the incident. Māwiyyah said, "Khubayb was imprisoned in Makkah in my home. I looked at him that day, and he had a bunch of grapes in his hand larger than his head which he was eating from. And in those days, not even a grape seed could be found in the land." Māwiyyah said, "Khubayb remained with the pagans as a prisoner until they agreed to kill him. He borrowed a razor from al-Ḥārith's daughter to shave his private area. After she gave him a razor, her small child crept to him while she was inattentive. When she came, she found him

[59] **Translator's note:** Abū 'Āmir ar-Rāhib, a Christian monk who refused the invitation to Islām and instead fought along with the Makkan pagans against Islām in the Battle of Uḥud.

alone, and the child was on his thigh and the razor was in his hand. She was terrified, and he realized its effect on her. He said, 'Do you fear that I shall kill him? I am not going to do that.'"[60] Māwiyyah embraced Islām and became a good Muslim.

❖ MUSAYKAH was a slave girl forced into prostitution by 'Abdullāh bin Ubayy, the leader of the hypocrites. Jābir said:

أَنَّ جَارِيَةً، لِعَبْدِ اللَّهِ بْنِ أُبَيٍّ ابْنِ سَلُولَ يُقَالُ لَهَا مُسَيْكَةُ وَأُخْرَى يُقَالُ لَهَا أُمَيْمَةُ فَكَانَ يُكْرِهُهُمَا عَلَى الزِّنَى فَشَكَتَا ذَلِكَ إِلَى النَّبِيِّ صلى الله عليه وسلم فَأَنْزَلَ اللَّهُ.

'Abdullāh bin Ubayy bin Salūl had two slave-girls; one was called Musaykah and the other one was called Umaymah. He forced them into prostitution. They made a complaint about this to the Messenger of Allāh ﷺ, and the verse was revealed:

﴿ وَلَا تُكْرِهُوا فَتَيَاتِكُمْ عَلَى الْبِغَاءِ إِنْ أَرَدْنَ تَحَصُّنًا لِّتَبْتَغُوا عَرَضَ الْحَيَاةِ الدُّنْيَا ۚ وَمَن يُكْرِههُّنَّ فَإِنَّ اللَّهَ مِن بَعْدِ إِكْرَاهِهِنَّ غَفُورٌ رَّحِيمٌ ﴾

And force not your maids to prostitution, if they desire chastity, in order that you may make a gain in the (perishable) goods of this worldly life. But if anyone compels them (to prostitution), then after such compulsion, Allāh is Oft-Forgiving, Most Merciful[61] (to those women).

[Sūrah an-Nūr 24:33]

❖ MULAYKAH al-Anṣāriyyah is the grandmother of Anas bin Mālik. Anas said that his grandmother Mulaykah invited the Messenger of Allāh ﷺ to a dinner which she had prepared. After he ate, he said, "Stand and I will lead you in prayer." Anas said:

---

[60] *Sunan Abī Dāwūd* 3112

[61] *Ṣaḥīḥ Muslim* 3029

فَقُمْتُ إِلَى حَصِيرٍ لَنَا قَدِ اسْوَدَّ مِنْ طُولِ مَا لُبِسَ فَنَضَحْتُهُ بِمَاءٍ فَقَامَ عَلَيْهِ رَسُولُ اللَّهِ صلى الله عليه وسلم وَصَفَفْتُ أَنَا وَالْيَتِيمُ وَرَاءَهُ وَالْعَجُوزُ مِنْ وَرَائِنَا فَصَلَّى لَنَا رَسُولُ اللَّهِ صلى الله عليه وسلم رَكْعَتَيْنِ ثُمَّ انْصَرَفَ.

I stood up on a palm-fiber mat belonging to us which had turned dark on account of its long use. I sprinkled water over it and the Messenger of Allāh ﷺ stood upon it. I and an orphan formed a row behind him, and the old woman was behind us. The Messenger of Allāh ﷺ led us in two *raka'āt* of prayer, and then he left.[62]

❖ MAWHIBAH was the freed slave of the Messenger of Allāh ﷺ. She milked the sheep for the non-Muslim guest of the Prophet ﷺ. Abū Hurayrah said, "The Messenger of Allāh ﷺ hosted a non-Muslim guest. The Messenger of Allāh ﷺ ordered a sheep to be brought for him, and it was milked. The man drank its milk. Then another came, and he drank it. Then another came, and he drank it until he had drunk the milk of seven sheep. In the morning, he became Muslim, and the Messenger of Allāh ﷺ ordered a sheep for him. It was milked, and he drank its milk. Then he ordered another for him, and he could not finish it. The Messenger of Allāh ﷺ said:

الْمُؤْمِنُ يَشْرَبُ فِي مِعًى وَاحِدٍ وَالْكَافِرُ يَشْرَبُ فِي سَبْعَةِ أَمْعَاءٍ.

" 'The believer drinks in one intestine, and the disbeliever drinks in seven intestines.' "[63]

NŪN – ن

❖ NĀ'ILAH bint al-Furāfiṣah was the wife of 'Uthmān bin 'Affān. She was with him when he was besieged in his home by the Khawārij. When they entered the home and killed 'Uthmān, Nā'ilah tried to shield him, and her fingers were cut off with a

[62] *Ṣaḥīḥ Muslim* 658

[63] *Muwaṭṭa' Mālik* 1683

sword.

❖ NAB'AH al-Ḥabashiyyah (the Ethiopian) was the servant of Umm Hāni' bint Abī Ṭālib, the cousin of the Messenger of Allāh ﷺ. Abū Ṣāliḥ, the freed slave of Umm Hāni', said that Umm Hāni' used to say, "He (the Prophet ﷺ) was taken to Jerusalem from my home while he was sleeping there that night. He prayed 'Ishā', then he slept. In the morning, he led us in the Fajr prayer and he said, 'O Umm Hāni', I prayed 'Ishā' prayer as you saw, and then I was taken to Bayt al-Maqdis and I prayed there; then I prayed Fajr prayer with you all.' The Prophet stood to leave, and I grabbed him by his garment and said to him, 'O Prophet of Allāh, do not tell anyone about this or they will belie you and harm you.' He said, 'By Allāh, I will surely tell them about it.' I said to my Ethiopian servant, whose name was Nab'ah, 'Follow the Messenger of Allāh ﷺ and listen to what he says to the people and what they say to him.' "

❖ NU'MĀ bint Ja'far bin Abī Ṭālib was the second cousin of the Messenger of Allāh ﷺ. The Messenger of Allāh ﷺ said to Nu'mā bint Ja'far:

مَا لِي أَرَى أَجْسَامَ بَنِي أَخِي ضَارِعَةً تُصِيبُهُمُ الْحَاجَةُ. قَالَتْ لاَ وَلَكِنِ الْعَيْنُ تُسْرِعُ إِلَيْهِمْ. قَالَ ارْقِيهِمْ. قَالَتْ فَعَرَضْتُ عَلَيْهِ فَقَالَ ارْقِيهِمْ.

"Why is this that I see the children of my brother lean? Are they not fed properly?" She said, "No, but they fall under the influence of an evil eye." He said, "Use incantation (*ruqyah*)." She recited (the words of incantation before him), whereupon he (by approving them) said, "Yes, use this incantation for them."[64]

❖ AN-NAHDIYYAH and her daughter were from the first and foremost to embrace Islām, and they are from the seven slaves freed by Abū Bakr. They belonged to a woman from Banū 'Abdud-Dār. The master sent them with some flour, and she said, "By Allāh, I will never set you free." Abū Bakr passed by them and said, "Set them

[64] *Ṣaḥīḥ Muslim* 2198

free, O Umm so-and-so." She said, "You corrupted them, so you set them free!" He said, "How much to purchase their freedom?" She said, "Such-and-such price." He said, "Then I have purchased them, and they are both free." He said to an-Nahdiyyah and her daughter, "Return her flour to her." They said, "Or can we complete the task and then return it?" He said, "As you like."[65]

HĀ' – ه

❖ HĀLAH bint Khuwaylid is the sister of Khadījah, the wife of the Prophet ﷺ. She is the mother of Abul-'Āṣ bin ar-Rabī'. 'Ā'ishah رضي الله عنها said, "Once, Hālah bint Khuwaylid, Khadījah's sister, asked the permission of the Prophet ﷺ to enter. On that, the Prophet ﷺ remembered the way Khadījah used to ask permission, and that stirred emotion within him. He said, 'O Allāh! Hālah!' So I became jealous and said, 'What makes you remember an old woman amongst the old women of Quraysh, an old woman (with a toothless mouth) of red gums who died long ago, and in whose place Allāh has given you somebody better than her?' "[66]

❖ HĀLAH bint 'Awf is the sister of 'Abdur-Raḥmān bin 'Awf, one of the 10 promised Paradise, and she was the wife of Bilāl bin Rabāḥ.

❖ HURAYRAH bint Zam'ah is the sister of Sawdah bint Zam'ah, the wife of the Messenger of Allāh ﷺ. She married Ma'bad bin Wahb. He fought in the Battle of Badr and became known for fighting with two swords.

❖ HUZAYLAH bint al-Ḥārith is the sister of Maymūnah bint al-Ḥārith, the wife of the Messenger of Allāh ﷺ. She is also the maternal aunt to Ibn 'Abbās and Khālid bin al-Walīd. Her *kunyah* is Umm Ḥufayd. 'Abdullāh bin 'Abbās said that he and Khālid bin

---

[65] Collected by Ibn Hishām in *The Prophetic Sīrah.*

[66] *Ṣaḥīḥ al-Bukhārī* 3821

al-Walīd visited Maymūnah, the wife of the Messenger of Allāh ﷺ, in the company of the Messenger of Allāh, and she was the maternal aunt of 'Abdullāh bin 'Abbās and Khālid. He found with her a roasted lizard, which her sister Umm Ḥufayd bint al-Ḥārith had brought from Najd, and she presented that lizard to the Messenger of Allāh ﷺ. It was rare that some food was presented to the Prophet ﷺ and it was not mentioned or named. When the Messenger of Allāh ﷺ was about to stretch forth his hand towards the lizard, a woman from amongst the women present there informed the Messenger of Allāh ﷺ what they had presented to him. They said, "O Messenger of Allāh, it is a lizard." The Messenger of Allāh ﷺ withdrew his hand, whereupon Khālid bin al-Walīd said:

يَا رَسُولَ اللَّهِ أَحَرَامٌ الضَّبُّ قَالَ لا وَلَكِنْ لَمْ يَكُنْ بِأَرْضِ قَوْمِي فَأَجِدُنِي أَعَافُهُ.

"O Messenger of Allāh, is lizard *ḥarām*?" He said, "No, but it is not known among my people, so I have a dislike for it."

So Khālid took some of the lizard meat and ate it while the Messenger of Allāh ﷺ looked on.[67]

Huzaylah bint al-Ḥārith embraced Islām after the migration, and she gave the pledge.

❖ HUZAYLAH bint 'Utbah is the mother of Zayd bin Khārijah, the man who spoke after his death during the era of 'Uthmān bin 'Affān.[68]

❖ HIND bint al-Ḥārith bin 'Abdul-Muṭṭalib is the paternal cousin of the Messenger of Allāh ﷺ.

❖ HIND bint Simāk was the wife of Sa'd bin Mu'ādh. The Messenger of Allāh ﷺ said:

---

[67] *Ṣaḥīḥ Muslim* 1946

[68] **Translator's note:** Imām al-Bayhaqī said that the chain of narration for this is authentic.

اهْتَزَّ العَرْشُ لِمَوْتِ سَعْدِ بْنِ مُعَاذٍ.

The Throne shook at the death of Sa'd bin Mu'ādh.[69]

❖ HIND bint Sahl al-Juhniyyah is the mother of Mu'ādh bin Jabal. This was mentioned by Ibn Sa'd. Likewise, she is mentioned among the five women who upheld the pledge along with Umm 'Aṭiyyah. Umm 'Aṭiyyah said, "We gave the pledge of allegiance to the Prophet ﷺ, and he recited to me the verse:

﴿ يَا أَيُّهَا النَّبِيُّ إِذَا جَاءَكَ الْمُؤْمِنَاتُ يُبَايِعْنَكَ عَلَىٰ أَن لَّا يُشْرِكْنَ بِاللَّهِ شَيْئًا وَلَا يَسْرِقْنَ وَلَا يَزْنِينَ وَلَا يَقْتُلْنَ أَوْلَادَهُنَّ وَلَا يَأْتِينَ بِبُهْتَانٍ يَفْتَرِينَهُ بَيْنَ أَيْدِيهِنَّ وَأَرْجُلِهِنَّ وَلَا يَعْصِينَكَ فِي مَعْرُوفٍ ۙ فَبَايِعْهُنَّ وَاسْتَغْفِرْ لَهُنَّ اللَّهَ ۖ إِنَّ اللَّهَ غَفُورٌ رَّحِيمٌ ﴾

"'O Prophet! When believing women come to you to give you the pledge that they will not associate anything in worship with Allāh, that they will not steal, that they will not commit illegal sexual intercourse, that they will not kill their children, that they will not utter slander, intentionally forging falsehood, and that they will not disobey you in any *ma'rūf* (Islamic monotheism and all that which Islām ordains), then accept their pledge and ask Allāh to forgive them. Verily, Allāh is Oft-Forgiving, Most Merciful.'

[Sūrah al-Mumtaḥanah 60:12]

"And he also prevented us from wailing and lamenting over the dead. A woman from us held her hand out and said, 'Such-and-such a woman cried over a dead person belonging to my family, and I want to compensate her for that crying.' The Prophet did not say anything in reply, and she left and returned. None of those women

[69] *Ṣaḥīḥ al-Bukhārī* 3803; *Ṣaḥīḥ Muslim* 2466

abided by her pledge except Umm Sulaym, Umm al-'Alā', Bint Abī Sabrah, the wife of Mu'ādh, and the mother of Mu'ādh."[70]

❖ HIND bint 'Utbah was the wife of Abū Sufyān bin Ḥarb and the mother of Mu'āwiyah. Her animosity towards the Muslims before she embraced Islām is well-known. She was present at the Battle of Uḥud and she did what she did to Ḥamzah. She was pitted against the Muslims until the conquest of Makkah; then her husband embraced Islām. Hind wanted to embrace Islām and give the pledge to the Messenger of Allāh ﷺ, but she was remorseful and afraid due to the harm she had caused the Muslims. Thus, she went to give the pledge while wearing the veil. After she embraced Islām and gave the pledge, she removed her veil, and she was accepted without any hostility.

Hind said to the Messenger of Allāh ﷺ:

إِنَّ أَبَا سُفْيَانَ رَجُلٌ شَحِيحٌ، فَهَلْ عَلَيَّ جُنَاحٌ أَنْ آخُذَ مِنْ مَالِهِ سِرًّا قَالَ خُذِي أَنْتِ وَبَنُوكِ مَا يَكْفِيكِ بِالْمَعْرُوفِ.

"Abū Sufyān is a miser. Am I allowed to take from his money secretly?" The Prophet ﷺ said to her, "You and your sons may take what is sufficient, reasonably and fairly."[71]

Hind bint 'Utbah died after her husband, during 'Uthmān bin 'Affān's caliphate.

❖ HIND bint 'Atīq bin 'Ā'idh is the daughter of Khadījah bint Khuwaylid from her previous marriage to 'Atīq. Thus, she is the stepdaughter of the Messenger of Allāh ﷺ. She married her paternal cousin, Ṣayfī bin Umayyah bin 'Ā'idh. She gave birth to their son Muḥammad bin Ṣayfī.

❖ HIND bint 'Amr is the paternal aunt of the well-known Companion Jābir bin 'Abdillāh.

[70] *Ṣaḥīḥ al-Bukhārī* 7215

[71] *Ṣaḥīḥ al-Bukhārī* 2211

❖ HIND al-Khawlāniyyah was the wife of Bilāl bin Rabāḥ. He married her when he moved to Shām. She was originally from Damascus.

WĀW – و

❖ WADDAH bint 'Uqbah Umm al-Ḥakam embraced Islām and gave the pledge to the Messenger of Allāh ﷺ.

❖ WAHIBAH bint Ubayy bin Khalaf. Her father, Ubayy bin Khalaf, was an enemy to Islām and the only person the Messenger of Allāh ﷺ killed with his own hand.

YĀ' – ي

❖ YUSAYRAH bint Mulaykah embraced Islām and gave the pledge.

❖ YUSAYRAH bint Yāsir embraced Islām, gave the pledge, and migrated with the first group of emigrants.

Those Known by Their Kunyah

From the Female Companions

Alif – أ

❖ UMM ABĀN bint ʻUtbah was previously married to the noble Companion Abān bin Saʻīd bin al-ʻĀṣ until he was killed in the battle against the Romans known as the Battle of Ajnādayn. When Umm Abān arrived from Shām, several men sought her hand in marriage, including ʻUmar, ʻAlī, az-Zubayr, and Ṭalḥah. She chose to marry Ṭalḥah.

❖ UMM IS'ḤĀQ al-Ghanawiyyah is from the noble Companions who migrated to Madīnah. Her freed slave Umm Ḥakīm bint Dīnār narrated her migration. Umm Is'ḥāq migrated from Makkah with her brother Is'ḥāq, headed towards Madīnah. When they reached a passage, her brother said to her, "Sit and wait here until I return from Makkah. I have to retrieve some provisions which I forgot there." Umm Is'ḥāq said, "I fear that if you return to Makkah, the evil one (meaning her husband) will kill you." Her brother left her and returned to Makkah. After three days, a rider passed by her and said, "Umm Is'ḥāq, why are you sitting here?" She said, "I am awaiting my brother Is'ḥāq." He replied, "There is no Is'ḥāq for you; he encountered your husband after leaving Makkah and [your husband] killed him."

Umm Is'ḥāq reached Madīnah and entered upon the Prophet ﷺ as he was performing *wuḍū'*. She said, "O Messenger of Allāh, Is'ḥāq (her brother) has been killed." The Prophet splashed a handful of water on his face. Umm Ḥakīm bint Dīnār, the narrator of the *ḥadīth*, said, "She had just been afflicted with a severe calamity, and you could see the tears in her eyes, but the tears were not streaming down her cheeks."

❖ UMM USAYD prepared food for the Prophet ﷺ when she married. Sahl said, "When Abū Usayd as-Sā'idī married, he invited the Prophet ﷺ and his Companions. None prepared the food for them and brought it to them except his wife. She soaked some dates in water in a stone pot overnight, and when the Prophet ﷺ had finished his food, she provided him with drink from the soaked dates."[1]

❖ UMM IYĀS bint Abil-Ḥaysar was the wife of 'Abdur-Raḥmān bin 'Awf. When 'Abdur-Raḥmān bin 'Awf married her, the Prophet ﷺ said:

أَوْلِمْ وَلَوْ بِشَاةٍ.

Hold a wedding feast, even if only with a sheep.[2]

❖ UMM AYMAN, the freed slave of Umm Ibrāhīm Māriyah the Coptic. She is not the Umm Ayman who was the caretaker of the Prophet ﷺ. Ja'far bin Muḥammad narrated from his father, "Umm Ayman was the freed slave of Māriyah the Coptic, the mother of Ibrāhīm the son of the Prophet ﷺ. When she would visit the Prophet ﷺ, she would greet him by saying:

---

[1] *Ṣaḥīḥ al-Bukhārī* 5182

[2] *Ṣaḥīḥ Muslim* 1427

سلام إلا عليكم.

" 'Peace except upon you.'

"And the Prophet ﷺ would excuse her because she was not able to say:

السّلام عليكم.

" 'Peace be upon you.' "

❖ UMM AYYŪB bint Qays was the wife of the well-known Companion Abū Ayyūb. The Prophet ﷺ stayed with them, and they prepared some food for him containing some legume vegetables. He disliked eating it, so he said to his Companions:

كُلُوهُ فَإِنِّي لَسْتُ كَأَحَدِكُمْ إِنِّي أَخَافُ أَنْ أُوذِيَ صَاحِبِي.

Eat it, for I am not like you are; I fear that I will offend my companion (meaning the angel).[3]

BĀ' – ب

❖ UMM BURDAH bint al-Mundhir nursed Ibrāhīm, the son of the Messenger of Allāh ﷺ, when Māriyah put him down. And she continued to nurse him until the day he died.

❖ UMM BISHR bint al-Barā' bin Ma'rūr came to Ka'b bin Mālik while he was dying and said, "O Abū 'Abdir-Raḥmān, if you meet my father, convey the *salām* to him on my behalf." He replied, "May Allāh forgive you, O Umm Bishr! We are too busy to think of that." She said, "O Abū 'Abdir-Raḥmān! Did you not hear the Messenger of Allāh ﷺ say:

إنّ أرواح المؤمنين نسمة تسرح في الجنّة حيث تشاء.

[3] *Jāmi' at-Tirmidhī* 1810

"'Verily, the souls of the believers are birds that fly in Paradise wherever they desire.'"

He said, "Certainly, I have heard this." She said, "That is what I mean."[4]

JĪM – ج

❖ UMM JUNDAB is the mother of Abū Dharr al-Ghifārī. She is mentioned in the story of his conversion to Islām. Abū Dharr said, "When I embraced Islām, I went to my mother and my brother and they said, "We have no aversion to your religion," and they both embraced Islām.[5]

ḤĀ' – ح

❖ UMM AL-ḤĀRITH from Banū Khazraj fought in the Battle of Ḥunayn with the Messenger of Allāh ﷺ, and she did not flee with those who fled.

❖ UMM ḤABĪB bint al-'Abbās is the first cousin of the Messenger of Allāh ﷺ.

❖ UMM AL-ḤAKAM bint az-Zubayr bin 'Abdul-Muṭṭalib is the paternal cousin of the Messenger of Allāh ﷺ, and his sister through nursing. The Prophet ﷺ would visit her in Madīnah. Umm al-Ḥakam said, "Some captives of war were brought to the Messenger of Allāh ﷺ. I and my sister Fāṭimah, daughter of the Messenger of Allāh ﷺ, went to him and complained to him about our existing condition. We asked him to give us some captives. The Messenger of Allāh ﷺ said, 'The orphans of the people who were

[4] *Sunan Ibn Mājah* 1516

[5] *Ṣaḥīḥ Muslim* 2473

killed in the Battle of Badr came before you (and they asked for the captives). But I will tell you something better than that. You should say:

تُكَبِّرْنَ اللَّهَ عَلَى أَثَرِ كُلِّ صَلاَةٍ ثَلاَثًا وَثَلاَثِينَ تَكْبِيرَةً وَثَلاَثًا وَثَلاَثِينَ تَسْبِيحَةً وَثَلاَثًا وَثَلاَثِينَ تَحْمِيدَةً وَلاَ إِلَهَ إِلاَّ اللَّهُ وَحْدَهُ لاَ شَرِيكَ لَهُ لَهُ الْمُلْكُ وَلَهُ الْحَمْدُ وَهُوَ عَلَى كُلِّ شَىْءٍ قَدِيرٌ.

" ' "Allāh is the Greatest" after each prayer 33 times, "Allāh is free from imperfection" 33 times, "Praise be to Allāh" 33 times, and "There is no god worthy of worship except Allāh alone, He has no associate, the Kingdom belongs to Him, praise is due to Him, and He has power over all things" (once).' "[6]

❖ UMM AL-ḤAKAM bint Abī Sufyān is the full sister of Mu'āwiyah, and the half-sister, by way of her father, to Umm Ḥabībah Ramlah bint Abī Sufyān, the wife of the Messenger of Allāh ﷺ.

❖ UMM ḤAKĪM bint al-Ḥārith became Muslim on the day of the conquest of Makkah, and her husband 'Ikrimah bin Abī Jahl fled from Islām as far as Yemen. Umm Ḥakīm set out after him until she came to him in Yemen, and she invited him to Islām and he became Muslim. He then went to the Messenger of Allāh ﷺ. When the Messenger of Allāh ﷺ saw him, he rushed to him in joy and did not bother to put on his cloak until he had made the pledge with him. Their marriage remained valid and they were not commanded to remarry.[7]

❖ UMM ḤUMAYD was the wife of Abū Ḥumayd as-Sā'idī. She came to the Prophet ﷺ and said, "O Messenger of Allāh, I love to pray with you." He said:

---

[6] *Sunan Abī Dāwūd* 2987

[7] *Muwaṭṭa' Mālik* 1141

قد علمت أنك تحبين الصلاة معي، وصلاتك في بيتك خير لك من صلاتك في حجرتك، وصلاتك في حجرتك خير من صلاتك في دارك، وصلاتك في دارك خير لك من صلاتك في مسجد قومك، وصلاتك في مسجد قومك خير لك من صلاتك في مسجدي.

I know that you love to pray with me, but praying in your house is better for you than praying in your courtyard, and praying in your courtyard is better for you than praying in the *masjid* of your people, and praying in the *masjid* of your people is better for you than praying in my *masjid*.

So she ordered that a prayer place be built for her in the furthest and darkest part of her house, and she always prayed there until she met Allāh (until she died).[8]

KHĀ' - خ

❖ UMM AL-KHAYR Salmā bint Ṣakhar is the mother of Abū Bakr aṣ-Ṣiddīq. She was from the first and foremost to embrace Islām. Aṭ-Ṭabarānī narrated that Ibn 'Abbās said, "Abū Bakr's mother embraced Islām, as did 'Uthmān's mother, az-Zubayr's mother, 'Abdur-Raḥmān bin 'Awf's mother, and 'Ammār bin Yāsir's mother." Abū Bakr brought his mother to the Messenger of Allāh ﷺ and said, "O Messenger of Allāh, this is my mother; invite her to Islām and supplicate for her." He supplicated for her and he invited her to Islām, and she embraced Islām.

DĀL – د

❖ UMM AD-DAḤDĀḤ is the wife of Abud-Daḥdāḥ. She was

[8] *Musnad Imām Aḥmad* 26550; classed as *ṣaḥīḥ* by Ibn Khuzaymah in his *Ṣaḥīḥ* (3/95), by Ibn Ḥibbān (5/595) and al-Albānī in *Ṣaḥīḥ at-Targhīb wat-Tarhīb* (1/135).

pleased with her husband preferring Paradise over the worldly life. Their story has been collected in *Ṣaḥīḥ Muslim*. Anas narrated, "An orphan disputed with Abū Lubābah[9] concerning a date tree. The orphan wanted to erect his wall, but the date tree belonging to Abū Lubābah was impeding this. The Prophet ﷺ ruled in favor of Abū Lubābah, and the orphan began to cry. The Prophet ﷺ said to Abū Lubābah, 'Give him your date tree.' But Abū Lubābah refused. The Prophet ﷺ said, 'Give him your date tree and you will have a date branch[10] in Paradise as compensation.' Abū Lubābah said, 'No.'

"Abud-Daḥdāḥ overheard the conversation and went to Abū Lubābah and said, 'Will you sell me your one date tree for my garden of date trees?' Abū Lubābah said, 'Yes.' Abud-Daḥdāḥ went to the Messenger of Allāh ﷺ and said, 'O Messenger of Allāh, if I give that date tree you requested for the orphan, will I have a date branch in Paradise?' The Messenger of Allāh ﷺ said, 'Yes.' Abud-Daḥdāḥ went to his wife said, 'Umm ad-Daḥdāḥ, leave the garden, because I have given it as a loan to my Lord the Exalted.' She said, 'That is a successful trade, O Abud-Daḥdāḥ.' She then moved her children and belongings to their new location."

Abud-Daḥdāḥ was killed in the Battle of Uḥud, and the Messenger of Allāh ﷺ said:

كَمْ مِنْ عِذْقٍ مُعَلَّقٍ فِي الْجَنَّةِ لِأَبِي الدَّحْدَاحِ.

How many hanging date branches will Abud-Daḥdāḥ have in Paradise![11]

Umm ad-Daḥdāḥ died during the lifetime of the Prophet ﷺ, and he led the Janāzah prayer for her.

---

[9] **Translator's note:** Abū Lubābah ﷺ is from the noble Companions. The Prophet ﷺ ordered him to guard Madīnah during the Battle of Badr, and he received the reward like those who attended the battle.

[10] **Translator's note:** Imām an-Nawawī said in his explanation of this *ḥadīth* that this word refers to a branch and not the entire date tree.

[11] *Ṣaḥīḥ Muslim* 965; *Musnad Imām Aḥmad* 12482

DHĀL – ذ

❖ UMM DHARR was the wife of Abū Dharr. She embraced Islām during the early days with her husband. Ibrāhīm bin al-Asyar narrated from his father that Umm Dharr said, "When death approached Abū Dharr, I cried. He said, 'Why are you crying?' I said, 'You are dying in the desert and I don't even have a garment large enough to cover you with.' He said, 'I give you glad tidings, so don't cry. I heard the Messenger of Allāh ﷺ saying to a group of men while I was among them, "A man from amongst you will die in the desert and his death will be witnessed by a group of believers." All of the men in the gathering that day died in a village, and I am the only one remaining. I have not lied nor was I lied to, so go to the road and look for those men.' I said, 'The pilgrims for Ḥajj have already gone and the road has been blocked.' Abū Dharr said, 'Go to the road and look for the men.' I went to the dune to look and then I returned, and he had become sicker.

"As we were in this state, all of a sudden, some men appeared on their riding beasts as though they were clouds. I motioned to them and they hurried to me until they reached me. They said, 'O female servant of Allāh, what is the matter?' I said, 'A Muslim is near death and he needs to be shrouded.' They said, 'Who is he?' I said, 'Abū Dharr.' They said, 'The Companion of the Messenger of Allāh?' I replied in the affirmative. They hurried to him and entered upon him. Abū Dharr said to them, 'I give you glad tidings; I heard the Messenger of Allāh ﷺ say, "A man from amongst you will die in the desert and a group of believers will witness." I was present in this group, and everyone else who was present in that gathering has died, and I am the only one remaining. I did not lie nor was I lied to. I do not have enough clothing to cover me and my wife. Thus, I implore you, by Allāh—I do not want a garment from a man among you if he is a ruler, corporal, courier, or monk.' There was only one young man among them who fit this description. He said, 'I will cover you with my waist wrap, O uncle; this garment was sewn with the thread of my mother.' Abū Dharr said, 'You are the one to shroud me.' Thus, the young man provided the shroud, and all the men buried him when he died."[12]

❖ UMM DHARRAH is from the noble Companions. She used to wrap 'Ā'ishah's head in musk and place amber in her *iḥrām*. She heard the Messenger of Allāh ﷺ say:

أَنَا وَكَافِلُ الْيَتِيمِ يَوْمُ الْقِيَامَةِ كَهَاتَيْنِ.

I and the one who takes care of the orphan will be like this on the Day of Judgment.

And he joined his middle and index finger together.[13]

RĀ' – ر

❖ UMM RŪMĀN bint 'Āmir bin 'Uwaymir was the wife of Abū Bakr aṣ-Ṣiddīq and the mother of 'Abdur-Raḥmān and 'Ā'ishah. The scholars differ concerning her name. Some say her name was Zaynab or Da'd. She was from the first and foremost to embrace Islām. 'Ā'ishah said:

لَمْ أَعْقِلْ أَبَوَيَّ قَطُّ إِلَّا وَهُمَا يَدِينَانِ الدِّينَ.

I do not remember my parents ever following anything but the true religion.[14]

She died in 6 AH, during the lifetime of the Messenger of Allāh ﷺ.

ZĀY – ز

❖ UMM ZAYD was a woman from the Anṣār. She had a disagree-

[12] *Zād al-Ma'ād* 3/534-535 and *Ṣaḥīḥ at-Targhīb* 3314; declared authentic by al-Albānī.

[13] *Ṣaḥīḥ al-Bukhārī* 5546

[14] *Ṣaḥīḥ al-Bukhārī* 3905

ment with her husband that led to a physical altercation between his family and her family. As the Prophet ﷺ went to resolve the issue, the following verse was revealed[15]:

﴿ وَإِن طَائِفَتَانِ مِنَ الْمُؤْمِنِينَ اقْتَتَلُوا فَأَصْلِحُوا بَيْنَهُمَا ۖ فَإِن بَغَتْ إِحْدَاهُمَا عَلَى الْأُخْرَىٰ فَقَاتِلُوا الَّتِي تَبْغِي حَتَّىٰ تَفِيءَ إِلَىٰ أَمْرِ اللَّهِ ۚ فَإِن فَاءَتْ فَأَصْلِحُوا بَيْنَهُمَا بِالْعَدْلِ وَأَقْسِطُوا ۖ إِنَّ اللَّهَ يُحِبُّ الْمُقْسِطِينَ ﴾

And if two parties or groups among the believers fall to fighting, then make peace between them both, but if one of them rebels against the other, then fight you (all) against the one that rebels till it complies with the command of Allāh; then if it complies, make reconciliation between them justly and be equitable. Verily! Allāh loves those who are equitable.

[Sūrah al-Ḥujurāt 49:9]

SĪN – س

❖ UMM SĀLIM was from the Companions of the Prophet ﷺ. Her son Sālim was the freed slave of Abū Ḥudhayfah. Her son is mentioned in the statement of the Messenger of Allāh ﷺ:

خُذُوا الْقُرْآنَ مِنْ أَرْبَعَةٍ مِنْ عَبْدِ اللَّهِ بْنِ مَسْعُودٍ وَسَالِمٍ وَمُعَاذٍ وَأُبَيِّ بْنِ كَعْبٍ.

Learn the Qur'ān from four people: 'Abdullāh bin Mas'ūd, Sālim, Mu'ādh bin Jabal, and Ubayy bin Ka'b.[16]

Sālim carried the flag during the Battle of Yamāmah. When his

[15] *Tafsīr aṭ-Ṭabarī,* Sūrah al-Ḥujurāt 49:9

[16] *Ṣaḥīḥ al-Bukhārī* 3808

right arm was cut off, he carried the flag with his left hand; when his left arm was cut off, he carried it with his neck until he was killed. ʻAbdullāh bin Shaddād said, "ʻUmar gave Umm Sālim the inheritance for her son when he was killed during the Battle of Yamāmah."

❖ UMM AS-SĀ'IB—also known as Umm al-Musayyib—is mentioned in the narration collected in *Ṣaḥīḥ Muslim*. Jābir bin ʻAbdillāh said that the Messenger of Allāh ﷺ visited her when she was sick and said:

مَا لَكِ يَا أُمَّ السَّائِبِ أَوْ يَا أُمَّ الْمُسَيَّبِ تُزَفْزِفِينَ. قَالَتِ الْحُمَّى لاَ بَارَكَ اللَّهُ فِيهَا. فَقَالَ لاَ تَسُبِّي الْحُمَّى فَإِنَّهَا تُذْهِبُ خَطَايَا بَنِي آدَمَ كَمَا يُذْهِبُ الْكِيرُ خَبَثَ الْحَدِيدِ.

"Umm as-Sā'ib or Umm al-Musayyib, why are you shivering?" She said, "It is fever, and may it not be blessed by Allāh," whereupon he (the Prophet) said, "Don't curse fever, for it expiates the sin of the children of Ādam just as a furnace removes the alloy of iron."[17]

❖ UMM SABRAH was from the Companions of the Messenger of Allāh ﷺ and a narrator of *ḥadīth*. Her son narrated that his mother heard the Prophet ﷺ say:

لاَ صَلاَةَ لِمَنْ لاَ وُضُوءَ لَهُ، وَلاَ وُضُوءَ لِمَنْ لَمْ يَذْكُرِ الله عَزَّ وَجَلَّ، وَلاَ يُؤْمِنَ بِي مَنْ لاَ يُحِبُّ الْأَنْصَارَ.

There is no prayer for the one who does not have *wuḍū'*, and there is no *wuḍū'* for the one who does not mention the name of Allāh the Exalted; and the person who does not love the Anṣār does not believe in me.[18]

❖ UMM SA'D was the mother of Sa'd bin Mu'ādh. The Messenger of Allāh ﷺ said:

---

[17] *Ṣaḥīḥ Muslim* 2575

[18] *Musnad Imām Aḥmad* 22152

اهْتَزَّ الْعَرْشُ لِمَوْتِ سَعْدِ بْنِ مُعَاذٍ.

The Throne shook at the death of Sa'd bin Mu'ādh.[19]

❖ UMM SA'D Jamīlah bint Sa'd bin ar-Rabī' al-Anṣārī was the wife of Zayd bin Thābit. Her father, Sa'd bin ar-Rabī', was killed during the Battle of Uḥud while her mother was pregnant with her. Her mother gave birth to her one month later. Umm Sa'd was raised as an orphan in the home of Abū Bakr aṣ-Ṣiddīq. Jābir bin 'Abdillāh said:

جَاءَتْ امْرَأَةُ سَعْدِ بْنِ الرَّبِيعِ بِابْنَتَيْهَا مِنْ سَعْدٍ إِلَى رَسُولِ اللَّهِ صَلَّى اللَّهُ عَلَيْهِ وَسَلَّمَ فَقَالَتْ يَا رَسُولَ اللَّهِ هَاتَانِ ابْنَتَا سَعْدِ بْنِ الرَّبِيعِ قُتِلَ أَبُوهُمَا مَعَكَ يَوْمَ أُحُدٍ شَهِيدًا وَإِنَّ عَمَّهُمَا أَخَذَ مَالَهُمَا فَلَمْ يَدَعْ لَهُمَا مَالًا وَلَا تُنْكَحَانِ إِلَّا وَلَهُمَا مَالٌ قَالَ يَقْضِي اللَّهُ فِي ذَلِكَ فَنَزَلَتْ آيَةُ الْمِيرَاثِ فَبَعَثَ رَسُولُ اللَّهِ صَلَّى اللَّهُ عَلَيْهِ وَسَلَّمَ إِلَى عَمِّهِمَا فَقَالَ أَعْطِ ابْنَتَيْ سَعْدٍ الثُّلُثَيْنِ وَأَعْطِ أُمَّهُمَا الثُّمُنَ وَمَا بَقِيَ فَهُوَ لَكَ.

The wife of Sa'd bin ar-Rabī' came with her two daughters from Sa'd to the Messenger of Allāh ﷺ and said, "O Messenger of Allāh, these two are daughters of Sa'd bin ar-Rabī', who fought along with you on the Day of Uḥud and was martyred. Their uncle took their wealth, without leaving any wealth for them, and they will not be married unless they have wealth." He said, "Allāh will decide on that matter." Thus, the verse about inheritance was revealed, so the Messenger of Allāh ﷺ sent word to their uncle, saying, "Give the two daughters of Sa'd two-thirds, and give their mother one-eighth, and whatever remains, then it is for you."[20]

❖ UMM SAYF was the wet nurse for Ibrāhīm, the son of the Messenger of Allāh ﷺ. She was married to Abū Sayf, the blacksmith. The Messenger of Allāh ﷺ said:

[19] *Ṣaḥīḥ al-Bukhārī* 3803; *Ṣaḥīḥ Muslim* 2466

[20] *Jāmi' at-Tirmidhī* 2236; Abū 'Īsā said it is *ḥasan ṣaḥīḥ*.

وُلِدَ لِي اللَّيْلَةَ غُلاَمٌ فَسَمَّيْتُه بِاسْمِ أَبِي إِبْرَاهِيمَ، وَدَفعتُه إِلَى أُمِّ سَيْفٍ امْرَأَةِ قَيْنٍ بِالْمَدِينَة، يُقَالُ لَهُ: أَبُو سَيْفٍ.

A child was born to me this night, and I named him after the name of my father Ibrāhīm. I then sent him to Umm Sayf, the wife of a blacksmith who was called Abū Sayf.

فَانْطَلَقَ يَأْتِيهِ وَاتَّبَعْتُهُ فَانْتَهَيْنَا إِلَى أَبِي سَيْفٍ وَهُوَ يَنْفُخُ بِكِيرِهِ قَدِ امْتَلأَ الْبَيْتُ دُخَانًا فَأَسْرَعْتُ الْمَشْىَ بَيْنَ يَدَىْ رَسُولِ اللَّهِ صلى الله عليه وسلم فَقُلْتُ يَا أَبَا سَيْفٍ أَمْسِكْ جَاءَ رَسُولُ اللَّهِ صلى الله عليه وسلم.

He (the Prophet) went to him and I (Anas, the narrator) followed him until we reached Abū Sayf, and he was blowing fire with the help of a blacksmith's bellows, and the house was filled with smoke. I hastened my step and went ahead of the Messenger of Allāh ﷺ and said, "Abū Sayf, stop it; the Messenger of Allāh ﷺ has arrived."

فَأَمْسَكَ فَدَعَا النَّبِيُّ صلى الله عليه وسلم بِالصَّبِيِّ فَضَمَّهُ إِلَيْهِ وَقَالَ مَا شَاءَ اللَّهُ أَنْ يَقُولَ . فَقَالَ أَنَسٌ لَقَدْ رَأَيْتُهُ وَهُوَ يَكِيدُ بِنَفْسِهِ بَيْنَ يَدَىْ رَسُولِ اللَّهِ صلى الله عليه وسلم فَدَمَعَتْ عَيْنَا رَسُولِ اللَّهِ صلى الله عليه وسلم فَقَالَ " تَدْمَعُ الْعَيْنُ وَيَحْزَنُ الْقَلْبُ وَلاَ نَقُولُ إِلاَّ مَا يَرْضَى رَبُّنَا وَاللَّهِ يَا إِبْرَاهِيمُ إِنَّا بِكَ لَمَحْزُونُونَ

He stopped, and the Messenger of Allāh ﷺ called for the child. He embraced him and said what Allāh had desired. Anas said, "I saw the boy breathe his last breath in the presence of Allāh's Messenger ﷺ. The eyes of the Messenger of Allāh shed tears and he said, 'Ibrāhīm, our eyes shed tears and our hearts are filled with grief, but we do not say anything except what Allāh is pleased with. O Ibrāhīm, we are grieved for you.' "[21]

[21] *Ṣaḥīḥ Muslim* 2315

SHĪN - ش

❖ UMM ASH-SHARĪD left a will bequeathal for her son ash-Sharīd to free a believing slave. Ash-Sharīd said:

أَتَيْتُ رَسُولَ اللَّهِ صلى الله عليه وسلم فَقُلْتُ إِنَّ أُمِّي أَوْصَتْ أَنْ تُعْتَقَ عَنْهَا رَقَبَةٌ وَإِنَّ عِنْدِي جَارِيَةً نُوبِيَّةً أَفَيُجْزِئُ عَنِّي أَنْ أَعْتِقَهَا عَنْهَا قَالَ "ائْتِنِي بِهَا". فَأَتَيْتُهُ بِهَا فَقَالَ لَهَا النَّبِيُّ صلى الله عليه وسلم "مَنْ رَبُّكِ". قَالَتِ اللَّهُ. قَالَ "مَنْ أَنَا". قَالَتْ أَنْتَ رَسُولُ اللَّهِ. قَالَ فَأَعْتِقْهَا فَإِنَّهَا مُؤْمِنَةٌ.

I came to the Messenger of Allāh and said, "My mother left a bequeathal saying that a slave should be freed on her behalf. I have a Nubian slave-girl; will it suffice if I free her on her behalf?" He said, "Bring her here." The Prophet said to her, "Who is your Lord?" She said, "Allāh." He said, "Who am I?" She said, "The Messenger of Allāh." He said, "Set her free, for she is a believer."[22]

❖ UMM SHARĪK was a wealthy woman from the Anṣār. She spent a lot of wealth for the cause of Allāh. Fāṭimah bint Qays said:

خَطَبَنِي عَبْدُ الرَّحْمَنِ بْنُ عَوْفٍ فِي نَفَرٍ مِنْ أَصْحَابِ مُحَمَّدٍ صلى الله عليه وسلم وَخَطَبَنِي رَسُولُ اللَّهِ صلى الله عليه وسلم عَلَى مَوْلاَهُ أُسَامَةَ بْنِ زَيْدٍ وَقَدْ كُنْتُ حُدِّثْتُ أَنَّ رَسُولَ اللَّهِ صلى الله عليه وسلم قَالَ مَنْ أَحَبَّنِي فَلْيُحِبَّ أُسَامَةَ.

'Abdur-Raḥmān bin 'Awf proposed marriage to me, along with others from the Companions of Muḥammad ﷺ. And the Messenger of Allāh ﷺ proposed that I marry his freed slave, Usāmah bin Zayd. I was told that the Messenger of Allāh had said, "Whoever loves me, let him love Usāmah."

[22] *Sunan an-Nasā'ī* 3653

فَلَمَّا كَلَّمَنِي رَسُولُ اللَّهِ صلى الله عليه وسلم قُلْتُ أَمْرِي بِيَدِكَ فَأَنْكِحْنِي مَنْ شِئْتَ.

When the Messenger of Allāh spoke to me, I said, "My affairs are in your hands; marry me to whomever you wish."

فَقَالَ انْطَلِقِي إِلَى أُمِّ شَرِيكٍ. وَأُمُّ شَرِيكٍ امْرَأَةٌ غَنِيَّةٌ مِنَ الأَنْصَارِ عَظِيمَةُ النَّفَقَةِ فِي سَبِيلِ اللَّهِ عَزَّ وَجَلَّ يَنْزِلُ عَلَيْهَا الضِّيفَانُ.

He said, "Go to Umm Sharīk." Umm Sharīk was a rich Anṣārī woman who used to spend a great deal in the cause of Allāh, and she always had a lot of guests.

فَقُلْتُ سَأَفْعَلُ. قَالَ "لاَ تَفْعَلِي فَإِنَّ أُمَّ شَرِيكٍ كَثِيرَةُ الضِّيفَانِ فَإِنِّي أَكْرَهُ أَنْ يَسْقُطَ عَنْكِ خِمَارُكِ أَوْ يَنْكَشِفَ الثَّوْبُ عَنْ سَاقَيْكِ فَيَرَى الْقَوْمُ مِنْكِ بَعْضَ مَا تَكْرَهِينَ وَلَكِنِ انْتَقِلِي إِلَى ابْنِ عَمِّكِ عَبْدِ اللَّهِ بْنِ عَمْرِو بْنِ أُمِّ مَكْتُومٍ". وَهُوَ رَجُلٌ مِنْ بَنِي فِهْرٍ فَانْتَقَلْتُ إِلَيْهِ.

I said, "I will do that." He said, "Do not do that, for Umm Sharīk has a lot of guests, and I would not like your *khimār* to fall off or your shins to become uncovered and the people to see something of you that you do not want them to see. Rather, go to your cousin 'Abdullāh bin 'Amr bin Umm Maktūm, who is a man of Banū Fihr." So I went to him.[23]

❖ UMM SHARĪK ad-Dawsiyyah Ghuzaylah embraced Islām during the month of Ramaḍān. Abū Hurayrah narrated her story, which has been collected by al-Bayhaqī. He said, "Umm Sharīk searched for someone to escort her to the Messenger of Allāh ﷺ in Madīnah. She encountered a Jewish man who said to her, 'What do you need, Umm Sharīk?' She said, 'I am looking for a man to escort me to the Messenger of Allāh ﷺ.' He said, 'Come; my wife and I will escort you.' She said, 'Wait for me until I fill my water-

[23] *Sunan an-Nasā'ī* 3237

skin with water.' He said, 'I have water, so you don't need to get water.' When the evening came, he took shelter and said, 'O Umm Sharīk, come and have dinner.' She said, 'I am thirsty. I can't eat until I drink some water.' He said, 'I will not pour you water until you become a Jew.' She said, 'May Allāh not reward you with good; you took me from my homeland and prevented me from bringing water.' He said, 'By Allāh, I will not pour you a drop of water until you become a Jew.' She replied, 'By Allāh, I will never become a Jew after being guided to Islām.'

"She tied up her camel and rested her head on its knees and went to sleep. She said, 'I was awakened by a cold pail which dropped by my side. I raised my head to see that it was water which was extremely white, whiter than milk, and sweeter than honey. I drank from it until my thirst was quenched. When the water was gone, the pail filled again, and I watched it as it ascended to the sky. When the morning came, the Jewish man came. I said to him, "Allāh has given me drink." He said, "Where did it come from? Did it descend from the sky?" I said, "Yes, by Allāh. Allāh the Exalted sent it down from the sky and then it ascended to the sky again." We continued our journey until we reached the Messenger of Allāh ﷺ and I narrated what had occurred to him.' "[24]

ṬĀ' – ط

❖ UMM ṬĀRIQ was the freed slave of Sa'd bin 'Ubādah, the chief of the Khazraj tribe. Sa'd bin 'Ubādah was killed by the *jinn* when he urinated in a hole that was their dwelling place, and they said:

نحن قتلنا سيد الخزرج سعد بن عباده، ورميناه بسهم فلم نخطئ فؤاده.

We have killed the leader of the Khazraj, Sa'd bin 'Ubādah; we struck him with an arrow, and we did not miss his heart.

---

[24] Collected by al-Bayhaqī (6/123).

❖ UMM ṬUFAYL was the wife of Ubayy bin Ka'b. Ubayy said, "Umar and I disputed concerning the waiting period for the woman whose husband dies while she is pregnant. I said that she is able to remarry after she gives birth. Umm Ṭufayl said, 'The Messenger of Allāh ﷺ gave Subay'ah al-Aslamiyyah permission to marry after she gave birth.'"

❖ UMM ṬALĪQ was the wife of Abū Ṭalīq. She said, "O Abū Ṭalīq, Ḥajj season has arrived." And Abū Ṭalīq had a she-camel and a camel. He used his she-camel for Ḥajj and his camel for battle. Umm Ṭalīq asked her husband to give her the camel so she could perform Ḥajj. He said, "Don't you know I use the camel for the path of Allāh?" She replied, "Ḥajj is in the path of Allāh, so give me the camel, may Allāh have mercy upon you." He refused to do so, so she said, "Then give me the she-camel and you can perform Ḥajj on the camel." He said, "I will not give you preference over myself." She said, "Give me provisions for Ḥajj." He said, "I do not have any extra other than what I have for myself and my family and what I have left for you all." She said, "If you give it to me, Allāh will replace it for you." The next day, she said to him, "When you see the Messenger of Allāh ﷺ, convey the greeting of *salām* to him from me and inform him of what I told you." Abū Ṭalīq went to the Messenger of Allāh ﷺ and conveyed the *salām* from his wife and informed him of what she said. The Messenger of Allāh ﷺ said:

صدقَتْ أم طَلِيق لو أعطيتها الجمل لكان في سبيل الله، ولو أعطيتها الناقة لكانت وكنْتَ في سبيل الله، ولو أعطيتها من نفقتك لأخلفها الله عليك.

Umm Ṭalīq has spoken the truth. If you would have given her the camel, it would have surely been in the path of Allāh, and if you would have given her the she-camel, it and you would have surely been in the path of Allāh. And if you would have given her the provision, Allāh would have surely replaced it for you.

Abū Ṭalīq said, "She asks, 'What is equivalent to Ḥajj?'" The Prophet ﷺ said:

عمرة في رمضان.

'Umrah during Ramaḍān.[25]

'AYN - ع

❖ UMM 'ĀMIR bint Abī Quḥāfah is the sister of Abū Bakr aṣ-Ṣiddīq. She married 'Āmir bin Abī Waqqāṣ.

❖ UMM 'ĀMIR al-Fihriyyah is the mother of Abū 'Ubaydah bin al-Jarrāḥ, one of the 10 promised Paradise. She was alive when the revelation was revealed, and she embraced Islām.

❖ UMM 'ĀMIR is the mother of Abuṭ-Ṭufayl 'Āmir bin Wāthilah. Abuṭ-Ṭufayl 'Āmir bin Wāthilah was the last Companion to die. He died in Makkah in 110 AH. Abuṭ-Ṭufayl said, "I saw the Messenger of Allāh ﷺ the day Makkah was conquered. I will never forget the whiteness of his face and the blackness of his hair. I said to my mother, 'Who is this?' She said, 'This is the Messenger of Allāh ﷺ.' "[26]

❖ UMM 'ABDILLĀH bint Aws al-Anṣāriyyah is the sister of Shaddād bin Aws. Umm 'Abdillāh narrated that she sent to the Messenger of Allāh ﷺ a bowl of milk to break his fast with after a long, hot day. The courier returned the milk to her and asked, "Where did you get this milk from?" She said, "From my sheep." The courier said, "Where did you get the sheep from?" She said, "I purchased it from my wealth." Thus, the courier accepted the milk. The next day, Umm 'Abdillāh went to the Messenger of Allāh ﷺ and said, "O Messenger of Allāh, yesterday I sent some milk to you and it was initially returned to me." The Prophet ﷺ said:

[25] Collected by Ibn Abī Shaybah with a good chain of narration.

[26] *Sunan Abī Dāwūd* 1/463

بِذَلِكَ أُمِرَتِ الرُّسُلُ أَلَّا تَأْكُلَ إِلَّا طَيِّبًا وَلَا تَعْمَلَ إِلَّا صَالِحًا.

This is what the Messengers have been commanded with: to only eat from the wholesome food and to only perform righteous actions.[27]

❖ UMM 'ABDILLĀH bint Ḥanẓalah bin Qasāmah is the wife of Nu'aym bin 'Abdillāh an-Naḥḥām, the tenth person to embrace Islām. 'Abdullāh bin 'Umar went to his father, 'Umar, and said, "I proposed to the daughter of Nu'aym an-Naḥḥām, and I want you to go with me and speak to him on my behalf." 'Umar said, "I know Nu'aym better than you. He has a nephew who is an orphan living with him. And he is not going to dust the people's skin and leave his own skin dusty."[28] Ibn 'Umar said, "Her mother has asked me to marry her." 'Umar said, "If you are determined to do so, then take your uncle Zayd bin al-Khaṭṭāb with you."

Zayd and Ibn 'Umar went to Nu'aym, and it was as though he had heard the speech of 'Umar. Nu'aym kindly welcomed them and honored them within his home. He said to them concerning Ibn 'Umar's proposal to marry his daughter, "I have a nephew who is an orphan, and I am not going to dust the skin of the people and leave my own skin dusty." Umm 'Abdillāh, the mother of his daughter, responded from the other end of the house, saying, "By Allāh, you are not going to marry her to your nephew until the Messenger of Allāh ﷺ judges between us. Are you going to hold her captive with an orphan from Banū 'Adī, your weak nephew?"

Then she went to the Messenger of Allāh ﷺ and informed him of what had occurred. He called for Nu'aym, and he explained what had occurred. The Messenger of Allāh ﷺ said to Nu'aym, "Keep the ties of kinship and make your orphan and the mother of your daughter happy, for surely both of them have a portion in this affair." Meaning: Nu'aym was not able to force his daughter to

[27] Collected by Imām Aḥmad in "The Book of Zuhd" (p. 398) and by Muslim (3/85); declared authentic by al-Albānī.

[28] **Translator's note:** Meaning, he will marry his daughter to his kin before marrying her to a non-relative.

marry his nephew.[29]

Nu'aym embraced Islām before 'Umar, but he did not migrate until shortly before the conquest of Makkah. That is because he financially supported the widows and orphans of Banū 'Adī. Thus, when he wanted to migrate to Madīnah, his people said to him, "Stay with us and practice any religion you want." Zubayr said, "When Nu'aym arrived in Madīnah, the Prophet ﷺ said to him, 'O Nu'aym, your people treated you better than my people.' Nu'aym said, 'On the contrary, your people treated you better, O Messenger of Allāh.' The Prophet ﷺ said, 'My people expelled me, while your people kept you.' Nu'aym said, 'O Messenger of Allāh, your people expelled you to migration, while my people kept me away from you.' "[30]

❖ UMM 'ABDILLĀH bint Abī Dūmī was the wife of Abū Mūsā. When Abū Mūsā was close to death, he fell unconscious. When he woke, his wife was crying in a raised voice, and he said to her, "Do you remember what the Messenger of Allāh ﷺ said?" She said, "Of course," and then she went silent. He said to her, "What did the Messenger of Allāh ﷺ say?" She said, "The Messenger of Allāh ﷺ said:

لَيْسَ مِنَّا مَنْ سَلَقَ وَحَلَقَ وَخَرَقَ.

" 'He is not one of us who raises his voice in lamentation, shaves his head, or rends his garments.' "[31]

❖ UMM 'ABDILLĀH bint 'Adī bin Khuwaylid is the niece of Khadījah, the wife of the Messenger of Allāh ﷺ.

❖ UMM 'ABDILLĀH bint Nubayh is the mother of 'Abdullāh bin 'Amr bin al-'Āṣ.

---

[29] Collected by al-Bayhaqī from the *ḥadīth* of 'Urwah, narrated by Ibn 'Umar.

[30] *Ṣaḥīḥ al-Bukhārī* 2313

[31] *Sunan an-Nasā'ī* 1865

❖ UMM 'ABD bint 'Abd Wudd bin Sawā' is the mother of 'Abdullāh bin Mas'ūd. Abū Mūsā said, "I used to believe that 'Abdullāh bin Mas'ūd and his mother were from the family of the Prophet ﷺ, due to them visiting him often."

❖ UMM 'UBAYS was from the first and foremost to embrace Islām, and she was severely punished by the pagans. She is from the seven slaves freed by Abū Bakr. Abū Bakr freed seven slaves who were punished in the path of Allāh: 'Āmir bin Fuhayrah, Bilāl, Zinnīrah, Umm 'Ubays, an-Nahdiyyah and her daughter, and Labībah (the slave of Banul-Mu'ammal).[32] She was married to Kurayz and gave birth to their son 'Ubays.

❖ UMM 'IṢMAH al-'Awṣiyyah was a narrator of *ḥadīth*. She was married to Ibn Qays. She said that the Messenger of Allāh ﷺ said:

مَا مِنْ مُسْلِمٍ يَعْمَلُ ذَنْبًا إِلاَّ وَقَفَ الْمَلَكُ الْمُوَكَّلُ بِإِحْصَاءِ ذُنُوبِهِ ثَلَاثَ سَاعَاتٍ، فَإِنِ اسْتَغْفَرَ الله مِنْ ذَنْبِهِ ذَلِكَ لَمْ يَرْفَعْهُ عَلَيْهِ يَوْمَ الْقِيَامَةِ.

There is no Muslim who commits a sin except that the angel entrusted to count his sins waits three hours. If he seeks Allāh's forgiveness from that sin, it will not be raised against him on the Day of Judgment.[33]

❖ UMM AL-'ALĀ' was a woman from the Anṣār. She gave the pledge of allegiance to the Prophet ﷺ. She said, "The emigrants were distributed amongst us by drawing lots, and we drew 'Uthmān bin Maẓ'ūn. We made him stay with us in our house. Then he suffered from a disease which proved fatal when he died, and he was given a bath and was shrouded in his clothes. The Messenger of Allāh ﷺ came and I said, 'May Allāh be merciful to you, O Abus-Sā'ib ('Uthmān bin Maẓ'ūn)! I testify that Allāh has honored you.' The Prophet ﷺ said:

[32] Collected by al-Ḥākim (5241).

[33] Collected by al-Ḥākim (4/262), with an authentic chain of narration.

وَمَا يُدْرِيكِ أَنَّ اللَّهَ قَدْ أَكْرَمَهُ؟

" 'How do you know that Allāh has honored him?'

"I replied, 'O Messenger of Allāh, let my father be sacrificed for you! On whom else shall Allāh bestow His honor?' The Prophet ﷺ said:

أَمَّا هُوَ فَقَدْ جَاءَهُ الْيَقِينُ، وَاللَّهِ إِنِّي لأَرْجُو لَهُ الْخَيْرَ، وَاللَّهِ مَا أَدْرِي - وَأَنَا رَسُولُ اللَّهِ - مَا يُفْعَلُ بِي.

" 'As for him, that which is certain came to him. By Allāh, I hope for him good, but by Allāh, I do not know what Allāh will do with me, though I am the Messenger of Allāh.' "

Umm al-'Alā' said, "By Allāh, I never attested to the piety of anyone after that."[34]

QĀF – ق

❖ UMM QAYS bint Miḥṣan is the sister of 'Ukāshah bin Miḥṣan. She was from the foremost to embrace Islām in Makkah, and then she migrated to Madīnah. She is the mother of the boy who urinated on the Messenger of Allāh ﷺ. Umm Qays bint Miḥṣan said, "I brought my young son, who had not started eating (ordinary food), to the Messenger of Allāh ﷺ, and he placed him in his lap. The child urinated on the garment of the Prophet ﷺ, so he asked for water and poured it over the soiled (area) and did not wash it."[35]

Umm Qays is likewise mentioned in the *ḥadīth* of prophetic medicine. Umm Qays bint Miḥṣan went to the Prophet ﷺ with her son, whose palate and tonsils she had pressed to treat a throat trouble. He said to her:

---

[34] *Ṣaḥīḥ al-Bukhārī* 1243

[35] *Ṣaḥīḥ al-Bukhārī* 223

اتَّقُوا اللَّهَ، عَلَى مَا تَدْغَرُونَ أَوْلاَدَكُمْ بِهَذِهِ الأَعْلاَقِ عَلَيْكُمْ بِهَذَا الْعُودِ الْهِنْدِيِّ، فَإِنَّ فِيهِ سَبْعَةَ أَشْفِيَةٍ، مِنْهَا ذَاتُ الْجَنْبِ.

Fear Allāh; why do you pain your children by having their tonsils pressed like that? You should use Indian aloeswood (*al-ʿūd al-hindī*), for in it are seven cures, one of which is pleurisy.[36]

KĀF – ك

❖ UMM KA'B al-Anṣāriyyah was from the noble Companions of the Messenger of Allāh ﷺ. She died during childbirth. Samurah bin Jundub said:

صَلَّيْتُ خَلْفَ النَّبِيِّ صلى الله عليه وسلم وَصَلَّى عَلَى أُمِّ كَعْبٍ مَاتَتْ وَهِيَ نُفَسَاءُ فَقَامَ رَسُولُ اللَّهِ صلى الله عليه وسلم لِلصَّلاَةِ عَلَيْهَا وَسَطَهَا.

I prayed behind the Messenger of Allāh ﷺ for Umm Ka'b. She died while giving birth. The Messenger of Allāh ﷺ stood in front of her waist to lead the prayer for her.[37]

MĪM – م

❖ UMM MĀLIK al-Anṣārī used to send clarified butter in a small skin to the Messenger of Allāh ﷺ. Her sons would ask her for condiments when they had none, and she would go to that skin and give them from its contents. Each time she would go to the skin, she would find it full with clarified butter, even though she had not added any butter to it, until one day she squeezed it completely empty. She went to the Prophet ﷺ and informed him of this. He said to her, "Did you squeeze it completely empty?" She said, "Yes." He said to her:

---

[36] *Ṣaḥīḥ al-Bukhārī* 5368; *Ṣaḥīḥ Muslim* 287

[37] *Ṣaḥīḥ Muslim* 964

لَوْ تَرَكْتِيهَا مَا زَالَ قَائِمًا.

If you would have left some, it would have continued to provide for you.[38]

❖ UMM MĀLIK al-Bahziyyah was from the noble Companions and was a narrator of *ḥadīth*. She narrated *aḥādīth* concerning the *fitnah* that would appear. Umm Mālik al-Bahziyyah narrated that the Messenger of Allāh ﷺ mentioned *fitnah*, such that it was drawing near. She said, "I said, 'O Messenger of Allāh, who is the best of people during this *fitnah*?' He said:

رَجُلٌ فِي مَاشِيَتِهِ يُؤَدِّي حَقَّهَا وَيَعْبُدُ رَبَّهُ وَرَجُلٌ آخِذٌ بِرَأْسِ فَرَسِهِ يُخِيفُ الْعَدُوَّ وَيُخِيفُونَهُ.

"'A man among his livestock who pays what is due on them and worships his Lord. And a man clutching the head of his horse, terrified of his enemy, and they are terrified of him.'"[39]

❖ UMM MUBASH'SHIR bint Bishr bin al-Barā' bin Ma'rūr al-Anṣārī is the daughter of the Companion who died after eating the poisoned sheep given to the Prophet ﷺ. Umm Mubash'shir said to the Prophet ﷺ, during the sickness of which he died, "To what do you attribute your illness, O Messenger of Allāh? I do not attribute the illness of my father except to the poisoned sheep of which he had eaten with you at Khaybar." The Messenger of Allāh ﷺ said:

وَأَنَا لاَ أَتَّهِمُ بِنَفْسِي إِلاَّ ذَلِكَ فَهَذَا أَوَانُ قَطَعَتْ أَبْهَرِي.

I only attribute my illness to that. And this is the time when it is cutting off my aorta.[40]

❖ UMM MA'BAD 'Ātikah bint Khālid al-Khuzā'iyyah is from the noble Companions. The Prophet ﷺ passed by her tent along

[38] *Ṣaḥīḥ Muslim* 2280

[39] *Jāmi' at-Tirmidhī* 2177

[40] *Sunan Abī Dāwūd* 4513

with Abū Bakr and Abū Bakr's freed slave, 'Āmir bin Fuhayrah, when they migrated to Madīnah. 'Ā'ishah narrated that the Prophet ﷺ and Abū Bakr hired a man who was a pagan from the tribe of Banud-Dīl as an expert guide ('Abdullāh bin Urayqiṭ). The Prophet ﷺ and Abū Bakr gave him their two riding camels and took a promise from him to bring their riding camels in the morning of the third day to the Cave of Thawr.[41]

Umm Ma'bad was known as a generous woman who would sit in her camp and feed the travelers who passed by. When the Messenger of Allāh and Abū Bakr passed by her tent, they asked her if she had food or drink they could purchase from her. Regretfully, she did not have any food or drink to provide for them. The Prophet ﷺ saw a scrawny goat which was being kept away from other sheep due to its weakness. He asked her if the goat had any milk. Umm Ma'bad replied that the goat was too scrawny to have milk. The Messenger of Allāh ﷺ said to her:

أتأذنين لي أن أحلبها؟

Do you give me permission to milk it[42]?

She said, "Yes, if you believe it has milk." The Prophet ﷺ rubbed the udder of the goat and said, "In the name of Allāh"; the udder swelled with milk, and the Prophet ﷺ called for a large vessel and filled it with milk. Then he milked the goat until Umm Ma'bad and his Companions drank her fill. He then said, "The one who holds the cup drinks last," and he drank his fill. Then he milked the goat a third time and filled the vessels of Umm Ma'bad, and they departed. Ibn Hishām said, "Umm Ma'bad was a Muslim during this day."

The goat which the Prophet ﷺ rubbed lived until the Year of Ashes, which was 18 AH. The Year of Ashes was so named due to the lack of rainfall.

---

[41] *Ṣaḥīḥ al-Bukhārī* 2264

[42] Collected by aṭ-Ṭabarānī (7/124).

When Umm Ma'bad's husband returned, he was amazed to see their vessels filled with milk. He said, "O Umm Ma'bad, where did you get this milk from?" She replied, "A blessed man passed by!"

Ḥubaysh bin Khālid is the brother of Umm Ma'bad and a Companion of the Messenger of Allāh ﷺ. He was killed during the conquest of Makkah. He narrated the description of the Prophet ﷺ given by his sister Umm Ma'bad. Although Umm Ma'bad only spent a short time hosting the Prophet ﷺ, she gave her husband a detailed description of him. Umm Ma'bad said:

رَأَيْتُ رَجُلا ظَاهِرَ الْوَضَاءَةِ، أَبْلَجَ الْوَجْهِ، حَسَنَ الْخَلْقِ، لَمْ تَعِبْهُ نُحْلَةٌ، وَلَمْ تُزْرِ بِهِ صَعْلَةٌ، وَسِيمٌ قَسِيمٌ، فِي عَيْنِهِ دَعَجٌ، وَفِي أَشْفَارِهِ غَطَفٌ، وَفِي صَوْتِهِ صَهَلٌ، وَفِي عُنُقِهِ سَطَعٌ، وَفِي لِحْيَتِهِ كَثَاثَةٌ، أَزَجُّ أَقْرَنُ، شديد سواد الشعر.

I saw a man who is distinctly handsome with a face that's bright. He is well-built, neither blemished by a big belly nor disfigured by an unusually small head. He is handsome and well-portioned. The pupils of his eyes are extremely black; his eyelashes are very long. His voice has raspiness. His neck is long and his beard is thick. His eyebrows are close and naturally arched. His hair is exceedingly black.

إِنْ صَمَتَ فَعَلَيْهِ الْوَقَارُ، وَإِنْ تَكَلَّمَ سَمَا وَعَلاهُ الْبَهَاءُ، أَجْمَلُ النَّاسِ وَأَبْهَاهُ مِنْ بَعِيدٍ، وَأَحْلاهُ وَأَحْسَنُهُ مِنْ قَرِيبٍ، حُلْوُ الْمِنْطِقِ، فَصْلٌ، لا نَذْرٌ وَلا هَذْرٌ، كَأَنَّ مَنْطِقَهُ خَرَزَاتُ نَظْمٍ يَنْحَدَّرْنَ.

When he is silent, he is enveloped in an aura of dignity. When he speaks, splendor is exhibited in his words. He is the most beautiful and splendid person from afar, and the most handsome and pleasant person from up close. His oration is sweet and deliberate, neither short nor long-winded. It is as though his speech is a string of pearls.

رَبْعَةً لا بَائِنٌ مِنْ طُولٍ، وَلا تَقْتَحِمُهُ عَيْنٌ مِنْ قِصَرٍ، غُصْنًا بَيْنَ غُصْنَيْنِ، فَهُوَ أَنْضَرُ الثَّلاثَةِ مَنْظَرًا، وَأَحْسَنُهُمْ قَدْرًا، لَهُ رُفَقَاءُ يَحُفُّونَ بِهِ، إِنْ قَالَ أَنْصَتُوا لِقَوْلِهِ، وَإِنْ أَمَرَ تَبَادَرُوا إِلَى أَمْرِهِ، مَحْفُودٌ مَحْشُودٌ، لا عَابِسٌ وَلا مُفْنِدٌ.

He is of medium height, not exceedingly tall or exceedingly short causing the eye to dip. He is like a branch between two branches. He is the most radiant of the three and the most respected of them. He has companions who surround him; when he speaks, they listen to his words, and when he commands, they hasten to carry out his order. They serve and gather around him. He neither frowns nor refuses.

Abū Ma'bad said, "That is the companion from the Quraysh; I will surely follow him if I am able."[43]

❖ UMM MA'BAD bint 'Abdillāh bin 'Umar bin Ḥarām is the sister of Jābir bin 'Abdillāh. Jābir bin 'Abdillāh said, "The Messenger of Allāh ﷺ used to visit the orchard of Umm Ma'bad, and he said to her:

يَا أُمَّ مَعْبَدٍ مَنْ غَرَسَ هَذَا النَّخْلَ أَمُسْلِمٌ أَمْ كَافِرٌ. فَقَالَتْ بَلْ مُسْلِمٌ. قَالَ فَلاَ يَغْرِسُ الْمُسْلِمُ غَرْسًا فَيَأْكُلَ مِنْهُ إِنْسَانٌ وَلاَ دَابَّةٌ وَلاَ طَيْرٌ إِلاَّ كَانَ لَهُ صَدَقَةً إِلَى يَوْمِ الْقِيَامَةِ.

"'O Umm Ma'bad, who has planted this tree—a Muslim or a non-Muslim?' She said, 'Of course, a Muslim.' The Prophet ﷺ said, 'No Muslim plants a tree and its fruits are eaten by human beings, beasts, or birds except that it will be charity for him on the Day of Judgment.'"[44]

❖ UMM MŪSĀ al-Lakhmiyyah is the mother of Mūsā bin Nuṣayr, the governor who led the conquest of Andalus. She partic-

[43] Collected by al-Bayhaqī in "Proof of Prophethood" (*ḥadīth* 255).

[44] *Ṣaḥīḥ Muslim* 1552

ipated in the Battle of Yarmūk with her husband Nuṣayr. During this battle, she killed a pagan and took his loot. She narrated the event, saying, "We were a group of women when some pagan men passed by. I saw one of the pagan men dragging a man from among the Muslims. So I grabbed a pole, creeped up close to him, and cracked his head. I began to take his loot, and the men helped me carry it."

WĀW – و

❖ UMM WARAQAH bint 'Abdillāh bin al-Ḥārith was nicknamed "the Martyr" by the Messenger of Allāh ﷺ while she was alive. She is also called Umm Waraqah bint Nawfal as an ascription to her great-great-grandfather. Umm Waraqah said to the Messenger of Allāh ﷺ:

يَا رَسُولَ اللَّهِ ائْذَنْ لِي فِي الْغَزْوِ مَعَكَ أُمَرِّضُ مَرْضَاكُمْ لَعَلَّ اللَّهَ أَنْ يَرْزُقَنِي شَهَادَةً.

O Messenger of Allāh, permit me to attend the battle (of Badr) with you so I may nurse you when you're sick, and perchance Allāh will bestow martyrdom upon me.

The Messenger of Allāh ﷺ said to her:

قِرِّي فِي بَيْتِكِ فَإِنَّ اللَّهَ تَعَالَى يَرْزُقُكِ الشَّهَادَةَ.

Remain in your home, for surely, Allāh the Exalted will bestow martyrdom upon you.

The narrator of the *ḥadīth*, 'Abdur-Raḥmān bin Khallād, said that, from that day forth, she was known as "the Martyr." She used to recite the Qur'ān in her home. She sought permission from the Prophet ﷺ to have a *mu'adh'dhin* in her house. Thus, he permitted her to do so. She announced that her slave and slave-girl would be free after her death. One night, they went to her and strangled her with a sheet of cloth until she died, and they ran away. The next day, 'Umar announced to the people that anyone who has knowledge about them or has seen them should bring them to him. After their arrest, 'Umar ordered that they be crucified. This was the first crucifixion in Madīnah.[45]

YĀ' – ي

❖ UMM YAḤYĀ was the wife of Usayd bin Khuḍayr. Her husband is mentioned in *Ṣaḥīḥ al-Bukhārī* in the chapter entitled "The merits of Usayd bin Khuḍayr and 'Abbād bin Bishr." Anas said:

أَنَّ رَجُلَيْنِ، خَرَجَا مِنْ عِنْدِ النَّبِيِّ صلى الله عليه وسلم فِي لَيْلَةٍ مُظْلِمَةٍ، وَإِذَا نُورٌ بَيْنَ أَيْدِيهِمَا حَتَّى تَفَرَّقَا، فَتَفَرَّقَ النُّورُ مَعَهُمَا.

Two men left the Prophet ﷺ on a very dark night. Suddenly, a light came in front of them, and when they separated, the light also separated along with them.[46]

'Ā'ishah said, "We returned from Ḥajj, and the announcement was given for the death of Usayd's wife, so he covered his face and began to cry."

❖ UMM YAḤYĀ bint Abī Ihāb married 'Uqbah bin al-Ḥārith. 'Uqbah said, "I married a woman, then a black woman came to us and said, 'I breastfed you both.' I went to the Prophet and said, 'I married so-and-so, and a black woman came to me and said, "I breastfed you both."' He turned away from me, so I came to him from the other side and said, 'She is lying.' The Messenger of Allāh ﷺ said:

وَكَيْفَ بِهَا وَقَدْ زَعَمَتْ أَنَّهَا قَدْ أَرْضَعَتْكُمَا دَعْهَا عَنْكَ.

---

[45] *Sunan Abī Dāwūd* 591; declared *ḥasan* by al-Albānī.

[46] *Ṣaḥīḥ al-Bukhārī* 3805

“‘How could you keep her as your wife when she (this woman) believes she breastfed you both? Leave her (divorce her).’ ”[47]

[47] *Sunan an-Nasā'ī* 3330

UNNAMED WOMEN

FROM THE FEMALE COMPANIONS

❖ THE SISTERS OF JĀBIR BIN 'ABDILLĀH AL-ANṢĀRĪ were from the Companions of the Messenger of Allāh ﷺ. The scholars differ concerning their number; some say he had seven sisters, some say nine. Jābir bin 'Abdillāh said, "I married a woman during the lifetime of the Messenger of Allāh ﷺ. When I came across him, he said:

يَا جَابِرُ تَزَوَّجْتَ؟

"'Jābir, have you married?'

قُلْتُ نَعَمْ. قَالَ "بِكْرٌ أَمْ ثَيِّبٌ". قُلْتُ ثَيِّبٌ. قَالَ "فَهَلاَّ بِكْرًا تُلاَعِبُهَا".

"I said, 'Yes.' He said, 'A virgin or one previously married?' I said, 'Previously married.' He said, 'Why did you not marry a virgin with whom to play together?'

قُلْتُ يَا رَسُولَ اللَّهِ إِنَّ لِي أَخَوَاتٍ فَخَشِيتُ أَنْ تَدْخُلَ بَيْنِي وَبَيْنَهُنَّ. قَالَ فَذَاكَ إِذًا. إِنَّ الْمَرْأَةَ تُنْكَحُ عَلَى دِينِهَا وَمَالِهَا وَجَمَالِهَا فَعَلَيْكَ بِذَاتِ الدِّينِ تَرِبَتْ يَدَاكَ.

"I said, 'O Messenger of Allāh, I have sisters, and I was afraid that

she (a virgin) might intervene between me and them.' He said, 'In that case, this is good. A woman is married for her religion, her wealth, and her beauty, so you should choose one with religion. May you prosper!' "[1]

❖ THE SISTER OF 'UQBAH BIN 'ĀMIR was from the Companions of the Messenger of Allāh ﷺ. 'Uqbah said:

نَذَرَتْ أُخْتِي أَنْ تَمْشِيَ، إِلَى بَيْتِ اللَّهِ فَأَمَرَتْنِي أَنْ أَسْتَفْتِيَ لَهَا رَسُولَ اللَّهِ صلى الله عليه وسلم فَاسْتَفْتَيْتُ لَهَا النَّبِيَّ صلى الله عليه وسلم فَقَالَ لِتَمْشِ وَلْتَرْكَبْ.

My sister vowed to walk to the House of Allāh, and she told me to ask the Messenger of Allāh about that. So I asked the Prophet for her and he said, "Let her walk, and let her ride."[2]

❖ THE SISTER OF NU'MĀN BIN BASHĪR is from the Companions of the Messenger of Allāh ﷺ. She witnessed one of the many miracles of the Prophet ﷺ. She said, "My mother, 'Amrah bint Rawāḥah, called me one day and gave me a handful of dates in a garment. She said, 'My dear daughter, go to your father and your uncle, 'Abdullāh bin Rawāḥah, with their lunch.' So I took the dates and headed towards them. I passed by the Messenger of Allāh ﷺ while seeking my father and my uncle. The Messenger of Allāh ﷺ said, 'Come here, dear child; what is this you have?' I said, 'O Messenger of Allāh, these are dates. My mother sent me to take them to my father, Bashīr bin Sa'd, and my uncle, 'Abdullāh bin Rawāḥah, for their lunch.' He said, 'Give them to me.' So I poured them into the palm of the Messenger of Allāh ﷺ. The dates were not enough to fill his palm. Then he asked for a garment, and he laid it out and spread the dates on top of it. The dates began to scatter and multiply on top of the garment. He said:

---

[1] *Ṣaḥīḥ Muslim* 715

[2] *Sunan an-Nasā'ī* 3814

أُصْرُخْ فِي أَهْلِ الْخَنْدَقِ: أَنْ هَلُمَّ إِلَى الْغَدَاءِ.

" 'Call the people of the trench to come quickly for their lunch.'

"The people of the trench gathered and began eating from it, and the dates began to increase until the dates were falling off the edge of the garment. There were 3,000 of them that day eating from the dates."[3]

❖ THE DAUGHTER OF KHABBĀB BIN AL-ARATT was from the Companions of the Messenger of Allāh ﷺ. She said, "Khabbāb went out on a mission, and the Messenger of Allāh ﷺ agreed to milk our goat for us. When he would milk our goat, its milk would overflow in abundance. When Khabbāb returned and milked the goat, its milk returned to normal. We said to Khabbāb:

كَانَ رَسُولُ اللَّهِ صَلَّى اللَّهُ عَلَيْهِ وَسَلَّمَ يَحْلُبُهَا حَتَّى تَمْتَلِئَ جَفْنَتُنَا، فَلَمَّا حَلَبْتَهَا نَقَصَ حِلَابُهَا.

" 'The Messenger of Allāh ﷺ used to milk her and our bowls would fill; when you began to milk her, our milk decreased.' "[4]

Her father Khabbāb is the narrator of the *ḥadīth* concerning the trial of the previous nations. Khabbāb said, "We complained to the Messenger of Allāh of the persecution inflicted on us by the pagans while he was sitting in the shade of the Ka'bah, leaning over his covering sheet. We said to him, 'Would you seek help for us? Would you pray to Allāh for us?' He said:

كَانَ الرَّجُلُ فِيمَنْ قَبْلَكُمْ يُحْفَرُ لَهُ فِي الأَرْضِ فَيُجْعَلُ فِيهِ، فَيُجَاءُ بِالْمِنْشَارِ، فَيُوضَعُ عَلَى رَأْسِهِ فَيُشَقُّ بِاثْنَتَيْنِ، وَمَا يَصُدُّهُ ذَلِكَ عَنْ دِينِهِ، وَيُمْشَطُ بِأَمْشَاطِ الْحَدِيدِ، مَا دُونَ لَحْمِهِ مِنْ عَظْمٍ أَوْ عَصَبٍ، وَمَا يَصُدُّهُ

[3] Collected by Ibn Kathīr in *Al-Bidāyah wan-Nihāyah* from the *ḥadīth* of Muḥammad bin Is'ḥāq from Sa'īd bin Mīnā from the daughter of Bashīr bin Sa'd.

[4] *Musnad Imām Aḥmad* 20159

ذَلِكَ عَنْ دِينِهِ، وَاللَّهِ لَيُتِمَّنَّ هَذَا الأَمْرَ حَتَّى يَسِيرَ الرَّاكِبُ مِنْ صَنْعَاءَ إِلَى حَضْرَمَوْتَ، لاَ يَخَافُ إِلاَّ اللَّهَ أَوِ الذِّئْبَ عَلَى غَنَمِهِ، وَلَكِنَّكُمْ تَسْتَعْجِلُونَ.

" 'Among the nations before you, a (believing) man would be put in a ditch that was dug for him, and a saw would be put over his head and he would be cut into two pieces; yet that (torture) would not make him give up his religion. His body would be combed with iron combs that would remove his flesh from the bones and nerves, yet that would not make him abandon his religion. By Allāh, this religion will prevail until a traveler from Ṣan'ā' (in Yemen) to Ḥaḍramawt will fear none but Allāh, or [fear] a wolf regarding his sheep; but you (people) are hasty.' "[5]

❖ THE GRANDMOTHER OF ḤASHRAJ BIN ZIYĀD was from the Companions of the Messenger of Allāh. Ḥashraj bin Ziyād narrated from his grandmother that she went out with the Messenger of Allāh ﷺ for the Battle of Khaybar. They were six in number, including herself. She said, "When the Messenger of Allāh ﷺ was informed about it, he sent for us. We came to him and found him angry. He said:

مَنْ خَرَجْتُنَّ وَبِإِذْنِ مَنْ خَرَجْتُنَّ؟

" 'With whom did you come out, and by whose permission did you come out?'

"We said, 'O Messenger of Allāh, we have come out to spin the hair, by which we provide aid in the cause of Allāh. We have medicine for the wounded, we hand arrows to the fighters, and we supply drink made of wheat or barley.' He said, 'Stand up.' When Allāh bestowed the victory of Khaybar on him, he allotted shares to us from spoils that he allotted to the men." Ḥashraj bin Ziyād said, "I said to her, 'Grandmother, what was that?' She replied, 'Dates.' "[6]

---

[5] *Ṣaḥīḥ al-Bukhārī* 3612

[6] *Musnad Imām Aḥmad* 3716

❖ THE GRANDMOTHER OF 'AMR BIN MU'ĀDH was from the Companions of the Messenger of Allāh ﷺ, and she was a narrator of *ḥadīth*. 'Amr bin Mu'ādh said, "A beggar came to our door and my grandmother said to us, 'Feed him.' We said, 'We don't have any food.' My grandmother said, 'Then give him something to drink, because I heard the Messenger of Allāh ﷺ say:

رُدُّوا السَّائِلَ وَلَوْ بِظِلْفٍ.

" 'Give something to the beggar, if even it's a cloven foot.' "[7]

❖ THE PATERNAL AUNT OF ḤUSAYN BIN MUḤSIN was from the Companions of the Messenger of Allāh ﷺ. Ḥusayn bin Muḥsin said that his paternal aunt went to the Messenger of Allāh ﷺ concerning some need; he met her need, then he said:

أَذَاتُ بَعْلٍ أَنْتِ؟ قَالَتْ: نَعَمْ. قَالَ: فَكَيْفَ أَنْتِ لَهُ؟ قَالَتْ: مَا آلُوهُ إِلا مَا عَجَزْتُ عَنْهُ. قَالَ: فَانْظُرِي كَيْفَ أَنْتِ لَهُ فَإِنَّهُ جَنَّتُكِ وَنَارُكِ.

"Do you have a husband?" She said, "Yes." He said, "How are you with him?" She said, "I do what he tells me, except what is beyond my capability." He said, "Look at how you are with him, for he is your Paradise and your Hell."[8]

❖ THE WOMAN FROM GHĀMID who was stoned for fornication is from the noble Companions of the Messenger of Allāh ﷺ. Buraydah said, "A woman of Ghāmid came to the Prophet ﷺ and said, 'I have committed fornication.' He said, 'Go back.' She returned, and on the next day she came to him again and said, 'Perhaps you want to send me back as you did to Mā'iz bin Mālik. I swear by Allāh, I am pregnant.' He said to her, 'Go back.' She then returned and came to him the next day. He said to her, 'Go back until you give birth to a child.' She then returned. When she gave birth to a child, she brought the child to him and said, 'Here it is! I have given birth to it.' He said, 'Go back, and suckle him until you

---

[7] *Sunan an-Nasā'ī* 2565

[8] *Musnad Imām Aḥmad* 4/341; classed as *ṣaḥīḥ* by al-Albānī in *Ṣaḥīḥ at-Targhīb* (1933).

wean him.' When she had weaned him, she brought him (the boy) to [the Prophet] with something in his hand which he was eating. The boy was then given to a certain man of the Muslims, and the Prophet ﷺ gave the command regarding her. So a pit was dug for her, and he gave the order and she was stoned to death.

"Khālid was one of those who were throwing stones at her. He threw a stone at her. When a drop blood fell on his cheeks, he insulted her. The Prophet ﷺ said to him:

مَهْلاً يَا خَالِدُ فَوَالَّذِي نَفْسِي بِيَدِهِ لَقَدْ تَابَتْ تَوْبَةً لَوْ تَابَهَا صَاحِبُ مَكْسٍ لَغُفِرَ لَهُ.

" 'Be easy, Khālid; I swear by Him in whose Hand is my soul, she has repented to such an extent that if one who wrongfully takes taxes were to repent to a similar extent, he would be forgiven.' Then she was prayed for and buried."[9]

❖ THE WOMAN CRYING AT THE GRAVE OF HER CHILD was from the noble Companions of the Messenger of Allāh ﷺ. Anas bin Mālik said, "The Prophet ﷺ passed by a woman who was weeping beside a grave. He said:

اتَّقِي اللَّهَ وَاصْبِرِي.

" 'Fear Allāh and be patient.'

"She said to him:

إِلَيْكَ عَنِّي، فَإِنَّكَ لَمْ تُصَبْ بِمُصِيبَتِي.

" 'Go away, for you have not been afflicted with a calamity like mine.'

"And she did not recognize him. Then she was informed that he was the Prophet ﷺ, so she went to his house, and she did not find any guard there. Then she said to him, 'I did not recognize you.' He said:

---

[9] *Sunan Abī Dāwūd* 4442

إِنَّمَا الصَّبْرُ عِنْدَ الصَّدْمَةِ الأُولَى.

" 'Verily, the patience is at the first stroke of a calamity.' "[10]

[10] *Ṣaḥīḥ al-Bukhārī* 1283